MONEY MAKES THE WORLD GO AROUND

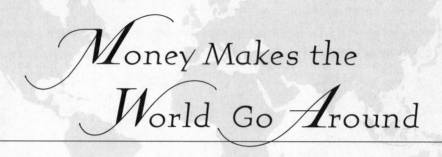

Money Makes the World Go Around

Barbara Garson

Viking

VIKING
Published by the Penguin Group
Penguin Putnam Inc., 375 Hudson Street,
New York, New York 10014, U.S.A.
Penguin Books Ltd, 27 Wrights Lane,
London W8 5TZ, England
Penguin Books Australia Ltd, Ringwood,
Victoria, Australia
Penguin Books Canada Ltd, 10 Alcorn Avenue,
Toronto, Ontario, Canada M4V 3B2
Penguin Books (N.Z.) Ltd, 182-190 Wairau Road,
Auckland 10, New Zealand

Penguin Books Ltd, Registered Offices:
Harmondsworth, Middlesex, England

First published in 2001 by Viking penguin,
a member of Penguin Putnam Inc.

1 3 5 7 9 10 8 6 4 2

AUTHOR'S NOTE
All the company names in this book are real and so are individual names except in Portland, Tennessee, and Biddeford, Maine. People in those towns were so unguarded in difficult situations what while no one seemed worried about my presence, I decided, on my own, to change their names.

Library of Congress Cataloging-in-Publication Data
Garson, Barbara
    Money makes the world go around : one investor tracks her cash through the
    global economy from Brooklyn to Bangkok and back / Barbara Garson
        p. cm.
    ISBN 0-670-86660-1
        1. Capital movements. 2. Mutual funds. 3. International finance. 4. Money. I.
    Title.

HG3891.G37 2001
332'.042—dc21   00-033558

This book is printed on acid-free paper. ∞

Printed in the United States of America
Set in FF Scala with Quartet and OPTI Lord Swash
Designed by Carla Bolte

AUTHOR'S NOTE

All the company names in this book are real. So are the individual names except in Portland, Tennessee, and Biddeford, Maine. In those two towns, people in difficult situations talked to me so unguardedly that while no one requested anonymity, I decided, on my own, to change most of their names.

CONTENTS

MONEY MAKES THE WORLD GO AROUND

One-world, a utopian phrase of my youth, suggested brotherhood, peace, Esperanto, the UN. Its current equivalent, the global village, suggests electronic banking and CNN. Sometime when I wasn't looking, the world had apparently become one, but under the ethos of Rupert Murdoch not Eleanor Roosevelt.

At first glance, the main rule of the new era seemed to be no rules at all—no impediments. Leave people alone to make as much money for themselves as they could and the system would work. The worst people operating from their worst motives will somehow bring about good. Not that good was the goal. Acting consciously for the common good was, in fact, the one way to slow things down. One Eleanor Roosevelt could stop the flow completely. For the global era was based on rapid and massive flows of money which should not and—more to the point—*could* not be purposefully slowed or redirected. The money itself, it seemed, was the fluid that had unified the planet.

What does it mean to live in a world united by, or immersed in, the free flow of capital? Is it anything new? As a matter of fact, is it anything at all? I'd certainly heard enough about information highways and unstoppable capital flows. But to change our daily lives, there must be a more tangible mechanism at work than a semi-mystical flow of electrons representing that even more abstract entity, money. I wanted to get beyond the global babble, if I could, and look at the mechanism close up. Even more, I wanted to find out from ordinary people how, or whether, the new economic order affected them personally.

Rather than interview everyone in the world, or even a representative sample, I decided to let chance, and the flow of capital itself, carry me to my subjects. Loans and investments are the two basic ways to finance economic activity. The corresponding places where Americans like me put their extra money, in those years, were banks and mutual funds. So I would make a bank deposit and a mutual fund investment and then explore the global economy by following my own money. But first, I needed the money to do it with.

It's common for book publishers to advance money to writers, and normal to dole out the agreed-upon book advance in installments as the work progresses. I proposed to my publisher that I would deposit the first half of their advance in a small bank, then follow that money as it flowed out of the bank and into the wider world.

If that worked out (I'm sure they had their doubts), the publisher would give me the next installment, which I would invest in a US mutual fund.

But money isn't like a pebble that you can mark before you toss it into the stream. Because money is fungible, which is a way of saying interchangeable, my money—whether I deposit it as cash, a check, or rolls of pennies—immediately becomes an indistinguishable part of an *amount* available to the bank or mutual fund for all its activities. I'd have to take responsibility for the range of things being done with that money, then follow a few representative uses in detail.

At the time that I made my bank deposit, money was pouring out of Europe, Japan, and the US into Southeast Asia. Even though I started at a one-branch, small-town bank, the flow soon carried my money to people who were borrowing to spend in Thailand, Malaysia, and Singapore. I tagged along, predisposed, I guess, to see Asian slums and sweatshops.

But the truth is, it was exhilarating. Rapid economic growth means the peasant becomes a laborer, the laborer becomes a welder, the welder becomes a foreman, the foreman becomes a contractor, the contractor becomes a merchant, and the merchant becomes a banker. They may be racing in circles to music they don't control. Still, it's musical chairs played with more chairs than people. That game can be invigorating.

Frankly, I was surprised that an economic statistic—8 percent growth—should translate so directly into something I could see and just about feel on the streets of Bangkok. Certainly many Thais were displaced and actually made poorer by the projects that I financed. Still, the closer people came to my money, the better their chances of being swept up into the ascending spiral.

After the Asian currency crash (I'm sorry if I'm giving away the plot) I was surprised again by the scale and speed at which substantial things, not just blips on a screen or entries in a ledger but real stuff like food, clothing, friends, and security, disappeared.

When I call my mother in Florida after any much-reported hurricane, I invariably find that in her area there was only heavy rain. No one she knows personally is ever affected. But after the baht crash *everyone* I could get back to in Thailand, from street vendor to CEO, was affected drastically. Suddenly they were playing musical chairs with many *fewer* chairs than people. That game feels desperate.

Gradually I came to understand how my money, transformed into capital, had produced so much exhilarating and painful change.

The mutual-fund investment that I made with the second part of my book advance kept me in the US, where my fund managers drew money out of American companies (that surprised me since I thought investing meant putting money in), then moved on to do the same in Europe. On both continents they pushed for "downsizing" and other policies that pulled chairs away while people were still sitting on them.

When I was writing about other people's insecurity, I was objective enough to consider that this might be a temporary period of creative destruction. But when my mutual fund bought a big stake in my book publisher's company, the insecurity came too close to home. I wanted off the roller coaster but that was no more possible for me than for anyone else.

Money like mine, though generally in larger chunks, exerted unrelenting pressure on bankers and fund managers; it had to be invested. That pressure had helped create the current global economy and might just cause it to crash, but no one seemed able to slow it down.

It took me the entire journey to see exactly how my money contributed to the insecurity and desperation so many people live with. To connect the financial mechanisms with personal lives, I had to go step by step, asking embarrassingly ignorant questions of Wall Street bankers, Bangkok food vendors, Malaysian jellyfish exporters, Chinese labor contractors, illegal Burmese migrants, British engineers, Texas oil-company treasurers, Maine electric blanket weavers, Singapore shippers, US mutual-fund managers, and scores more, all drawn together by my money. They were sometimes hard to get to, but once I found them they almost always gave me direct answers. I'm still not sure why.

I started out, I must admit, with a head full of clichés about these people. But when they spoke they told me things I never could have imagined, but knew to be true as soon as I heard them. Everyone I met was surprising, but no one exotic. In that sense, we already live in one world.

I found that world so full of wonders that I'd hate for us to revert to a preglobal or postglobal provincialism. But what was exciting for a touring investor could be rough on the people I met along the way. And though I didn't start out with much environmental sensitivity, I couldn't help noticing that my global investments were also rough on the great globe itself. Toward the end of my travels I could see practical possibilities for a kind of globalism that might be less harsh. But I couldn't think about changes until I'd followed my own money at ground level and seen precisely how it works close up.

The *B*ank Deposit

So there I stood with a check for $29,500—half my book advance minus the agent's fee. If the earth's economy were truly one, like its oceans, this money would eventually reach everyone, everywhere. It shouldn't matter where I started. But to be as fair as I could, I determined to find a sound little bank that exemplified the most useful and decent banking principles. Yet it had to be typical—not some goody-good, socially relevant credit union.

Eventually I explained my requirements to a New York State bank examiner named Turhan Tirana, who gave me the names of three good small banks. He didn't say he had a favorite, but he got nostalgic when he remembered his visits to the Bank of Millbrook.

"It's an excellent small bank in horse country, an hour and a half up the Hudson [from New York City]. They've been around for a hundred years and they're privately owned, so they don't have to show increased earnings to shareholders every quarter. They can look at the long term; they don't have to crank out bad loans when times are tough. I find I can also tell how the local economy is doing," Tirana gave me a tip, "by stopping in at the tack shop on Main Street [Franklin Avenue]."

I wrote to all three banks, asking if they'd accept my deposit and spend an hour or two explaining where my money would go. To make it even more fair, I determined to give the honor to whoever said yes first. I'm not sure what I would have done if I didn't like the results. But the first and only response came from George T. Whalen III of the Bank of Millbrook.

Turhan Tirana had described the rolling countryside and the wealthy little village, but he hadn't prepared me for the bank itself. It was one of the most beautiful small buildings I'd ever seen.

Bank of Millbrook; small office of George T. Whalen III—midmorning

George T. Whalen III was the son of the bank's current president, George T. Whalen, Jr., and grandson of its previous president, George T. Whalen. "When you put your money in the Bank of Millbrook," young George informed me, "we make community loans, most of them in a five-mile radius of the bank."

My deposit would be unusual not only because I was writing a book, but because the bank didn't normally solicit out-of-town customers.

"Oh, we have some customers from out of our territory, even from New York [City], but that's misleading because Millbrook is a weekend community for some New Yorkers, so they have their household accounts here. They may pay the estate employees from these accounts because they couldn't cash his Citibank checks around here. Some of these people's household accounts are bigger than my main account," George volunteered. That was the first time I'd heard of a "household account."

"No," he answered my next question, "the bank of Millbrook would not become involved in loans to such a customer's weekday corporation. It couldn't even make the mortgage loan on a typical Millbrook estate, especially to an outsider.

"Let's say a stockbroker from New York making six hundred thousand a year buys a house in Millbrook. He loses his job. Is he going to get another six-hundred-thousand-dollar job?" George had no way of knowing. "So if he says 'George, I want an eight-hundred-thousand-dollar mortgage on my house,' I say 'That's just too big for us.' But if he's a weekend New Yorker and he wants to buy the next-door cottage, we'll put up seventy thousand toward it."

"Would the Bank of Millbrook ever syndicate a large loan?" I asked, using my brand-new banking vocabulary. "Perhaps with one of its correspondent banks?"

As a matter of law, no US bank can lend more than 15 percent of its capital to one borrower. As a matter of good sense, few would lend anything near that percent. So when large companies need big loans, a lead bank like Citibank or Chase rounds up other banks to participate in what's called a syndicated loan.

Small banks like Millbrook all have a special "correspondent" relationship with at least one money-center bank that can provide them with services like check clearing and foreign exchange. I was wondering whether the Bank of Millbrook might parcel out or "syndicate" an oversized loan through its correspondent bank.

"No," George answered. "The Bank of Millbrook is not in a position to do such a thing. What is too big for us to do alone might be too small for them to consider at all. What we would have," he explained, "is not correspondent banks, but friends. If we have a loan we'd like to do but it's too big, I might send half or a third of it to the Stissing National Bank of Pine Plains, which is about one-third our size but they have a similar philosophy to us. Robert Whalen is their president."

"That's your . . . ?"

"Uncle. So if we have a four-hundred-thousand-dollar loan—a little bigger than we'd like—I'll send a package to Pine Plains and my Uncle Bob will review it. Basically we invest in three things: local loans, Federal funds—no, four—US government securities, local bonds."

The most important of those, George stressed, were the local loans that he could make because he knew his community.

"If someone wants to start a—pizza place," George gestured letting me know that this was just a for-instance, "and he needs fifteen thousand dollars, he comes to me, shows me his business plan. I know him; I know the town. I can make the loan even if it's unsecured. Our bread and butter is the local full-time resident—the Main Street commercial loan.

"When no one else is coming in the door [for a loan], we invest in various financial instruments. The most liquidity is Federal funds, which we sell overnight to our correspondent banks. If a wealthy depositor wants us to wire all his funds out, we can get that money right back." The Federal-funds option is something I'd learn a great deal more about as I followed my money.

Senior Vice President Ron Mosca handled investments like government securities and Federal funds, George told me.

"My job is lending—and many other things. I originate the loans, sell them, actually negotiate the deals. But it's too small to say I'm going to do loans and that's it, because if Mrs. Jones comes in and says 'George, you have to help me balance my checkbook,' I also might be shoveling snow.

"But our basic bread and butter," George repeated in summary, "is the local Main Street loan."

The Bank of Millbrook was perfect. Only one thing worried me. Would it still be there when I finished my story?

"Have there been offers to buy the bank?" I asked.

"There have been people interested, but they know we're not for sale."

"What about a . . . a takeover?" I suggested reluctantly. The banking industry was consolidating at the time. Large banks were merging and small banks disappearing.

"Sixty-five percent of the stock is owned by the Whalens," George said. "So people know they can't buy the bank."

Because of bank licensing laws, I didn't have to worry that a large bank would open a branch in Millbrook and drive them out of business. In New York State, small banks serving communities of under fifty thousand people were deliberately protected from competition. The way the law was written, no large bank could open a branch in Millbrook unless it managed to buy the little bank's license. The justification for this interference with the market was that local banks tended to make more local loans, while branches of large banks tended to gather up local savings and send them out of town. The ultimate beneficiaries of the special protection were envisaged not as small-town bankers but as the New England fisherman who needed a boat loan and the Midwestern farmer who needed a seed loan.

But the Bank of Millbrook had the exclusive license to serve a community of tax-write-off horse-breeding estates. That ought to make its license so valuable, it seemed to me, that even family members might be tempted to sell.

"The Rockefellers sold Rockefeller Center," I reminded George. "The cousins needed the cash."

He recognized the problem. "When my grandfather ran the bank, he paid out very few dividends. He was the major shareholder, and his idea was to plow it back into the business because he'd just have to pay income tax on it. We have a similar philosophy now, but it's different because there are lots of

Whalens owning the stock and they have differing personal needs. But the Board of Directors are local businessmen and retired businessmen," George assured me. "I think we could say the Bank will be around."

The next week I deposited my $29,500—1,000 in a checking account and 28,500 in a savings account that paid under 3 percent interest. Then I strolled up Franklin Avenue past Reardon-Brigg's Hardware (est. 1907), past George T. Whalen, Inc., Real Estate Insurance with its own new building, and stopped at the tack shop, as Tirana had suggested.

"Horse breeding has had its ups and downs," the proprietor told me. "Ten years ago the Arabs came in and paid millions for yearlings. It subsided. Maybe the recession. Now it's coming back. Lots of people with regular jobs are riding now."

"Weekenders?" I asked, thinking of that six-hundred-thousand-a-year stockbroker.

"Yes, luncheon rides, you get to see the countryside, like a very tall trail walk, then you come back for the lunch.... Pony clubs, you start children young, then at college they meet the other pony-club people. It's a good way to make contacts."

That's just what I had to do. Now that I was a Millbrook depositor, I needed to contact borrowers.

The Pizza Puzzle

George had mentioned that he could lend $15,000 without collateral for a new pizzeria if he knew the owner and his business plan. That was, of course, a hypothetical pizzeria. No third-generation banker would discuss a particular customer's financial situation. But I also knew, after only an hour's acquaintance, that young George was not a fanciful person. Not that I'd want him to be. You don't want your dentist to start imagining he's a world-renowned surgeon and you don't want your banker to imagine, even for a moment, that he's a great venture capitalist. Let him take the money in at 3 percent and buy government bonds at 5 percent, never lend over 15 percent to any one entity, and never let his fancy wander enough to think, "but it's nine percent, it's J. P. Morgan, it's only overnight, just this once..." That's how honest banks get in trouble.

Weighing George Whalen III's balance of the two bankerly virtues, discretion and lack of imagination, I figured he must recently have lent not fifteen thousand to a pizzeria, but twenty thousand to a hamburger stand.

So I went up to the public library on the corner of Franklin and Friendly to browse through back issues of the local weekly, the Millbrook *Round Table*. The bank, I read in the *Round Table*, was seeking Planning Board approval for construction of a drive-through ATM. I also read that George III's father, George Whalen Jr. (who looks as distinguished as the movie version of himself) had accepted an award from the Boy Scouts, acknowledging with grace that he himself had never been a scout. But nothing about hamburgers. Wait. . .

A small picture on the front page of last week's paper showed a jaunty man in a baker's outfit. "His specialty is Pie," said the caption. "Pizza, that is. Denny Tyner follows up success in Stanfordville by opening Millbrook Pizza."

> "I opened this place because I know a lot of people in Millbrook" he said. "It's a nice little town and we wanted to get away from Poughkeepsie." His roots here extend to the early 1980's when Tyner started serving drinks at the Cottonwood Inn. Also, *his mother Millie cared for George Whalen Jr.'s deceased mother."* [Emphasis mine]

Well I'll be . . . son of faithful old retainer set up in life by grateful squire's son. But what about confidentiality? How could George have all but told me that Denny Tyner needed $15,000 and didn't have any security?

I went over to Millbrook Pizza, ordered a stuffed slice, and asked Denny about his new business.

It was his third pizzeria, he told me. "Two I'm running now and one that's still using my equipment. I paid ten thousand for all this," he pointed to the mixers and oven.

"Good buy." The other $5,000 must have gone into start-up costs, I thought, still assuming the $15,000 loan. "I saw in the paper that your mother took care of Mrs. Whalen."

Tyner searched his memory for a second, then "Oh, yeah. She made meals for her."

"So I guess you went to them for the loan?"

"Nah. I wouldn't go there."

"Oh?"

"I went to Poughkeepsie. That's where I do my business."

"Poughkeepsie? Hey, this is delicious!" It really was. "I'm sorry I don't have room to try your white pizza."

Then we got to talking about the fresh mozzarella and fresh ricotta you could get on Arthur Avenue in the Bronx.

"I use fresh *mozarel*," Denny said, "but fresh ricotta.... What they like here, you go into any of the galleries?" I nodded yes. "New antiques and phony art. There aren't enough Italians around here."

The next time I saw George Whalen I explained how I'd read that the mother of the fellow who opened the new pizzeria had nursed George's grandmother and I'd mistakenly assumed that George had been the match-maker who found the right person to fill the empty store. ("An empty store on Main Street is like a missing tooth in a smile," goes the expression.)

"No," said George. "We actually had another guy all set up who had a pizza shop in another town. But not Denny. No. But I'll have lunch there once in a while."

So George's hypothetical example had been an elliptical reference to a painful regret—the loan that got away.

Solving the pizza puzzle taught me several things. First and most important, *don't be a smart aleck.* However prosaic a person's words, they connect back to a web of references unique to each human being. If the reader will re-member this later when we speak to Asian peasants, I'll try to remember it when we speak to Wall Street Bankers.

The pizza puzzle also reminded me that loan opportunities in Millbrook are scarce and precious. Millbrook is a long-established and stable commu-nity. The shops may change hands from time to time, but the basic struc-tures are already built. It's what economists call a mature economy. That's one of the things that makes it such a nice place to live. But it makes it a dif-ficult place to sell loans.

Loans are in demand when new things are going up or when existing businesses are expanding so fast that they can't finance their growth them-selves. In more stable times many businesses can finance most of their op-erating expenses out of cash flow, so a dynamic banker looks for areas where things are growing or changing hands.

There had been another pizzeria at the location that was now Denny Tyner's. It had closed due to damage that occurred when the proprietor went away for too long. George didn't wait passively to see if someone else might take it over. He felt the town could support the shop (it hadn't closed for lack of business), so he went out and found someone with experience and energy who needed just a little capital to make it work. Unfortunately the owner of the property gave the lease to an outsider who didn't need the Bank of Millbrook. Or so he thought. (There was still a twist or two left in the pizza plot.)

The Merritt Bookstore

A wealthy, horsey, antiquing town is not necessarily a reading town. Yet Millbrook supported a spacious, two-floor, independent bookstore with a children's section as inviting and well used as the public libraries should be. Its proprietor, Scott Meyer, had been a substitute teacher who sometimes sold books outside the corner magazine store.

"Then a store opened up and the owner said, 'Scott, just go in and use it. I'll take ten percent of your profit.' I gave him twenty-one dollars for four months."

But Scott stayed in the book business, and "at the end of 1987 George Whalen the Third rented this store to me for three hundred dollars a month." Scott was speaking to me upstairs in an out-of-the-way corner, but people stopped often to say hello or ask him for recommendations.

I asked Scott about other dealings with the Bank of Millbrook. "Here," he said, pulling out papers each of which reminded him of a different connection to the bank. "I have my personal checking account with about fifteen dollars in it; two store checking accounts; I took out a business loan, twelve thousand dollars for bookstore fixtures; our personal savings; my son's savings. He's three and a half, but he knows about going to the bank.

"When publishers ask me for credit references I just say, 'call my bank, we have various accounts.' When I was having trouble getting a visa/mastercard—they turned me down because I have no credit history—Ron said, 'Don't worry, I'll write you a letter.' And I got it. And Ron said to me, 'You know, I had to write a letter for [he named a man reputed to be one of the richest people in town, whose family had been on the bank board for three generations] because he can't prove he works either.'

"They know me; they know my business. That can be a negative. But it can be good. If they know you, they can support you."

"Like how?" I asked.

"My wife and I decided it was time to buy a house. So I went into the bank and said, 'Could I get a mortgage?' I was dealing with Ron. He said, 'Okay, no problem, how much would you need?' I think George came over, too. So they walked me through the forms. Like, I didn't have enough money to get a hundred-and-fifty-thousand-dollar loan, so they said, 'How much do you think the goodwill of the store is worth? We'll pick a number to make it work.'

"Another advantage of their knowing my business if I have to order a single book from a publisher, I can send a blank check and let them fill in the price. I don't have to worry because if the bank sees a check like that come back filled in 'two thousand dollars,' they stop it. They know it's going to be under a hundred unless I call them to say otherwise.

"An independent bookstore and an independent bank, it's a perfect match," Scott enthused. "It's also a sounding board. I go to Ron and George, 'I've got this idea, will it fly?' "

"Like what kind of idea?"

"Like starting another bookstore. I'm negotiating with someone in Pine Plains. They told me call Bob Whalen [George's uncle who runs the bank there]. Some people approached us from another town, they desperately want a bookstore. If I do it, they're giving me the building to start and some money, and the school district will buy all their textbooks through us. . . . But Ron said to be very careful about that offer. It has a heavy debt. 'Be careful it isn't just real estate people that want you to take it over, but the town fathers are really behind you.'"

There was no end, it seemed, to the things the bank officers would do to help a local business.

"Once I needed something notarized when the bank was closed and Ron was there and he said, 'Sure, come over.'

"They have four thousand statements that go out every month. They said they'd put a flier in from us announcing future author appearances. By the way, when your book comes out . . .

"They work things out with people. They give employment to people who owe them money, I won't tell you who but ... you have the feeling if you called the Bank of Millbrook when you were away on holiday and you needed money, they'd just help you."

"Do they help you by buying books?" I asked.

"Not ... really. George is always saying he doesn't read. But George's wife comes in, and Ron's wife."

"If I didn't have the bank and people like George Whalen the Third, I might not be here, because they gave me a space from '88 to '92 at three hundred dollars a month, which is all the rent I could have afforded then; they knew my figures. And now," he summed up with great pride, "I'm paying a thousand three hundred and fifty dollars and paying off all these loans."

By helping Scott Meyer with loans, graduated rents, cautious business advice, advertisement—everything short of actually reading books—the officers of the Bank of Millbrook had developed a good tenant and a good loan customer. They'd also helped create a civic-minded businessman in their own image and, most miraculous to me, a thriving independent bookstore. Even if my book turns out not to suit Millbrook's reading public and Scott thinks better of his invitation for an author's appearance, every author is still grateful for every independent outlet for books.

How splendidly the bank of Millbrook fulfills its special role. Some people have spare money, other people have a use for it. Bankers *intermediate* between the two groups. I wouldn't have guessed that Scott Meyer could make an independent bookstore work in Millbrook. Besides, I couldn't risk lending him my book-advance money no matter how much confidence I had in his plan. But the Bank of Millbrook decided that he was creditworthy, and took on the risk themselves. Through their intermediation my money became a part of a pool available to Scott and other Millbrook entrepreneurs, even while the bank guarantees to return it to me—in full, with interest, whenever I ask—no matter how those businesses fare.

Not only that, but by a special arrangement with the US government, banks are authorized to create and lend out about ten times the amount of money that they take in in deposits. And all the money they create, within those limits, will be recognized as legal tender US currency. So my $29,500 could be leveraged into more than a quarter of a million dollars that people like Scott might use to create wealth for themselves and others. (The Merritt Bookstore employs three and a half permanent staff and eight to ten high school students.) I hope the bank makes more such loans, now that they have my money.

Of course a bank also fulfills its intermediation roll when it refuses a loan.

The Wild One

Ed Lodi is an architect with a small office in a corner of the Whalen Real Estate building. He's a slim, well-dressed man with a slight accent that I couldn't place.

"I've banked with Millbrook maybe twenty years," he told me. "I would have banked with them since I came to this part of the world thirty years ago, [It's a Hungarian accent, I realized—post-uprising?] but for my first experience.

"I set up a meeting about a mortgage. I showed up on my motorcycle with a helmet and I didn't get the mortgage. I didn't even get responded to.

"I went to Pauling [the bank in a nearby town] and got it without any trouble. Eventually I got to know the Whalens and I kid George Whalen about it now. But I refused to walk into the bank for about ten years."

Perhaps the bank was overcautious on the mortgage loan (or a little stodgy if the motorcycle was really the reason). Later, at the height of a real-estate boom, Lodi—by then a prizewinning regional architect—needed some money toward a $650,000 house he was building on speculation. The Bank of Millbrook turned him down again. "It was too risky for them. But this time I met with the Senior V.P. and George came in personally to give me the ax. I was very impressed with the way he did it."

"Yes, we got the loan from another bank," he answered my question. "And yes, it was paid back but we got singed on that business. Back in the 1980's everyone got singed on real estate and the banks ended up collecting property they didn't want. But not the Bank of Millbrook.

"I'll say this: if I had dealt with the Bank of Millbrook, I would have avoided that one because they pretty well analyzed the deal themselves. 'It's risky and I won't be part of it.' Of course if there's a killing to be made and it's risky, they won't be a part of that, either."

Though the bank eschewed Ed Lodi's risky propositions, they hired him as the architect on the parking lot that they were expanding for the town's use.

The real estate boom and subsequent crash that Lodi referred to hit major banks like Chase Manhattan and Citibank hard. In fact, bad real estate loans compounded by bad LDC (Less Developed Country) loans left Citibank technically bankrupt in the 1980's.*

Why, I wondered, had the Bank of Millbrook come so smoothly through a boom and bust that affected bigger banks so badly? One reason, the one George Whalen III would probably give first, is that the bank knows its community. But doesn't Chase Manhattan know Manhattan? Can't someone there sense when there'll be no more tenants to move into the last unneeded office building just as easily as the bank of Millbrook officers can guess when home building in the valley has gone far enough?

I once asked a model airplane flier how many turns to put on the rubber band and he said, "Go 'til it breaks, then do one less." For over a hundred years, there's been someone at the Bank of Millbrook with the economic intuition to stop before the rubber band breaks. They may also have been guided by a resident's esthetic sense. George III mentioned that his father tried to keep malls and giant discount stores out of the area. If he justified that in terms of economic self interest—protecting the bank's Main Street loans—George Whalen, Jr. would be on strong bankerly moral grounds. But if he consistently stopped several turns before the rubber band broke because he didn't want the area to change too fast, he would be faulted as an overcautious banker for impeding the full development of the area. Bank regulators actually look for a bad loan or two as a sign that a bank isn't too conservative.

Did the Whalen family consciously cultivate the kind of personal moderation that makes you stop with a dollar less than you might make? Did they consciously modulate the pace of change in Millbrook? Whalen character and caution certainly contributed to the bank's fine loan record. But there

---

*Many analysts say that US banks were brought through the decade by government policies that allowed them to take money from depositors at artificially low rates and use it to buy government securities at rates set high enough to guarantee safe profits—if they did nothing else.

must be some structural reason why the Bank of Millbrook can stop one turn short while the big banks cyclically break rubber bands and require rescuing.

Pizza Mystery Coda (flash forward)

Less than a year after I made my deposit, I read that Millbrook Pizza had changed hands again. The new owner, 22-year-old former manager, Lou Portaro, got his 15 minutes of fame in the *Round Table*, too. But he wasn't shown tossing the dough cockily like Denny. Lou's photo showed an earnest lad concentrating hard on spreading the cheese out evenly.

"How did you manage to buy the business?" I asked.

"I got a ten-thousand-dollar loan."

"Was it hard to get?"

Lou shrugged. "It's who you know in this town."

The landlord had gone to the Bank of Millbrook to initiate the loan for Lou.

"How come Denny sold it?" I asked.

"He didn't do too well."

"Well, if he didn't do too well, how will you?"

"I know everyone in this town, they like me. . . . My father owned the pizzeria around the corner, where Rocco's is now."

"They buy pizza if they like you?"

"It's who you know in this town."

I couldn't engage Lou in a conversation about ricotta, and I was surprised to hear that he would be changing Denny's recipes. But I guess he knew Millbrook tastes, because less than a year later, he moved—with another bank loan—from the take-out place to the vacated ice cream parlor across the street where he could serve meals. On weekdays his mother would help him. "She cooks on one of the estates, weekends," Lou told me. She would leave some prepared dishes on those days.

Perhaps Denny Tyner's Millbrook venture would have turned out better if he'd used the local bank. Not just opened an account, but sought their advice and contacts, respected their knowledge of the community, and been more, not exactly 'umble but . . . Lou Portaro wasn't embarrassed to say that his mother cooked on one of the Millbrook estates, but Denny had seemingly forgotten that his mother had cared for Mrs. Whalen. In Millbrook these things may matter more than a good crust.

Lou Portaro and Scott Meyer are the kind of positive young people I'd be pleased to have as neighbors. Why, then, do I have such sympathy for a guy like Denny Tyner? Partly, I suppose, because I liked his pizza. I also sense that if I'd grown up near Millbrook, I too would have felt like an outsider. Even if I'd been raised as part of the *household-account* class, I'd probably have been too prickly, at least when younger, to accept Whalen beneficence graciously.

So the nice people drove the grump out of Happy Valley. No, that's not a fair way to look at it. People have the right to buy the pizza they like in the atmosphere they choose. Market forces replaced an out-of-towner with a Bank of Millbrook borrower. But the bank did nothing unethical to increase its dominance in the pizza sector.

I also found the bank blameless in the only thing resembling a financial scandal I came across in the area.

A couple of months after I made my deposit, I read the Millbrook *Round Table* headline, "Union Vale Residents Demand Vote on New Town Hall Plan." Union Vale was another town in Millbrook's county. George had mentioned the Union Vale town hall loan several times. It was one of the bank's biggest deals. But the *Round Table* article, accompanied by a photo of grim citizens seated shoulder-to-shoulder on folding chairs, explained that the proposed $750,000 town hall loan would raise local taxes by about 30 percent.

About a hundred Union Vale citizens, who didn't look as affluent as Millbrookians, were listening to a North Clove resident whose trim beard, gleaming dome, narrow tie, and dark vest made him look remarkably like Lenin, at least in the photo.

"We fought a revolution over taxation without representation," he was quoted as saying. "We want a vote on this issue."

It turns out that a town hall proposal had been voted down by referendum five years earlier. But the current project didn't legally require a referendum, because the entire loan would be paid back in five years. That's why the temporary tax increase had to be so steep. Since residents had already voted down a new town hall, they felt that a bit of fancy financing was being used to rob them of their right to decide.

There was another side to the story, of course. The town government had been asked to vacate its temporary headquarters in Tymor's barn, and paying the loan back in five years instead of thirty would more than halve the cost. I didn't know enough to have an opinion about the need for a new building. But I understood that the expense being crammed down people's throats was one of the biggest yet safest loans that the bank of Millbrook had going, and by this time my money would be in the mix.

When I went to investigate the bank's role in the deal, I found the ex-supervisor—the power broker attacked by town hall opponents—and the woman who'd replaced him chatting in her office in the already-completed new town hall. (You can act quickly when you don't need popular consent.) She sat demure and erect, like a visitor, while he sprawled large, Tammany-ish, and very much at home.

In answer to my carefully neutral question, the new supervisor explained that the town hall was financed by a Tax Anticipation Note to be paid back $150,000 a year plus 5 percent of the balance. The money would come directly out of tax revenues on which the bank had first claim. (That's what made it such a safe loan.) The Bank of Millbrook had given them "fantastic" terms on the loan, the current supervisor was explaining, when the ex-supervisor just had to interrupt.

"When you pay something off in five years, you're not subject to a referendum. Judy will tell you, there's a lot of people didn't want this town hall." He paused to make sure I copied that down. The antidemocratic maneuver I'd been careful not to accuse them of was the very accomplishment this political pro didn't want left out of the story.

"Was the Bank of Millbrook helpful in getting it through?" I asked.

"THEM?" he laughed. "Nah, they wouldn't get involved with that."

That laugh answered all of my questions, but I probed a little further.

"You mean because they're from the next town and they don't have any influence to use here?"

"I don't think they would've even if they were in this town," he said dismissively.

"I believe some people wrote them letters telling them not to make the loan," said Judy. "I know who it was."

"But it went through," said the ex-supervisor victoriously. "This," indicating the edifice, which looked and smelled like the inside of a swimming pool, "will be free and clear in five years."

It takes one to know one, they say. Well, it also takes one to know who's *not* one. That politician's laugh was all the proof I needed that the Bank of Millbrook was as decent and straightforward as it seemed.

I've never had any reason to change that opinion. In the course of my travels I would encounter larger banks working with more powerful politicians to foist my money onto communities in the form of questionable, costly loans. But I was never ashamed of anything the Bank of Millbrook did locally with my deposit. As a matter of fact, I keep a small account in Millbrook to this day. My story might have started and ended there, too, except for one problem. The Bank of Millbrook can't find enough interest-paying local uses for my money.

Not that there weren't needs. The neighboring town of Dover Plains was a poor, scruffy place that might have been improved by a bookstore. It was the end of the line for the train I took to the bank and the taxi drivers who took me on to Millbrook were generally overeducated. One woman had been a social worker at a local hospital until it closed. She might have liked the atmosphere at the Merritt Bookstore, but she wouldn't have bought very many hardcover books at list prices.

Dover Plains was just too poor to support enterprises like the Merritt Bookstore. If it was hard to make good loans in the wealthy, mature economy of Millbrook, it was even harder in poor, underdeveloped Dover Plains.

My money could only stay on earning interest in Millbrook, because the bank, while keeping it fully available to me, passed it along at the same time (another banking miracle) for other banks to lend out. They did this through the vehicle Ron and George referred to as Fed funds.

Fed Funds

Every bank that does business in the US is required to keep an account with a certain minimum—it's calculated in a complicated manner but amounts to about 3 percent of deposits—at the Federal Reserve Bank. This account doesn't receive any interest, so banks don't like to keep more money, more Federal funds, as this money is called, in their Federal Reserve accounts than they have to. On the other hand, if they fall below their reserve requirement, there are severe penalties. Being overdrawn at the Fed is such a taboo that no banker I asked even knew what the penalties were.

The goal of every bank, therefore, is to meet its reserve requirement (which changes with each day's inflows and outgoes) while having as little extra in the account as possible. It's tricky. One way banks solve the problem is to lend and borrow (sell and buy) the uninvested money among themselves. In other words, there's a market among banks for their extra Fed funds.

Small-town banks like Millbrook, which receive a lot of deposits but can find only limited uses for their money on Main Street, usually wind up with more unused cash than they need at the end of the day. Banks like Citi or Chase, which lend to multinational corporations, have regular though not entirely predictable needs for extra money to balance their Fed-funds account.

The small banks generally sell money to their correspondent banks. I knew when I started this study that any small bank I choose would have a correspondent among the major Wall Street banks. I assumed, for no good reason, that Millbrook's would be Citibank. I'd been trying, with some success, to line up contacts at Citi's fortresslike public-relations department.

As it turned out, the Bank of Millbrook had had a correspondent relationship with Citibank until recently. When I asked George why they had broken it off, he answered that "they might have broken off with us. We might have been too small-potatoes for them."

Chase was now Millbrook's primary correspondent bank. It was a very important relationship—so important and so new that Ron asked if I would refrain from mentioning Millbrook's name when I first went up to Chase. He realized that I would eventually use Millbrook's name in my book, but asked that for the meantime I "just say 'one of your correspondents.' They have thousands."

Fed funds are sold on a daily basis. During the period covered by this book, Millbrook was lending Chase between one and three million dollars a day (generally closer to, or slightly over three million.) So the very day that I made my deposit, that night to be exact, a chunk of my money went over to Chase Manhattan.

Using those dollars to meet its reserve requirements, Chase could send many more times that money out into the world. Those multiples of my money might leave Chase through many different exits, but it was at the Fed-funds desk that I could watch my money come into the Chase system.

I was lucky enough to make contact with the unpretentious senior vice president who ran the Chase Fed-funds desk. His job was to keep track of all Chase's inflows and outgoes and, on that basis, buy or sell enough Fed funds from other banks to keep the Chase Federal reserve account *just* balanced. He invited me to spend a day watching how he did it.

Wall Street area, Chase Manhattan Plaza, 35th-floor trading room—weekday morning

"Bearlike," I scribbled in my notebook when Gardner Young met me at the elevator. Shambling and hearty is what I meant. I'd called the day before to ask how a Fed-funds desk works, and Gardner had plunged in right on the phone.

"People filter in numbers from all over the bank, I get on a computer with a spread sheet... fourteen phone lines... I'm talking to you on a head set ... notes come in, tickets ... "

The basic job of a Federal-funds desk is to keep track of inflows and outgoes from all parts of the bank and then buy or sell enough money so that Chase meets its reserve requirement with as little extra money as possible lying around earning no interest. Gardner had invited me up to the trading room for a day to see how he did that. Now he continued the explanation in person as he led me across the trading floor.

"We get the numbers on asset-backs—they close out about one o'clock; we get the loans made and repaid; gross figures for real estate come in in the morning—we look at the delta, the changes. Today it's two billion [all the other bankers I'd met at Chase had been graciously vague]... we do commodities, TT and L accounts, we downstream money to Chase Delaware, which is our credit card bank, we get the ... " It was a relief to meet a big banker so proud of what he does.

But I had a hard time getting it down while walking and looking up, for Gardner was also pointing out the security traders, currency traders (much quieter than I'd imagined), and scores more who sat in front of computers, buying and selling.

"All this," he gestured around the enormous trading room, "that also feeds into us."

Us, I saw when we got to the Fed-funds desk, was Mark, Phil, and Gardner, all wearing polos and chinos (the uniform for dress-down Friday) plus Marie who managed to look like she really was dressed down for a backyard barbecue. They all sat family-style on one side of a long table.

"And that's where *your* money comes in." Gardner pointed to the other side of the table and introduced me to Robert and Warren. "They handle the small banks. They get the aggregate and it's filtered into my numbers along with all the other elements. It's about six hundred million."

That figure, which included the Bank of Millbrook's three million, was one of the most predictable of Gardner's inputs.

"Even if we're long on money that day [if they had more than enough deposits to meet their reserve requirement] we still buy Fed funds from our correspondent banks. It's a service. But to close our position, we buy or sell from brokers in lots of twenty-five million.

"Right now,"—Gardner pressed a few keys to get a number on his spreadsheet—"we estimate that we're three billion dollars long."

That meant that despite buying three million from the Bank of Millbrook, the basic task of the day was to unload three billion dollars.

"It's up to us, at the end of the day, to make sure that we're solvent but not so solvent we have money sitting idle."

And he sat down with the others to do it.

There was nothing tense about their trading. I heard many have-a-nice-weekends and same-heres. At the end of most calls, the speaker usually wrote up a ticket (a sell or buy order) and tore it off one of the small, colored order pads. A lot of unfamiliar phrases were coming at me from many directions, but it sounded like Gardner's team was dealing not in the twenty-five-million-dollar lots he'd mentioned but in the low millions, and talking to regular companies, as opposed to other banks.

Technically, private companies can't trade in Fed funds. But Gardner could, he explained, buy idle money from the bank's good customers as a favor.

"This, for instance, is a corporate telephone asset." He held back one of the slips headed for a spindle. Yes, Fed-fund orders in the millions were scribbled by hand and spiked onto old-fashioned metal spindles. "The company deposits dollars with Chase Nassau over the weekend. Twelve million, see, 8/5 to 8/8." He pointed out the dates on the slip, Friday to Monday, and the amount, which was $12,471,008.72. "Monday it will be reversed with interest."

"How do you know the dollars are really there?" I asked, wondering if I could earn three days' interest on twelve and a half million nonexistent dollars simply by calling late on a Friday and saying, "Hold it for me over the weekend."

"If we go to debit their account at Chase and it's not there, we won't pay it back with interest," Gardner answered. "It happens on a regular basis that people forget to make a deposit or send it to the wrong bank. It leaves us a little short-funded but it's not a big deal. So they were supposed to send a few million to Chase and they sent it to Chem instead."

"Oh, I see. You have to already have put the money in the bank." I'd had the same unoriginal thought as everyone else who came close to money creation: "Why not create a little extra for me? Just say it's there." My own streak of larceny was so humble that all I wanted was the interest on my imaginary money. Still, it had diverted me from a truly significant aspect of that twelve-million-dollar transaction. Fortunately I caught the last phrase of another routine transaction: "Okay. Put it in Chase Nassau," Gardner said—and this time it rang a bell.

"What was that thing about Nassau?"

The treasurer of a small hospital wanted to sell (lend) Chase $1,350,000 over the weekend. Gardner had said he'd take it. "Maybe they just got a Medicare payment," he speculated as he wrote up the ticket. "This money is their cash flow. If they have to pay an electric bill, it goes down. But they don't want it sitting idle over the weekend."

The problem is that it's illegal to pay interest on corporate checking accounts. That regulation was put in place during the great depression of the 1930's to keep the convalescing banks from competing too strenuously for money. It may or may not have been in their own best interest then, but it was a nuisance now. To get around that US law, the hospital must make its deposit in Nassau.

"The federal government stops twelve miles offshore," Gardner reminded me.

"Will that make it a Eurodollar dollar?" I asked, trying to sound casual.

"Yes," he answered.

Wait! Stop! This is a Eurodollar; this is offshore banking! This is the most powerful, most subversive, most global force in the entire global economy! A little background is in order.

Eurodollars

Before Eurodollars (before the 1960's, say), if that hospital had wanted to get around a US law or take advantage of higher interest rates abroad, it would first change its US dollars into the local currency. In this case they would then have had an account denominated in Nassau dollars. When they wanted the money back there'd be another currency exchange. But the exchange rates could easily have fluctuated enough to wipe out the weekend's interest. They might even have lost money. The small hospital would have been taking on an exchange risk frightening enough to discourage most such transactions. All that changed with the Eurodollar.

There are conflicting legends about who "invented" the Eurodollar. But all Euro-lore starts with the Cold War. In the late 1940's, when the Soviet and Chinese Communist governments sold goods in the US, they accumulated dollars in their New York bank accounts. It would have been silly to change that money into rubles, renminbi, or any other currency when so much of what they wanted in the world could only be bought for dollars. But as the Cold War intensified, it also began to seem silly—in fact dangerous—to leave their money where the US government could seize or freeze it. They needed a bank outside the US that would accept that money *as dollars,* and pay interest on it.

According to one origin myth, the first Eurodollar was created, or booked, for the Soviets at their own Narodny Bank in Paris. I like that version because, Chase Manhattan was Narodny's main correspondent bank at the time. That would mean that someone from Chase must have helped the Soviet Union transfer that first Eurodollar. The Narodny Bank story is the one Martin Mayer tells in *The Bankers*.

But others trace it back to the Chinese, who in 1949 managed to move almost all of their US dollars to the Soviet-owned Banque Commercial Pour L'Europe du Nord, also in Paris. According to this version, the Chinese not only created their Eurodollars first, but did it through a series of transfers that kept the ownership secret. They did it just in time, too. In 1950 (The Korean War), the US government froze all that was left in Chinese accounts in the US.

But the important thing is not who booked the first Eurodollars, but who began trading them. Walter Wriston, arch-foe of government intervention (except when it bails his bank out), was head of Citibank during the years in which Eurodollars grew from an anomaly used to meet odd needs like the Soviets' to become the dominant world currency.

In *The Twilight of Sovereignty*, he too traces Eurodollars back to Communist governments keeping their dollar deposits abroad. But for Wriston, the big breakthrough came in the mid-1950's when the Soviets went looking for better interest rates and convinced an Italian banking cartel to give them more interest than those dollars could legally have earned if they were still deposited in the US.

That meant that the Italian bankers had to find customers ready to borrow the Soviets' dollars and pay above the US's legal interest-rate caps for their use. And they did. From then on the gloves—and the caps—were off. If the US (or any other government, for there were soon Euromarks, Euroyens, etc.) set interest rates too high or too low, people could buy or sell their currency outside the home country for what this new Euromarket, not some bureaucrat, determined. If a government passed some pesky law about interest on corporate checking accounts, a corporation could deposit its dollars, *as dollars*, in some sovereign state that did not have such a law.

One of the first and still most important victories for the new currency occurred in the 1960's, when US companies were starting to expand abroad so rapidly that they created a chronic balance of payments deficit (more money going out than coming in). To slow the process, the Kennedy administration enacted a series of regulations of the kind called *capital controls*. These made it more difficult or more expensive to spend or invest dollars abroad. So banks like Chase and Citi helped US companies send their money out of the country as Eurodollars. That way they could lend, buy, set up foreign sub-sidiaries, move factories abroad, and so on, free from both currency risk and the US government's capital controls.

This was quite a bit more important to US companies than the right to get interest on their spare cash over the weekend. It was more important to US citizens as well: This was the start of the era when the US dollar not only *could* move abroad freely but *did*.

Starting in the 1970's and continuing to this day, American firms began to close US factories and either move them abroad or pay foreign contractors to make part or all of their products. This involves the transfer of a great deal of money abroad, but no US capital controls could seemingly impede the flow because it was moved as Eurodollars. So the Eurodollar was the main in-strument that facilitated, though it did not cause, what is exaggeratedly called the deindustrialization of America.

By the 1990's, The Federal Reserve estimated that about two-thirds of US currency was held abroad as Eurodollars. I find it hard to imagine how the Fed makes their estimates now that I've seen how fast the hospital's dollars move offshore and back. Despite the difficulty of keeping tabs, everyone agrees that the Euromarket is vast and, more to the point, can be increased instantly if any "sovereign" state passes regulations that are unpalatable to people who have lots of money.

Unlike Citibank, the Soviets had no plot to subvert capitalist govern-ments. But "by initiating these transactions," wrote Walter Wriston, "the Sovi-ets were among the fathers of the Euromarket." Eurodollars and Euromarket are "by their very existence," Wriston declared, "symbols of the growing fu-tility of government attempts to regulate capital."

So this is stateless capital. When economists worry (or, in Wriston's case, gloat) that nations are now powerless before global capital, Eurodollars are the kind of instrument that they have in mind. And I had just seen millions of them created. Indeed, some of my own money would be Eurodollars by the afternoon.

Of course, the hospital's 1.35 million is a very small Eurodollar deposit. The hospital treasurer wasn't going offshore to discipline governments, deindustrialize nations, or even escape taxes. He just wanted to collect a little interest over the weekend to look like he was earning his pay.

"When you tell a corporate treasurer to put it in Nassau, what does he physically do?" I asked. "I mean, where is it?"

"He doesn't physically do anything," Gardner laughed. "It's what we call book activity. It's an entry in our general ledger."

"But where are the books?"

"It's run out of New York."

"A special Eurodollar branch?"

"For all I know there may be a teepee or a trailer downstairs."

"But nobody in Nassau?" I'd imagined a Bahamian lawyer—a bit of a sharpie but good-natured—with the licenses for the Nassau branches of all the world's money-center banks hanging on the wall behind his desk. "Not even a clerk in Nassau?" I asked, disappointed.

"If we say put it in Chase London, well, there is a London. And there *may* also be a Chase bank in Nassau, as it happens. But it's a bookkeeping entry. It's a paper creation. Something the government set up for us."

"Something the US government set up? I thought the government was against..."

"Gardner, a hundred million." We were interrupted by a dulcet voice on the intercom and Gardner had to attend to more money coming in.

My Money

While Gardner was occupied, I drew up a chair at the side of the Fed-funds desk where Robert, dignified, sad, and slightly cross-eyed, and Warren, who looked like a mole, handled the small banks. Under their Good Till Changed program, a preset amount, in Millbrook's case around three million, was moved from each small bank's account into Chase's account at night, then moved back the next morning automatically, *till* such time as the small bank's instructions about the amount were changed.

"The small banks, they produce about six hundred million in core funding every day," Robert told me. "Five years ago it was over a billion but because of consolidation of banks..."

Robert was leading me through a typical Good Till Changed transaction. "Six million, three hundred fifty thousand. It's transferred back with the interest that's, let's see [getting a bank's record on the screen] seven hundred forty-nine dollars and sixty-five cents is the net increase to their account. That happens every business day if they don't call..." My attention was caught by Warren, speaking on the telephone. Actually it wasn't his words that caught my attention, but his pauses.

"Oh...so that means...you're not going to...[his mouth puckered, quivered] sell me any more? Yeah, but..."

"Another bank buyout," Robert muttered to me in a tone that meant "par for the course." Some large bank had just annexed one of Warren's small bank customers. Now the small bank would no longer need the Chase relationship. That had become very common as large banks merged and small banks like Millbrook disappeared. But Warren sounded as if his wife of 30 years had announced with no warning that she was going off with someone else.

"B of A in San Francisco?"

"Yeah, but...but we gave you good rates, John."

"No....Oh....Oh.... Are you changing your name then, too?"

Warren just couldn't grasp that it was over.

"Well, I mean, if there's a possibility they might let you sell funds to us...or is everything going to go to B of A?"

"Funny...you know, I was going to call you because we noticed you sold us a million in April, May, and June and not July, and we wondered...so I was going to call...."

"All right, John. Good luck."

"God ..." He set the receiver into its cradle. "Bank of America, Hawaii."

Most countries have long had a few large nationwide banks. But until recently, US banks were legally limited to operate only within state lines or even smaller boundaries. At the time I was writing, those restrictions were falling by the wayside. Large and medium-sized banks were consolidating to form what, I assume, will be a handful of dominant national banks by the time you read this book.

As a small bank in a small town, Millbrook was still protected by the licensing law that made it necessary for a larger bank to buy the smaller bank if they wanted to do business in that town. But many of the remaining small banks left in the US turned out to have a price.

A few years before my visit, Bob and Warren serviced more than 300 small banks. But Good Till Changed had shrunk to 152—now 151—as banks like the Liberty Bank of Honolulu became branches of Bank of America.

Some of the shrinkage had been accomplished by Chase itself. When New York regulations eased, Chase had bought many of the independent upstate banks that Robert used to handle. "We would say to little banks like yours, 'This is money.'" He made a come-hither expression while thumbing an imaginary wad of bills. But Millbrook shareholders had thus far resisted the temptation.

I was increasingly proud of my little bank and sorry that I was pledged not to mention its name. I had only told the people at the Fed-funds desk that I was following my money from a bank with about 70 million in assets. (Chase assets at the time were 116 billion.)

"Seventy-five," someone called teasingly to me from the other side of the desk, as he wrote up the ticket for the sale of 75 million dollars to another money-center bank. "I just moved more than your bank's total assets—in one transaction."

About time, I thought. When I'd arrived at 9:30 A.M., Gardner told me he was three billion long. When the Federal Reserve called him at 11:00 he was three and a half billion long. A half-billion more to get rid of if we wanted to neatly balance. I was getting worried.

Every day at about 11:00, The Federal Reserve called Gardner and his counterparts at several other money-center banks to ask their *positions*— were they short or long, not how they felt about free speech in Afghanistan. The Fed also asked Gardner his *view*.

"That means, how will we handle that position," he explained. "The interest on Fed funds was four and a quarter this morning." Banks receive no interest for the money in their Fed-funds accounts, but they do charge each other for the Fed funds that they lend or borrow to meet reserve requirements. That rate hovers around a number set by the Federal Reserve, but it fluctuates within a narrow band. "If we're thinking rates will go up, we'll hold onto the money and wait till it goes to four and three-eighths to sell it. They call to find out what the market is thinking."

I was impressed. I knew by then that Gardner was smart and articulate. But I looked at him a little differently when I realized that the Central Bank of the United States of America regarded Gardner Young as "the market" and phoned daily to assess his thinking.

One reason that the Federal Reserve Bank consulted the market, in the person of Gardner Young, was to find out about the demand for the Fed's own products—US money and credit. If banks were short, the Fed could lower reserve requirements. Then banks could lend greater multiples of my money. With the present reserve requirements, the US banking system could legally lend out about ten times the amount of the deposits it took in.

The Fed could also affect how freely credit and money flow around the country by indirectly raising or lowering the interest rate on Fed funds. When reporters say that the markets are poised waiting to see if the Federal Reserve Bank will raise interest rates, it's the Fed funds' rate they're referring to. Yes, the Fed funds that we've been talking about, the money that Millbrook lends to Chase, create that all important "benchmark" that the Federal Reserve Bank fools around with when they want to stimulate or restrain the economy.

But it's not something they'd do simply to help Gardner Young with his day's task. He still had to dump three and a half billion dollars. That's why I thought "About time" when I started to hear numbers like 50 and 75 instead of five and six. It's amazing how quickly one's sense of scale expands. Everyone at the Fed-funds desk, including me after only one morning, meant *million* when we said five or six. The scale shrunk back, however, when one went out the trading room door.

"The profit-sharing envelopes are out at the desk," Marie reported, returning from the ladies' room. Suddenly zeroes dropped off. People were now concerned with the difference between five or six *hundred* in their own profit-sharing bonus. Someone joked that "Warren will need a wheelbarrow for his share, he's been here so long." So perhaps we were talking thousand or even tens of thousands in some cases. I didn't dare ask. Everyone was being so open with me about millions and billions, but I knew they'd clam up if I asked about real money.

"Thank you, M—!" Warren put down the phone, beaming.

One of his small banks had called to sell Chase two million dollars every night for a fixed term of 185 days at a fixed rate. Immediately there came a call from a second bank placing a different amount for the same term. This time Warren jumped, literally jumped lightly several times for joy.

"What are you doing over there," Gardner joked, "giving away toasters?"

"They must have talked to each other," Warren said and he wrote up the tickets in a large round hand with a big black felt pen. "M— is my best customer."

Buying money was Warren's job. He and Robert would be unemployed if it wasn't for the small banks. But no one else seemed particularly enthusiastic about their success.

"We don't make anything on this product," Robert had explained to me about Good Till Changed. "It costs about seven or eight dollars a ticket every night. But our correspondents will purchase other services [like foreign-exchange trading or investment services] down the line. That's how we justify maintaining it. It's an accommodation."

Meanwhile, Gardner had just told his co-worker Phil to accept 22.3 (meaning millions or course) from a company, also as an accommodation.

"But, but, but . . . " I spluttered. I couldn't understand why they were taking more money when they had three billion to get rid of that day.

"They're a good customer," Gardner explained. "I can sell it though the brokers. Don't worry, it works out."

I felt certain that Gardner knew his business. Still, the bulk of the morning's transactions, at least those I could follow, seemed to involve buying money, not selling it, usually as a favor to some good corporate customer.

But by the afternoon the calls were coming from other banks, either directly or through brokers, and they were buying. By 3:00 P.M., yellow slips jogged past with numbers like 25 and 35. After 4:00, the callers were all banks and the mix more international. The sums were vast now and the names so illustrious that they resonated like the catalogue of ships in the Iliad.

All the big banks in the world are Chase's Fed-funds partners. Their names are not secret, and borrowing Fed funds is nothing to be ashamed of. As a matter of fact, it's an indication that a bank has big customers with real need for money. Still, I had promised Gardner that I wouldn't use customers' names when describing *specific* transactions.

But God is in the details and, for me, in the rhythms. Maybe I can convey the epic grandeur of the afternoon's global crescendos with simulated names.

"Banco de Paella, eighty at three-eighths."

"The Dashi Bank of Tokyo, eighty at five-eighths."

"The Frankfurter, Hamburger and Koenigsberger Klopse, one hundred million at four and five-eighths!"

No use. You need the real names.

"We haven't heard from mighty Aetna yet," Phil said at 6:15. "Nor Merrill," Gardner added. Surely I can name *non*-customers. But then the phone rang at 6:29 [Fed-funds trading closed at 6:30]. "What's this late? Only Morgan," Phil speculated.

"—million is what they have on their line," Gardner reminded him, flipping through the printout that assigned a credit limit to all the banks they might conceivably deal with.

I can't tell you whether that final customer of the day was in fact the Morgan Bank, nor what Morgan's credit line was, nor how much was left on it. But even for the venerable house of Morgan, Gardner would not have exceeded the assigned credit limit, because a Fed-funds sale is an unsecured, overnight loan. If a bank went broke by morning—it's happened—Chase would be out real money.

But within these credit limits, the banks of the world pass my money around freely, and much faster than ever before. What would happen to the flow, some experts wondered, if dozens of banks went bankrupt at the same time? With everyone buying and selling money from everyone else continuously, it would be hard simply to figure out who owed what to whom. But there had already been some bank failures in the electronic era, and computers didn't seem to be either the problem or the solution. So far, things had come out okay because governments had made up the losses.

Gardner had arrived at seven in the morning. He closed the Fed-funds desk at 6:30 in the evening. As we left the trading room, the Foreign Exchange desk was still trading intensely.

Bank brochures explain that these money traders facilitate commerce by helping customers to purchase the foreign currency they'll need to do business abroad. Foreign-currency fluctuation can be tricky. A manufacturer agrees to pay so many deutsche marks for a shipment of parts that he'll need six months from now. But if the relative value of the dollar and the deutsche mark changes, he may need more dollars than he'd thought. No sound businessman agrees to buy something for an unknown price. He can't offer his customer a price now when he doesn't know what the components will cost him until later. To take the gamble out of the deal, the bank may arrange a futures contract. You agree now to pay so many dollars six months from now for the deutsche marks you'll need then.

That's not about making a profit on exchange-rate fluctuations, it's about allowing a businessman to know in advance what it will cost, in his own currency, to produce his product. This is a very useful service. And the explanation is true, although only for about 2 percent of the foreign-exchange transactions.

The other 98 percent of currency trading is done in an attempt to profit from the constant changes in exchange rates. Buy deutsche marks for dollars, hold them for six minutes (six minutes is not a short-term, but a medium-term trade), exchange them at a prearranged rate for baht or pesos, make a small profit (a hundred thousand here, a hundred thousand there, it adds up), then proceed to the next trade.

Unlike the trade in goods and services, where orders stimulate production that didn't exist before and thereby make the world richer, this speculative currency trading is a purely I win/you lose (or vice versa) gambling game. Unfortunately, there could be a hundred million losers who never even placed a bet. But that's something I learned later.

Gardner's own Fed-fund trading would soon be expanded to 18 hours a day, he told me. He was looking forward to that, he said, because, "then they'll *have* to have two shifts."

When we said goodbye near the basement candy stand (Gardner was headed to the underground parking garage and I to the subway), Chase was still a billion dollars long. But it wasn't quite the problem I thought because banks settle with the Fed every other Wednesday, not every day. That meant that they only had to have met their average daily reserve requirements over the two-week period. Those biweekly Settlement Wednesdays are the really hectic days when all banks are lending and borrowing to make sure their reserve accounts were retroactively "just" balanced.

So the desk had done well enough, that day, by moving two and a half billion. Especially since we'd started out buying money from the small banks at four and one quarter (Good Till Changed customers always got the morning's opening price) and wound up selling it to big banks at the end of the day for two or three eighths more. Wait a minute, who's *we?* How quickly I begin rooting for the team I'm sitting with, no matter what the game.

Actually, the Fed fund's desk isn't primarily a trading game, and Gardner's principal mandate was neither to outmaneuver the Bank of Millbrook nor to make a huge profit. I could never have spent a day kibitzing at a high-pressure, high-turnover, buy-cheap-sell-dear profit center like the foreign-exchange desk. Nor would I be invited to watch "a day in the life of" at a department where urbane bankers woo big borrowers and set policy by structuring highly negotiable deals.

Though Gardner was as senior as any other senior vice president, a Fed-funds desk is less about trading or lending than about *compliance.* Its primary function is to keep a bank in compliance with US Federal Reserve regulations.

Which brings me to a question that had been troubling me since I first saw Gardner create Eurodollars. Why do banks bother to comply? At the time of my visit, Chase's reserve requirement, though a surprisingly small percent of its deposits, averaged about 450 million dollars a day. (Millbrook's was about half a million.) It's expensive to keep 450 million dollars in a non-interest-paying account. But there are no reserve requirements on Eurodollars, and no Federal Deposit Insurance premiums either. So why doesn't Chase thumb its nose at reserve and insurance requirements the same way it thumbs its nose at US regulations about interest on corporate checking accounts? Why doesn't it do all its business through Nassau?

One tentative answer I came up with is that banks *like* reserve requirements. Or at least they accept them in the same way that most of us accept traffic laws. We may be tempted to go through a long red light, on an empty street, in the middle of the night—just this once. (The Bank of Millbrook never would, of course.) But we accept and usually follow the rules because we appreciate the convenience of safely flowing traffic.

It's extremely convenient for banks to be able to pass money around freely through their Federal Reserve accounts. But with all those blips streaming so rapidly through the wires, any crash would mean a horrendous multibank pileup. Reserve requirements and their equivalents in other banking systems keep the banks from lending infinite multiples of the money taken in, and thus slow traffic to a safe speed. But if it were a significant impediment, it would be honored like that rule about interest on corporate checking accounts.

Does that mean that at this point in history, banks can only be made to follow those laws that are purely in the interest of smooth banking? Are banks only pretending when they complain that governments force them to comply with costly and onerous regulations? Or are governments only pretending when they lament that they can no longer force global capital to comply with regulations for the common good? My sense is that they're lamenting and pretending together in carefully sustained contrapuntal harmony while the conductorship is still in flux.

As I rode home on the subway thinking about these problems, the Chase balance sheet was still in flux, too. Each of the numbers that filter into Gardner's spreadsheet is a still shot extracted from a running total that was squared off and captured at a particular moment. But the cutoff times—days, nights, alternate Wednesday—are as arbitrary as the dividing line between your earlobe and your elbow. The action is continuous. The sun never sets on the Chase Manhattan spreadsheet.

The Hot Potato

When Gardner Young accepted money from Chase corporate customers, he was doing them a favor. They would bring the bank interest or fee-paying business down the line. The same applied to the small banks. Chase was taking their money as an "accommodation."

The Bank of Millbrook, by contrast, had seemed positively happy to take my money. One reason, I suppose, is that they knew they could pay me $2\frac{1}{4}$ percent and sell it to Chase at $4\frac{1}{4}$ percent.

Chase should have been equally happy to take Millbrook's money. That steady 600 million from the small banks was a solid stake (money in the bank, so to speak) ready to be loaned or invested. If, that is, they had loans or investments to make.

When I made the deposit that started this story, I thought of my money as the raw material that banks need and want in order to make more money.

But I was beginning to sense, however fuzzily, that it could also be a hot potato that Millbrook passed to Chase and Chase had to pass quickly to the next guy. Whoever held it, even for a second, had to pay interest. Which means he had to be able to collect interest. If he couldn't, he got burned.

This hot-potato notion was only vague at the time. According to the text-books* money-center banks draw money thirstily from small-town and regional banks in order to fund national and international loans. I happened to have visited the Fed-funds desk on a day that Chase was long. But there were many days when they were short of money. There were even days, Gardner had told me, when they started way long, sold as much as they could, then had to scramble to buy money back in order to finance big loans or other profitable opportunities that suddenly turned up.

On a short day at the Fed-funds desk Chase would be thirsty and I'd have gotten caught up rooting "come, come, come" as I watched the money trickle from small branches into regional rivers and finally empty into the vast Chase delta. That's how the flow is often described, and that, minus the thirst, is what I'd seen.

The next step was to follow my money out into the open sea.

---

*For instance, *The Money Market*, by Marcia Stigum, Business One Irwin, Homewood, IL, 3rd edition, 1990.

The Manhattan Bank was founded in 1799 by Aaron Burr, largely, it seems, to spite Alexander Hamilton. (It was one of a series of spites that led to their duel and Hamilton's death.) Burr's Manhattan Bank soon became a great commercial bank that financed such projects as the Erie Canal. The Chase bank wasn't founded until 1877, but by the 1920's it was the leading lender to American corporations, and under David Rockefeller, it became an international commercial bank.

Joined a century later as Chase Manhattan, it made its share of home mortgage, auto, and prodigiously profitable consumer credit-card loans. But it was still a venerable commercial bank. I decided to illustrate Chase's traditional function by following two classic commercial loans. To be representative, one should go to a powerful multinational, the other to the kind of midsized company that my mother used to work for as a bookkeeper. Her fabric importers, lamp-fittings plants, and shoelace manufacturers always needed a few hundred thousand dollars to finance operations between the time the orders came in and the time they got paid.

The multinational's loan would meet essentially the same need, I assumed. But I had only a vague idea how big a big loan might be, and what kind of relationship a multinational has with its bank.

I began by studying tombstones. Those are the narrow (or sometimes wide) boxed ads in papers like the *Wall Street Journal*, where financial institutions announce some of the prestigious deals they've just made. Chase made the *Journal* regularly as the leader or coleader of large syndicated loans. But all their loans seemed to be for mergers and acquisitions (M&A), which meant that they helped one company buy another company's stock.

I immediately rejected M&A loans, not for ideological, but for dramatic reasons. I wanted to show my money at work in the world. But when ownership changes, nothing moves but a few billion electrons.

I broadened the search to periodicals like a banker's tip sheet called the *LPC* (Loan Pricing Corporation) *Gold Sheets*. Based on inside contacts, the *Gold Sheets* listed as many as they could unearth of the large loans being negotiated each week, with information on the up-front fees, the spreads (interest above what the banks pay each other), and the purposes of the loans.

Tradition and prudence in banking suggest that commercial loans should be made for specific short-term purposes, such as seed money until the harvest or start-up costs on construction. Of course these have to be profitable purposes, or how would the loan be paid back?

It's also increasingly common to give creditworthy companies loans for "general corporate purposes." These are rolled over automatically as long as the interest is paid. Such nonspecific loans are used to finance the day-to-day operations of what, again, must be a profit-making enterprise.

The kinds of loan purposes that I looked for in the *Gold Sheets* were "working capital," "general corporate purposes," and "project finance." There were some of those, but the more common purposes were "LBO" (leveraged buyout), "takeover," "aquis program," and "stock buyback"—all forms of ownership transfer.

Surely big borrowers had to be doing something besides buying and selling each other. That something is the productive process capitalism is justly proud of. I'd started this book with the best small bank that I could find, and I felt duty-bound to illustrate the most productive uses Chase would now make of my money.

But I was running out of credible addresses from which to send for sample *Gold Sheets,* and a subscription would cost over $2,000. For a couple of weeks I wandered into the *Gold Sheets* offices, "discovered" that I was in the wrong place, and wandered out, casually taking the current issue from the waiting-room coffee table. But one time the receptionist gave chase. Seeing by the indicator light that the elevators were too many floors away, I ducked into the stairwell. This was getting ridiculous.

Chase is a bank; banks make loans. And they can't all be for mergers and acquisitions. I'd just have to go up there and ask people what kinds of loans they were making.

A Liquid Elephant

Chase had 34,000 employees working in departments with names like Global Financial Services, Global Specialized Finance, Global Financial Services Marketing, Global Corporate Client Management, Global Payments and Treasury Services, Global Securities Services, Global Corporate Markets, and Global Markets, just to select from among the G's. I felt like the blind man groping my way around the elephant.

The bank assigned me to a PR man who didn't seem to know any better than I did who among the Globals might make a loan. So I fell back on the friends-of-friends method, asking everyone "Do you happen to know anyone who works at Chase?" Surprisingly, this landed me not too low but too high, at first, to find a loan. The bankers I met on the upper floors at Chase Manhattan Plaza didn't want to make loans and collect interest, they wanted to underwrite offerings and collect fees. The real money, I learned, was in helping corporate clients float bonds or issue stocks. Unless these guys were number-dropping to impress me, up-front fees for these services started at around five million dollars.

"But how can one-time fees pay as much over the long run as interest?" I asked.

"Morgan Stanley has survived; Goldman Sachs has survived," my informant said, naming the leading investment banks. "I'm not feeling sorry for either of them."

According to the would-be investment bankers, the kind of project loan I was looking for was not only less lucrative and less prestigious, but downright bad for the bank. "No one wants an asset on their books; liquidity is everything to a money-center bank," one said. Another told me that such loans "should be made only to the twenty largest companies in each country—known quantities." That way, he explained, the debt could be chopped up into chunks and sold on the Euromarket.

Lend to the people that everyone already knows? What happened to inter-mediation? You don't need bankers to find the twenty biggest companies. How will a Merritt Bookstore or Millbrook Pizza get loans? And what about the growing, but not yet blue-chip companies around the world?

At slightly lower levels I met people who didn't scorn traditional loans; they were trying to make them. The problem, a couple of loan salesmen insisted, was that large corporations didn't need their money. Since salesmen always complain about their product and their territory, I wasn't going to accept at face value that money was a hard sell. So I checked it out with some likely customers.

Awash

Several corporate financial officers confirmed that if their banks were making any money, they were making it in fees, not interest. "The loan is the bank's loss leader," according to an Assistant Treasurer at ITT (a Chase customer).

This particular man happened to be arranging complicated leveraged financing to buy Madison Square Garden (more M&A). But when it came to the plain vanilla loan, "It's a buyer's market. Credit is a commodity. Right now the demand is so much less than the supply that ITT pays as little as five BPs for a 364-day commitment. If they draw it down, it's as little as LIBOR plus 25 BPs. [LIBOR, the London Interbank Offered Rate, is the rate at which banks get money in the Euromarket. 100 BPs (basis points) means one percent. An interest rate of 25 BPs is therefore only one quarter of one percent above what the bank pays for the money.] The loan is a loss leader to get our fee-based business."

The assistant treasurer explained that ITT didn't really need bank loans because it was usually "awash" in cash. When they did need money quickly, they could issue commercial paper. These are short-term IOUs that a company sells directly to individual investors, skipping over the bank. Only the largest companies with top credit ratings (the "known quantities") could issue commercial paper. But for those who could, there were always buyers (lenders) for the exact amount and duration needed. "It's great stuff, commercial paper," the assistant treasurer enthused.

Nevertheless, for very large sums, ITT would select a lead bank to round up the money from other commercial banks. Between leads, co-leads, and the many tiers of contributors, there could be a score of banks in on one syndicated loan.

"It's like a Lincoln Center Theater program," the assistant treasurer joked. "Friends, donors, patrons, moguls." They rushed to lend at ridiculously small markups, he felt, to get a crack at the fee-earning roles. "So we have a stable of banks that are constantly trying to be on our short list . . . The banks are no better than cold callers or the Fuller Brush Man—literally. They come knocking at your door."

"But aren't you busy?"

"That's why they all want to be part of the credit line. It gives them the entitlement to come talk to you about the progress of the loan, and while they're there they can show you their new products. It gives them the foot in the door."

So the money salesmen hadn't been exaggerating. The territory was glutted with their product. The striking word in many of these interviews was *awash*. Banks were *awash* in deposits; large corporations were so *awash* in profits that they could be their own banks; investors—mutual funds, other corporations, or just wealthy individuals—were so *awash* that ITT had no difficulty finding matches for any commercial paper they issued.

A couple of deregulated decades had concentrated huge globs of money under the control of companies and individuals who seemed to be having increasing trouble finding anything to do with it besides buying and selling each other.

Because of this, bankers who once held power by dangling money before industrialists were now reduced to performing services for fees—working for tips. How did it happen that companies had so much money? Where had all the money come from, and how come I never noticed it until I started nosing around lower Manhattan? I made a note to come back to these questions, though in fact they came back on their own, repeatedly.

Looking for Señor Good Loan

In the meantime I turned my attention to the one place where Chase was surely making large loans. The financial press of the time was gaga over what they called "The Emerging-Market Whiz Kids." The US loan market may have been slow, but the real go-getters were selling dollars at big markups in Latin America. So hot were these Emerging Markets that it was even rumored that the woman in charge of Latin American lending at Chase would become the first female head of a money-center bank. I wasn't far enough inside to know if this was ever seriously considered. I can only report that it was a genuine rumor. Latin America was hot.

So, using the friends-of-friends method again, I found myself on the 16th floor, at GLOBAL CORPORATE FINANCE, following the signs to:

SECTOR MANAGEMENT

EMERGING MARKET GROUPS

LDC PORTFOLIO MANAGEMENT

If I'd paid more attention to that three-letter abbreviation, LDC, I might have remembered what happened last time Latin America was hot.

Alan Delsman offered me a cup of tea, which he prepared himself in the kitchenette. Once in his office he turned his full and warm attention on me. I explained my scheme for following my Chase deposit to Latin America, volunteering that I'd like to go to Chile, if possible, because I'd met so many gracious Chileans.

"Chile is a bad example of the use of bank funds," Delsman responded. "This is one country—because of their economic policies—where the dollar isn't that important."

"They don't want dollars?"

"You'd prefer to borrow in your own currency," he explained. "You take an additional risk if you borrow in dollars."

"Oh, yes, currency risk."

"Now in Mexico or Argentina they can't get a seven- or nine-year loan in the country, so they'll take the risk. But in Chile, that's a developed economy. The guy can go out and borrow in pesos."

"So in a stronger economy like Chile, they don't want dollars?"

"The government doesn't want them to take dollars. We don't have any natural advantage there. [I think he meant legal, not natural, advantage. The Chilean government required businesses to pay a small tax on money borrowed from abroad for less than a year. This discouragement was a form of capital control, like the capital controls that the US government declared itself helpless to enforce after about 1974. Only US capital controls were designed to keep dollars inside the country, while Chilean capital controls were designed to keep dollars out. At least if they came in short-term.] Just the opposite of Mexico or Argentina," Delsman explained.

"Well then, what kinds of loans are we making in Mexico and Argentina?"

"Briefly, to give you a little background, for twenty-five years the policies in those countries have been protectionist—developing local products to foster import substitutions."

"Oh, yes," I said, "local steel mills and all that."

"Reversing that has meant a radical change for countries like Argentina. Here," he handed me a flier, "you can hear Carlos Menem." The flier announced a talk by the president of Argentina. "So what everyone is financing now is the sale of those public-sector enterprises in Brazil, Argentina. They're selling airlines, banks, phone companies . . . I've been trying to get ahold of this guy all day." He excused himself to take a phone call.

[Delsman, into Phone] ". . . I took the liberty of reducing the . . . it was four hundred basis points. I approved to basically a half of that in the light of that they really wanted to win the mandate, blah-blah-blah." [Mandate! This could be one of these privatization deals.] I went to two hundred, which would be for a risk-rated six." [I hope I got those numbers right. I was glancing around the room pretending to be studying the decor.] "Now they won the deal and they still want to reduce it even further. . . . I tried to explain to him, supposing your mother was a Chase shareholder, how would I justify such a deal to her? . . . Yeah," Delsman chuckled, "we'll make it up in volume. . . . So I wanted to warn you, we're already way below the required pricing for an RR of seven. . . . Yes, that's another fifty million. . . . I priced down because they wanted to win the mandate. Now they've got it. . . . "

It sounded like they agreed on leaving it at 200. If that meant 200 basis points above LIBOR (the rate at which international banks could get money from each other), they were talking about real interest, ten times above what the bank netted on those loss-leader loans to ITT.

Maybe I was in the right office this time. Privatization was almost as hot, at that moment, as Emerging Markets. And Mr. Delsman did both. In fact, that's what it sounded like he was talking about on the phone—a loan to a company that had won the mandate to buy and run some formerly government-owned utility in an emerging-market country.

"So let me make sure I understand this. We lend money to people who are actually buying telephone companies?" Delsman confirmd that. "And the money they borrow from us, five hundred million dollars or whatever—will go in the form of . . . ?"

"All cash, up front . . . they are literally selling dams, power projects, telephone companies. All for better management. . . . Now, when you buy a telephone company, you've got to promise to install four hundred thousand telephones a year," he said, giving a for-instance, ". . . for so many years to get the guys in charge to say we'll keep it a monopoly." [I thought we favored competition. Oh, well.] "So there'll be requirements for further capital for lines."

"I suppose those governments have been running the telephone companies pretty inefficiently," I said, offering up what I knew to be the usual justification for privatization.

"Obviously there's a level of inefficiency," he replied. "But another problem is these Latin American governments have been shut off from capital since 1981, so how will they raise money to do any expansion?"

The year of the LDC crisis (those initials again) was 1981. LDCs, less-developed countries, were roughly the same nations now called Emerging Markets. The dated abbreviation was still used by bank departments that handled the collection operations left over from loans made the last time Latin America was hot. If Mr. Delsman was correct, those earlier loans were one reason that Latin American governments couldn't run their own dams, power projects, and phone companies now. I should have asked more about the LDC loans, but Delsman was explaining the different ways that Chase participated, two decades later, in Emerging Markets privatizations.

First, for a nonrefundable advisory fee, Chase used their long experience and many contacts in Latin America to help a consortium put together its bid for one of these phone companies. "We might be backing two or three of them."

"Isn't that a conflict of interest?" I couldn't help asking.

"We have separate teams. The second part is to give a loan to the winning consortium."

Now we were getting to my part, I thought. Once the property is bought and the government paid, the Chase borrower would start putting in new phone lines, repairing the dam, upgrading the airline, whatever.

"So I could go to Argentina and watch my money putting people to work?"

Well, not quite. "Our loan for the acquisition was short-term, for the capital expenditure. The long-term *take-outs* are done by the Euromarket—private insurance companies, US mutual funds, et cetera."

Once Chase had made a loan for a merger or acquisition, it might then, for another large fee, help the purchaser float bonds, issue stocks, or otherwise raise long-term money to "grow" their new business. But that was down the line, if ever. The immediate use of the take-out loan was to repay, or *take out* the short-term lender, Chase. So, like other M&A loans, Chase privatization loans financed only the transfer of ownership.

I asked the patient Mr. Delsman if there was any way in which my Chase deposit directly financed development in Latin America. (Maybe I was at the wrong bank entirely.)

"In Mexico, because of the Free Trade Agreement and the end of tariffs, you couldn't be competitive unless you made your plant more efficient. Since the long-term financing was not available, they couldn't borrow pesos. They had to borrow dollars to make their steel mills more efficient. So megaplayers from Mexico would come to us, and it's case-by-case. It's no different than if he comes from Omaha. He says 'I need the money because if I don't do these things, I cannot compete with the US. So here's what I want the money for.'"

At last, Mexican companies borrowing money from Chase to modernize and compete! I didn't feel I could ask Mr. Delsman about specific pending large loans. The *Gold Sheets* charged over $2,000 a year for such bits of information. Besides, he couldn't divulge the details of a client's financial situation. Or if he could, he wasn't going to do it for me, I sensed. But knowing such loans were out there, I could now look for them myself.

I began wangling my way into events given for Latin American businessmen. I set my sights on one of the hardest for me to crash, the Third Annual Conference on the Americas, subtitled "Advances in the Americas: Can the Momentum Be Maintained?" It was held at the Waldorf Astoria Hotel and sponsored by AT&T, Citibank, Banco del Progreso, and Promperu.

The Waldorf Astoria Hotel: a ballroom set up for a conference plenary—a weekday morning

The opening panel, hosted by Dow Jones, was called "Latin America: One Year after NAFTA [The North American Free Trade Agreement]." I took my china teacup to a table with a pink tablecloth in time to hear Dr. Sylvia Ostry, a Canadian with a gruff smoker's voice and the only woman panelist in the entire conference, warning about a particularly insidious threat to free trade—"Transformational Coalitions." "They live in cyberspace, their transnational operations are extraordinary. We are familiar with traditional lobbies jockeying for different-sized pieces of the pie. But *they* want to tell *us* what should go into the pie, and how it should be baked."

Who are these powerful transformational coalitions, I wondered. And who is the *us* who rightfully determine how the pie should be baked?

While I was wondering, another panelist, Robert Reich, then US secretary of labor, was taking credit, on behalf of the Clinton administration, for passing NAFTA. Reich didn't mention transformational coalitions, but he joined Ms. Ostry in warning that free trade has powerful enemies—"The Buchanans and the Perots of left and right." "US wages have been going down for twenty years," he reminded the audience. "When Americans feel threatened they turn isolationist, protectionist."

When Reich was through, the moderator, David Asman, reminded the next two speakers—the finance minister of Venezuela and the chairman of the board of the Peruvian Telephone Company—to stick to their eight minutes because "The Secretary has to leave at 10:30 and I *don't* want him to escape without being questioned."

The questioning turned into a roast. Audience members universally attacked Reich for allowing labor and environmental items on to the agenda of an up-and-coming hemispheric trade summit. Reich assured them that trade would be the true focus of the meeting, though the workers' fears must be addressed somehow. But he didn't get through. You cannot explain window dressing to autocrats.

"We're worried," says the chairman of the Peruvian Telephone Company. No one is debating Reich, just sending him a message. Asman hurls those very words as the departing secretary scurries up the isle. "We'll send you a message!"

The next morning Asman brandished the message. It was printed in the day's *Wall Street Journal*, in the column Asman edited, and it was headed "The Miami Vision Thing: An Agenda for the Summit." It derided the administration's "list of worthy causes that include combating corruption and prompting democracy, human rights, and environmental protection." It suggested instead a no-nonsense, trade-focused agenda. The column listed sample trade-agenda items, each one framed by an industry spokesman. First, for example, was the drug industry's item:

> Says Pfizer Vice President Mike Hodin: "One of the preconditions for research-based pharmaceutical companies is to develop first-rate patent laws as reflected in the standards of NAFTA."

Here's what that means. Until NAFTA's patent standards went into effect, drugs had been cheaper in Canada and Mexico than in the US in part because Canadian and Mexican patent laws gave drug manufacturers shorter monopolies on newly patented drugs. NAFTA's free trade didn't mean opening the doors so that those cheaper Canadian and Mexican drugs could compete in the US. It means, instead, that Canada and Mexico had to move toward the longer US patents. The result was that drug prices to Canada's National Health Service went up about a third, forcing cutbacks in medical care. Drug companies made the expected larger profits, and now, in the name of free trade, they wanted the restrictive rules expanded to all of the Americas.

The other proposed agenda items were similarly undisguised demands from each industry to be able to make more money through new regulations only tenuously related to anything that an ordinary English speaker would call "free trade." I was shocked by the stark-naked selfishness of the demands. I was also surprised at the rude way that the gathering had treated a cabinet member. I assumed that the rule among the powerful would be "talk softly and carry a big check."

Of course, the panel people weren't really *them*, the men with the big checkbooks. These were just their ... employees, I guess I'll say. (The memory of Asman snapping at the legs of the rapidly departing Reich called the clichéd "running dog" unwelcomed to my mind.)

"One Year after NAFTA" was the liveliest panel of the two days. For the most part we listened peacefully to speakers like Roger Dorf, AT&T's president, Caribbean and Latin America on the topic "Opportunities for Investment in Latin America."

> Virtually all of Latin America is rich with opportunity in almost any industry. . . . The wave of democracy that has swept through Latin America . . . government privatization of many former state-owned industries . . . telecommunications . . . transportation . . . energy . . . airlines . . . Chile . . . $11 billion was poured in. . . . Argentina . . . privatization has brought in $24 billion in cash . . . inflation slashed from twenty-three hundred to four percent . . . in Brazil some one-point-two million people want phone services and have the money to pay for it. . . . Colombia, eight hundred thousand people on the waiting list . . . Venezuela, about six hundred thousand . . . The value of this waiting list is astronomical, probably in the realm of multiple billions of dollars . . . consortium that will invest more than seven hundred million dollars . . . so in summary, Latin America and the Caribbean appear to be one of the hot emerging markets of the 1990's and beyond.

Waves of millions and billions wafted soothingly over us for two full days. On the second morning, at "Tapping International Capital Markets," William R. Rhodes, now CEO of Citibank, took a statesmanlike historical overview.

> [last year] The returns investors gained from emerging markets greatly exceeded what investors realized in the so-called developed market. . . . Brazil's market rose one hundred and fifteen percent, Mexico's forty-eight percent, Colombia's thirty-nine percent, Argentina thirty-six-point-five percent, and Chile's twenty-eight percent . . . stalled in early February . . . has now recovered, particularly in countries that have demonstrated positive economic reform policies . . .
>
> . . . differences between the investment climate today in Latin America and conditions existing in the 1970's and 1980's prior to the LDC debt crises [those initials again] . . . major structural and economic reforms . . . privitizations, deregulation, trade liberalization and tax reforms . . . expansion of regional trade . . . passage of NAFTA. . . . independent central banks. . .
>
> In closing . . . word of caution . . . risks inherent . . . [but] . . . reforms well under way . . . in the main, irreversible . . . barring of course unforeseen catastro-

phes ... most Latin American countries have come a long way over the past decade—but many still have a way to go.

In the sleepy late afternoon there was a panel on "The Social Consequences of Rapid Economic Development," in which we heard some sobering words from the editor (Chilean) of Dow Jones' Latin American magazine.

Effects of the rapid move toward a market-driven economy in Latin America ... entire regions and industries destroyed ... poverty and unemployment increases ... opportunities cannot be seized by many ... industries are destroyed faster than they are rebuilt [*He must be exaggerating a little*, I thought] ... "Rapid" growth is not that rapid and an underclass is emerging ... but *eventually* [emphasis mine}, growth starts decreasing unemployment and raises salaries.

In the meantime, the articulate editor suggested inflation control, if and where achieved, might be the one meaningful benefit for all classes from the rapid movement to a market-driven economy.

This talk so infuriated the man sitting next to me (his badge identified him as the head of Philip Morris International, Ecuador) that he rose to demand, "Why are we talking about the negatives?! There can be only good consequences from rapid development!"

Which reminds me, *Why am I overreporting the one negative panel?* Most people snoozed or networked through "Social Consequences." The conference was generally a stream of positive statistics highlighted by talks from the presidents of Bolivia and Peru, who told us how well things were going in their countries.

Heads of state tend to ignore poor people, I know. Still, some of the millions must trickle down. The world might be more pleasant if someone was deliberately directing all this capital to make life more equitable—someone other than Chase, AT&T, and Citibank. But even *their* capital flows had to be better for poor countries than stagnation, I came to feel after two full days of talks.

Anyway, I had a job to do at the conference and it wasn't evaluating the speeches. I was there to find a Latin American businessman who had bor-

rowed some of my money from Chase. A lot of the delegates' badges read
"Jefe" or "Presidente," so I waylaid as many Latin CEOs as I could during the
breaks and asked if their companies had borrowed money from Citibank or
Chase. Not one of them had (or could, some added), except for the man from
Philip Morris. But he scared me too much to confess my real mission.

By 4:00 on the last day, I was discouraged and very hungry. The other reporters—I'd made it to the conference as press—grumbled that there were
no sandwiches in the pressroom that year, even though we were excluded
from the luncheons while expected to cover the luncheon speeches from
chairs in the rear. ("The benefits of rapid economic development are sometimes unequally distributed," as we heard from the podium.) So, hungry, ir-
ritable, limping toward the exit on high heels, I made my last try.

As I left the Waldorf, Julio Berdegue Aznar, the white-bearded, black-
eyebrowed president of El Cid Mega Resort and head of a group of Mexican
companies active in hotel, marina, golf course, shrimp aquaculture, and real
estate development, strode back in.

"Can you go into Citibank or Chase and get a loan?" I asked.

"No."

"But this whole conference? The capital flows? The millions? The billions?"

"It's a bunch of rich people getting together to tell each other how beautiful the world is!"

"Wait! Can I interview you?"

But Señor Aznar had to meet someone right away and he was flying home
that very evening. *Probably a case of sour grapes,* I thought sour-grapishly. A
man with a dozen development companies in the fire is too small-time to
borrow from international banks.

But who *was* getting those loans? I didn't entirely trust Citibank or AT&T,
but there was no way they were making up the numbers. Capital was flowing
by the billions into Latin America, yet I couldn't find one single old-
fashioned capital-development loan.

And this wasn't the first conference I'd gone to. I'd even asked on the Internet, "Is your company sending you to Latin America?" I got a couple of
missionaries, a man working with a Peruvian Indian confederation, and an
engineer whose company might be sending him to Chile to teach road

builders how to use a Falling Weight Deflectometer. But neither the Chilean nor the American company was using my money.

I left the conference convinced that I'd have to go back to the Bank of Millbrook, withdraw my money, and return it to the publisher. Apparently, economic research couldn't be done on the ground, at least not by me. The capital was flowing freely but I couldn't find a single recipient.

What stopped me was a sudden crash—a crash of pesos, followed by a crash of stock markets, followed by crashes of businesses and banks, and after the crashes a sustained wail. There were dozens of conflicting explanations as Mexico, the model Emerging Market, crashed. There was no way, then, that I could have waded through the muck of accusations: this was my first time around. But in the wake of the crash a great deal of information about lenders, borrowers, and investments surfaced and it became obvious why I hadn't found my model loan. It didn't exist.

Part of the problem was my limited conception of a loan. I thought a loan had to be *for* something. I was looking for a resort, a bottling plant, a phone company that hired operators or even just fired operators with my money. To me it seemed only logical that borrowed money had to be used to build or expand or at least streamline a business. How else could the money be paid back with interest?

But it turned out that the great capital flow into Latin America involved almost none of that kind of investment. Most of the Chase loans had gone to governments or to banks, while most of the equity investments worked like the loans that I'd rejected as too static: nothing moved but electrons. The billions I'd been hearing about purchased stocks or bonds from the people who already owned them. That made the price of the securities go up. And since they were appreciating so fast—the Mexican stock market went up 436 percent in the four years before the crash—more money flowed in and the same stocks and bonds were sold over and over at rising prices.

Every change of ownership sent the electrons whirling. Some of them had spun out and back to Chase and Citi because many of the Mexicans personally enriched by the capital flow thought that those were good places to keep their money. (*Flight capital*, it's called.) Between a third to a half of the billions that went into Mexico in its LDC days had come out that way. No one was sure yet how much it was this time—it's hard to keep track.

But very little went to people who used it to build new and productive or even *destructive* businesses like golf courses or shrimp farms. To put it in terms I was starting to learn from the financial pages, the great capital flow turned out to be all *portfolio investment.* And the money moving so fast, though by no means stolen, was the kind they call *hot money.*

It was lucky that I hadn't found the model loan I was looking for, because it wouldn't have been representative. It wasn't just lucky, of course. It was a confirmation of my research theory that you usually find what's usual or, in this case, its negative corollary: if it's hard to find, maybe it isn't that common.

———

I decided to forget the Latin American Emerging Market fad, or fluke, or whatever it had been, and move on to something solid. There could be nothing faddish about the growth and the development that was going on in Asia. From then on I asked about money going East instead of South. I also abandoned the upper floors of Chase Plaza and decided to start with the small loan that I understood.

Someone among Chase's 34,000 employees must be lending a few million to a local merchant or manufacturer for specific, short-term purposes. If Asian production and trade were real, then someone at that level would be lending my money to facilitate it.

My assigned PR aide didn't know of such a person, offhand, but I saw an ad in the *Wall Street Journal* that said:

> Chase believes middle market companies shouldn't have to call ten people to get answers. That's why at Chase you have a Relationship Manager.... one person who is trained to understand every detail of your business.... To meet a Chase Relationship Manager, call one of the following Middle Market Managers.

I called all five. Leonard Walker, Middle Market Manager for the Brooklyn, Queens, and Staten Island region, was the first to call back.

A Real Relationship at Last

Metro Tech Center, downtown Brooklyn—late morning

Leonard Walker's offices in downtown Brooklyn were comfortably drab compared to Chase Plaza or the Waldorf. On our way to his desk he introduced me informally to a couple of loan salesmen and their shared secretary. I felt closer already to my mother's fabric importer or shoelace manufacturer.

But as soon as I took out my notebook, "We like what we call, relationships," Mr. Walker became formal. "Our group attempts to become the relationship bank for the people we do business with. My people are team players trained to lend money and sell services. The services may belong to some other area of the bank.... We provide financial services that become the focal point for the full banking relationship...." Leonard Walker was speaking Mission Statement.

You could hear the same language at annual meetings from Chase CEO Labrecque. "Our collaboration enables customers to enjoy a single window into Chase," or "Our emphasis on teamwork will enable us to maximize relationships."

Back in those days it was the custom for large corporations to pay consultants upwards of a million dollars to help them articulate their missions. Chase had bought not just a mission but a vision. Once the official vision was formulated, small meetings were held all over the bank to inculcate it. However obvious and awkward they sounded, million-dollar mission/vision statements generally highlighted some concept that wasn't entirely meaningless (when translated). "Relationship" had its own operational significance at Chase.

Mr. Walker's Middle Market team sold loans to companies with revenues of between 10 million and 500 million dollars a year. Such firms pay large fees for letters of credit, pension-plan management, currency hedging, and other bank services. (Unlike big companies, Middle Market companies also pay well for loans.) So it was natural for Chase to long for a "full relationship" that would bring them all the client's business. On his end, Mr. Walker embraced the relationship concept not just to be loyal or to quote the Mission Statement but because, as a salesman, it gave him something to sell.

What a loan officer sells is money. But his money is exactly like everyone else's. He can't clinch a sale by spreading samples out on the table. So what can he pitch? As every good salesmen knows, you don't sell the steak, you sell the sizzle. Relationship is the intangible sizzle on an invisible steak.

I asked Mr. Walker about the types of companies he had relationships with.

"One of my RMs [Relationship Managers] has a relationship with a customer in Russia who sells overruns of products that might compete with Revlon. [This coy reference reminded me that Leonard Walker, like George Whalen, is not free to name his clients. How would I get around that?] Where it's difficult to take out hard currency, the products might be exchanged for other things. They might take vodka out of Russia or India and ... "

"Everything in Russia is so convoluted and unique," I said. (I didn't want to chase another fluke) "Is there such a thing as a straightforward, typical ... ?"

"We have a customer who brings frozen seafood from Asia. We provide him with a line of credit with which he procures shrimp and—"

The phone rang.

[Asia!]

"Leonard Walker." He answered his phone himself.

[I prefer scallops to shrimp, but ...]

"I'll send it to you," Walker said as he scanned a document on his desk, "but to give you the quick and dirty: _____ million at two point two three." He seemed to be informing someone that Chase would grant his loan at 2.23 percent above LIBOR. After two more brief exchanges, Mr. Walker turned back to me.

"Do the RMs use standard loan application forms?" I asked. "Take that shrimp man ... " Was it too much to hope that he might show me his application?

"Each loan in middle-market is custom-made. We have no credit applications; we create them as we go. Each business is different. For example, the gentleman I was just talking to. He wants to buy a business." Walker swiveled to a shelf behind him and pulled down two heavy file boxes full of folders and documents. "Here's his credit application." He dropped the lot on his desk. "Handcrafted. We build it from scratch."

"You must know almost as much about the business as he does," I said, looking at the pile of documents. "By the way, it was very impressive how you had those loan figures at hand."

"I have excellent support," he said modestly.

Excellent and expensive, I thought.

"What's the minimum-size loan that could be profitable?" I asked. "Considering your overhead."

"I will look at it if it's at least a half a million dollars. Anything less than that, it's clearly an accommodation. I've made fifty thousand but I can't afford to because my people are highly trained." And highly paid too, I thought. "Someone with a different overhead would come up with a different figure for a minimum profitable loan. I'm most comfortable at one million and above."

I thought about the Bank of Millbrook's profitable loan of $10,000 to buy pizzeria equipment. Walker would on no account lend to a restaurant, he told me. "It's not the proprietor's fault, but tastes change too much."

"On this loan," he indicated the pile, "my fee will be half a million off the bat." I must have looked startled, perhaps even disapproving.

"Any less," he explained, "it would be difficult to have an adequate return for our shareholders who are requiring fifteen to twenty percent."

"Fifteen to twenty percent!"

Millbrook shareholders were getting 9 percent. And there was a long waiting list for shares. Perhaps the Bank of Millbrook can make small loans profitably because George and his cousins define "profitable" differently than Chase shareholders. Hey, why have I been worrying about overhead and salaries? Why did it take a banker to remind a socialist that dividends can be the big drain on a business? But 20 percent!? Who makes 20 percent? [See Part II: The Investment.]

"About these loans with foreign tie-ins?" I was hoping to bring us back to Asia. Instead we got into an informative discussion about country and currency risks, during which I worked up the courage to broach my real question.

"I know you can't tell me the names of your loan clients, but do you suppose it might be possible to give my name to some Brooklyn, Queens, or Staten Island borrower who would enjoy being interviewed for a book?"

"We have a man in Brooklyn who might be that. I'll have his RM ask. If I don't get back to you in a couple of days, call Sean O'Conner."

"Thank you," I said, amazed at how easy that had been. "Do you want my number?"

"I have it right here." The printout under the glass on Walker's desk showed him the time of our appointment (now nearly up) with my phone number.

"You have terrific support," I said as we rode down in the elevator. (He was off to a meeting.) "But you must be very well organized, yourself, to handle everything." He accepted the compliment noncommittally. "Are you able to fit in time with your family?"

He said that he lived in Princeton, New Jersey, and usually got home in time to read his daughter her bedtime story. But he had lots of weekend work. "We are committed as a team to provide financial services that enhance our customers and our communities," Walker concluded, reverting for just a moment to Mission-speak. "Good luck."

A few days later I found this message on my answering machine.

"Hi, Barbara, this is Sean O'Conner from Chase Manhattan Bank. I'm returning your phone call to me earlier. I've spoken to my client and he's agreed to talk to you.... The client's name is James and Charles Domino Wholesale Sea Food, Incorporated—sometimes known as JC Seafoods. They're located in Brooklyn on _____Street between _____ and _____Avenues. The person you want to talk to is the president. His name is James Domino or Jimmy.... He uses money that he borrows from Chase. . . to purchase seafood coming out of India and various locations in Asia. You'll find him approachable and usually quite a lot of fun. He can be reached at area code 718____. Just ask for Jimmy Domino and tell him you were referred to him by Sean O'Conner and Leonard Walker. I don't think you'll have any difficulty. If you do give me a call 718____. Good luck, bye-bye."

Everyone should have a Relationship Manager at Chase!

Trading Prawns with a Letter of Credit

The basic elements of a trade are so simple that it can even be negotiated between species. I have something in my hand that you might want. I hold it out to show you. You hold out something I might want in return. We look, we nod, we edge toward each other. Then I touch what's in your hand, you touch what's in my hand, and at exactly the same instant, we both let go. Now *you* hold what *I* had and *I* hold what *you* had. The trade occurred at the moment we let go together.

But supposing we're too far away to see each other. We can agree by message what we'd be willing to swap for what. But how do we know that the other guy let go? How does a man holding out dollars in Brooklyn know that a man in Singapore really put forty thousand pounds of frozen shrimp on a boat? How can the man in Singapore, who has to buy, pack, freeze, and ship the shrimp, be certain that the check is really in the mail? The man in Brooklyn, Jimmy Domino, and the man in Singapore, Mr. Ravindran, use a medieval banking instrument called a letter of credit to take the risk out of letting go.

Brooklyn industrial area—offices above a cold storage warehouse—morning
Domino's company, JC Seafoods, started as a fish store in Brooklyn. After it burned down during a 1968 race riot, James and Charles, Jimmy's father and uncle, never reopened the retail store, but they continued distributing fish to local restaurants. After Jimmy got out of the army, he expanded the business from distributing to importing. "That was basically a matter of survival," he told me. "The chain of command was breaking down. The bigger importers were selling directly to my customers—restaurants and supermarkets. So I evolved from a distributor to an importer/distributor."

Today he's an importer/distributor/broker/trader doing 35 million dollars of business a year. Still, the JC Seafood Group (there are three corporations) is head-quartered in a couple of functionally furnished rooms above his warehouse. The office of Asia Pacific Seafoods in Singapore (which I was to see much sooner than I expected) were also located above the company's cold-storage facility. There Mr. Ravidran, Ravi as everyone called him, traded by phone and fax in a similar space decorated with the same calendar from the Sealand Shipping Agency and the same poster of "The Commercial Fish of India."

JC Seafoods and Ravidran's Asia Pacific Seafoods are fair-sized firms in the fish-trading business, but neither has the resources to check the other's current financial situation or to go to court in a foreign country if one party lets go and the other doesn't. So, after they negotiate the specifics of a trade—26 to 31's (shrimp per pound), eleven-fifty (US dollars per kilogram), Burmas (the source)—Jimmy buys a Letter of Credit from Chase. The letter promises that Chase, not JC Seafoods, will pay Mr. Ravidran as soon as he brings papers to *his* bank showing that he's sent off the shrimp. In the fish business, the papers are generally an inspection statement from someone like Llyods of London indicating that the exporter packed what he said he would, and a bill of lading from a port authority confirming that he then let go. When Ravidran's bank in Singapore informs someone at Chase that it has the documents, Chase sends the money. The two banks have to know and trust each other, but they don't have to know anything about fish or even about the two fish companies. They simply verify that they both let go.

In some cases Chase not only creates the letter of credit for Domino, it lends him the money to buy it. That's what happens when JC draws down on its three-and-a-half-million-dollar line of credit to import seafood.

"These are baby lobster tails that I will sell to Red Lobster," Jimmy Domino said, pointing to a photo in his album. "It's a deep-sea lobster. We probably bring in about ninety percent of the catch that comes into the country. Red Lobster buys eighty percent of them from us."

Domino was very busy; his fiscal year ended in a few days. "But then it will be something else," he'd apologized on the phone. "You'd better just come out." I said I didn't mind sitting around, so he'd given me his photo album to look at while he took care of a few things.

In one snapshot, women in chartreuse dresses and orange sweaters (the colors must look better in the Indian sun) were packing fish at shiny metal tables in a cold room.

"It's very clean-looking," I commented when Jimmy popped back into the glassed-in conference area.

"But we have problems with the FDA on India. A person like this [pointing to one of the women] that makes maybe a dollar a day, how can they understand what 'global standards' means? This particular guy, he has a trick: once a week he makes everybody eat what they package."

"How does he *make* them eat it?"

"They take out random packages and they have them eat the fish they packed."

Another of Domino's pictures (he was the photographer and the pictures were very good), showed what looked like boys sitting and kneeling around fish trays. "The kids on the floor, they pack our fish," Jimmy said. "Now this is a problem.

"But here, Chulka Lake, the area is fascinating. We buy a lot of their fish and it's beautiful."

Jimmy Domino is the only seafood tourist I know of, besides myself. When I visited a friend's mother in Venice, she wrote back scandalized that "that American" had been to the fish market before the Academia. But Titians are reproduced in books. Where else could I have seen sweet-fleshed cannochie with bright pink "eyes" at their tails?

"Do your suppliers buy from these people?" I asked, pointing to a rustic bamboo structure off a lakeshore.

"The poles are weighted to lower and raise the net," Jimmy explained. "They leave it in for a few hours and then they lift the fish out. It's for local consumption," he said, with a half-amused, half-pitying smile. "Our fish come from boats." (I understood the smile when I encountered the giant trawlers and massive industrial shrimp farms that are JC's "fishermen.")

Jimmy had things to attend to. After he left I slowly began to make sense out of the trading operations in the next room.

"Are you doing anything on tigers?" someone said into the phone. "Like big. I got eight to twelves [eight to twelve prawns per pound]. Singapores! [That, I could tell, meant top of the line.] I got a hundred and ninety cases on the East Coast. I'm asking [X] dollars. They're packed one to six."

Jim (as opposed to Jimmy) was trading black tiger prawns from his desk outside the conference area. Next he concluded a call that seemed to be about trash removal. "I just got off the phone with these boxes and they said they're gonna pick it up. Same as yesterday, same as the day before. Anybody see that movie *Groundhog Day?*"

Since everybody else was too busy to answer, I joined Jim at his desk and he explained how he uses LCs (Letters of Credit). "First we strike a deal with the supplier on the fax —quantity, price. In the fish business it's a little simpler because the world price is in dollars. Then he'll tell us, 'I need you to open an LC.' So we fill in the form. I got a stack of blanks. I know what I want to buy and what I want to say. The bank tells me 'You say it this way for a Letter of Credit.' Then the bank fills in their part. You could have an LC fifteen pages long. Then Chase sends it to their Letter of Credit department and assigns it a number. We fax the number over to them. I could do a deal right

now with people I know personally. We still have to do an LC. They won't
load anything 'til they have that LC number."

Letters of Credit are fast, and they facilitate trade between all sizes of businesses. But they give a special boost to the new or small trader, because it's
safe to send him goods even if you don't know him. Conversely, there's no
safe way to grab his goods and thumb your nose, no matter how much bigger you are. So LCs let the new guy get into the game. Still, quality and timely
supply depend on the kind of contacts people like Jim, Jimmy, and Roy
Matthews, at the far desk, have built up over the years.

"Bring it baby, bring it!" came a supplication that sounded like a crap-
shooter's prayer over the dice. "My memory is shot," he reaches for a paper.
"Ooohh, they cannot release it!"

They was apparently the United States Food and Drug Administration. Or
perhaps not. It may merely have been my open notebook that evoked Roy's
execration of the FDA.

"The law is a hundred years old! Japan is different than a hundred years
ago! . . . Thailand, Singapore, they have facilities newer, cleaner, better than
here . . . but India in the past leans toward Russia so they break their chops.
Now Pakistan is building an A-bomb so they hold up a forty-thousand-pound
container of fish. How do you reject two, three hundred thousand dollars
worth of fish because you found a hair? . . . They're passing along a political
message at our expense. Let them do it through the embassy!"

The dyspeptic trader from Cochin, India, already batty from a day's business, is further crazed when I ask him what the FDA is checking for.

"All the frozen seafood that comes into this country is to be cooked!
Ninety percent of the *domestic* product has salmonella. There should be a
law—stamp on each box, 'MUST BE COOKED BEFORE EATING.' One rubber
stamp—cheaper and better than all the inspectors!

"Okay, they test for salmonella, decomposition, and filth. Decomp, there's
no proven method of detecting it. They smell it by the nose. So if the guy has
a cold . . . " Roy raises his hands and eyes, calling on a higher power to witness the absurdity.

"Like human beings, all the different species have different smells. The
fish I bring in is for ethnic communities. Not just white-table restaurants or
white people eat it. These people eat fish every day, they know the smell!"

JC distributes ethnic specialties like Rohu. "It's a fish like a carp," Jimmy Domino had explained to me. "Indians and Pakistanis and Bangladeshis love it. The name means heart or soul. It's important to them, like turkey on Thanksgiving." Jimmy had also shown me bags of dried cuttlefish and tiny dried anchovies. "They eat them like you and I eat popcorn." JC distributes such specialties to Asian stores all over the US, Canada, and parts of the Caribbean. The company has a Korean and a black salesman. "It's a real United Nations," says Jimmy, modestly and sincerely giving his mixed staff and foreign associates credit for his global reach.

"I have product that came in *January* 27th and today is *March* 27th!" Roy continues his tirade. "I still don't have a release from the government. That's four months [sic] I'm paying for the storage! The law is a hundred years old: the people who work for them are stupid! . . . People don't want to ship to this country. It's easier to get fish into Europe or Japan!"

"Roy wants to go back to India but his wife doesn't want to," Jimmy said, perhaps to explain the man's ire. "She was born in India but she's more American than you or I."

"I'm very intelligent, very educated," Roy stated factually. "Right now I can make more money in India than here. It's the most booming economy in the world. But this is a saturated economy. There's nothing to devleop." Does that explain the prevalence of M&A loans?

"Here," Roy said, photocopying several business cards for me. "The one in Thailand doesn't speak English. Fax their office in Malaysia. P'ng speaks good English. Go there."

On my way out, Jimmy introduced me to the Mexican who was hosing the cement floor outside the freezer room. It was 3:30 P.M. after a day that had begun at midnight (they load their trucks and send out fish around 5:30 A.M.), yet even the filleting room didn't smell fishy. I patted a tuna rat goodbye— anything under eighty pounds is a rat—and my hand smelled sweet. "But if you work in this building all day, you come home smelling like fish," Jim warned me. "It gets into your clothing, so hang them out." But when I got home, I didn't notice. I was too excited about my first contacts in Asia.

I left the seafood firm with the names of their suppliers in Thailand, Malaysia, and Singapore. The same week my mother mentioned that her old friends' son was meeting his wife in Hong Kong on his way back from a business trip to Thailand and Singapore.

These friends of my parents were so close that we called them aunt and uncle when we were little. That should have made their children cousins. The problem was that my mother's every mention of these naturalized cousins included reference to their jobs—real jobs as opposed to writing— and to their lovely homes. Who knows what they heard about me?

So of course I never remembered where Al lived or what he did. All I knew was that he worked for some big corporation that sent him around the world to places where his wife could have a horse.

When I phoned after 35 years, Al was perfectly friendly. His company turned out to be Caltex, and he was a chemical engineer who'd worked on petroleum construction projects in Asia and the Middle East (hence the Arabian horses) and had now moved into oversight, which meant evaluating other people's projects.

"It's partly like a building inspector. You ask 'did you actually do all the things you said you were going to?' But also, you're a successful playwright, right? [So that's what *his* mother rubbed in.] You might say to a friend who's a playright, 'We've been living with this for a year and a half. We can't see what's in front of us. Would you take a walk around the set? See if you notice any potential trouble areas.'"

"Absolutely," I agreed. "Actually, we'd do a complete run-through for him. Because you never know what's going to happen when you put it together."

"That's just what I do! We try to take them back over the whole process, what could go wrong when you go on line."

The trip I'd heard about from my mother would take Al first to Beijing— "No business there. It's just the most central location for the CEO's retirement party"—then to Singapore, where the company was expanding an existing refinery. Then he'd take a "snoop team" to Thailand to check out a brand-new refinery in progress. In the past Al had been stationed abroad to oversee similar large construction projects. But this inspection or "run-through" visit would only take about a week. Then he'd return to Caltex headquarters in Texas.

The refinery he was checking out would refine oil for Thailand's domestic use. Oil, Al pointed out, was a sensitive barometer of economic activity. I realized how fast the Thai economy must be growing when Al told me that this was the first time in 25 years that Caltex, or any other major oil company, was building a new refinery from scratch, "grass roots."

"Would there be something to see if I went there now?" I was thinking of those billion-dollar merger-and-acquisition loans where nothing shifted but electrons.

"There are over nine thousand people working there. We just passed the twenty million work-hours mark with not one hour lost due to an injury."

"Congratulations."

"They had a ceremony with speeches in six languages."

"Wow."

"There are over fifteen languages on the Thai site. And in Singapore— you'll like this—do you remember the Love Boat? The *Habiba* I think it's actually called. They used it to house troops during the Gulf War?" According to Al, there were now some 1,600 Bangladeshi, Thai, Indian, and other migrant laborers living on the ship while they worked on the Singapore refinery. "They have five separate kitchens—Muslim, Thai, Chinese, vegetarian, Western . . . "

"Do you happen to know if either of those projects involve Chase loans?"

"I don't know. Ask the treasurer." He gave me his number. "And I've got a tape that will give you some idea of what's involved. I'll send it."

The tape arrived at my door the next day. When one of my poor filmmaker friends sends me his latest documentary opposing, say, oil refineries, he borrows a second VCR to make a copy, he pastes a label over a used mailing envelope retrieved from the wastepaper basket, and I pick it up at the post office ten days later with a bill for $8.00 to cover postage and the blank tape. Al must have simply phoned the secretary or perhaps scribbled my address on a FedEx envelope and walked it down to the mail room himself. (Engineers are informal.) This was my first experience of being on the Caltex team. I could get used to it. And the tape was very helpful.

It was a progress report from the project in Thailand covering the very quarter in which my money started its nightly movement from the Bank of Millbrook to Chase. The Caltex treasurer had confirmed that Chase was a major participant in both the Thai and Singapore refinery loans. Like the Bank of Millbrook, Chase officers couldn't ethically tell me who they loaned to for what. But borrowers were under no such constraint, and the treasurer told me with great enthusiasm about the money he'd saved the company in Singapore by arranging a special "tax sparing" loan that went through Chase Australia to Caltex Singapore. In addition to the big Thai and Singapore project-finance loans, Caltex had a Chase line of credit that it could draw on for home-office expenses including, I suppose, the cost of sending me the videotape.

During the quarter covered by the tape, my money had financed the erection of an 81-meter, 450-ton crude oil processing column. The camera followed the massive column's gliding arrival on a barge from Japan and then the long, slow lift, which took four hours. I can't believe the video crew wasn't consciously lapsing into pornography as they focused in on the groove around the column's head. Another accomplishment of that quarter was laying the piles for the pier where tankers would bring in the crude oil. But to me the most interesting task was hydro-testing a tank. Before putting oil into new tanks, they do a run-through (flow-through?) with water to make sure there are no leaks. A man in a hard hat squinted into the sun and described how, at the rate of 400 cubic feet (half an Olympic-size swimming pool) an hour, it took 18 days and 18 nights to fill the tank. Negotiating with local Thai officials to use that much water had been difficult, and Caltex had had to promise to store and reuse the water for testing the remaining 88 tanks.

"Gee," I said to Al, "I've driven past oil tanks hundreds of times and I never thought of finding the water for hydro-testing as one of those jobs you have to assign to someone wherever you build."

"You're not supposed to," he said. "But we have to. I'm sure there are jobs like that in getting a play on."

He was right. When the curtain goes up no one in the audience asks "Hey, how did those people get to the right place on stage in the dark?" There's a standard procedure for setting out luminous tape to guide the actors to their positions. And there's a person in charge of recording those positions and making sure the tape is set before each performance.

"One more question," I said. "Why is it cheaper to build a refinery in the US?" Al himself (not so much heavier after 35 years) had appeared on the video as chief technical advisor to congratulate the Thai project team for building the refinery for less than it would cost in the United States. "And as we all know, it's typically more expensive to build abroad," he'd said.

"First, infrastructure," Al answered. "Here, you can send things by truck. You don't have to put them on a railroad car to get them to a port and then put them on a boat. And if something breaks and you need another, you can just get on the phone. Abroad, it will take time, so you always bring extras. But the main thing that makes it cost more abroad is labor."

"But I thought US workers were so expensive!"

"Yes, but they're also very productive. You'll see nine thousand people camped around the site when you get to Thailand. We'd never use more than three thousand in the US. They're easier to supervise, they speak the same language, they know what they're doing."

That's the part that sold me. Caltex isn't in Thailand like some fly-by-night shirt or shoe company to use the cheap labor while it lasts. They're there to supply power for Thailand's growth (or Bangkok's traffic jams). Either way, they're an integral part of the Thai economy. Once again, I wanted to pick the best not the worst cases.

But I still wasn't certain. I mentioned that I was leaning toward telecommunications as my sample big loan because it was so global, so "where it's at."

Energy, Al assured me, is not only where it's at but where it's going, as long as anything physical has to be moved either in production or transportation. And oil would be a major source of energy for the foreseeable future. He was right. The computer and telephone communications industries are like railroads 150 years ago. New technologies create new fortunes for people who act at the right moment and bet on the right track width—or bandwidth. But after the building spurt, the economy is what's carried on the rails or wires. Telecommunications was about transporting information and instructions; that is, about bookkeeping and control. Oil was about making and transporting the real stuff.

Besides, all of the Chase telecommunications loans I'd come across were for mergers and acquisitions—loans to buy and sell existing facilities, not to create anything new. But Caltex was borrowing three hundred million in Singapore and over a billion in Thailand—for real capital expansion. There'd be something to see when I got there.

"Well . . . " I still hesitated.

"Round trip to Singapore is cheap—two thousand dollars."

"Oh."

"Then you can cross the causeway to JB."

"Huh?"

"Johor Bahru, in Malaysia.'"

"Hey, one of my shrimp farms is there!"

"And take the train to Bangkok." He really wants me to come. "I'll be in Thailand from the 12th to the 22nd. Send a fax to Nigel Carlin. He's the project director. I'll tell him to expect you."

Map Ta Phut, Thailand—a chauffeur-driven car rides through a
bulldozed industrial desert one hundred miles southeast of Bangkok

As the car approached them, the Erector Set-like structures in the distance grew huge and I could see that building a refinery is not like staging a play; it's like filming an epic movie.

The project director's office inside a long, low, temporary building

Nigel Carlin, a taut Yorkshireman, picked up immediately on the rehearsal analogy. "In the last fifteen years, only two grass-roots refineries have been built by private companies: this, and the one down the road being built by Shell. Before that, for Caltex, it's been twenty-five years since we were involved in a grass-roots . . . In Korea. So there's no recent experience. You plan every detail in advance, but whenever you do something for the first time there are bound to be things you don't think of.

"For instance, I ordered a generator made by GE in a factory near Toronto. They were going to ship it out of Halifax. It wasn't particularly big. But it turned out it was too big to take on the roads with those wide-load restrictions in the eastern provinces. Now they made the things all the time. They just never shipped one to Sweden. In this case what they forgot was so simple that it was embarrassing. So they came up with a more complicated story."

"Why was it going to Sweden, by the way?"

"To be tested with the gas turbine that drives it. Let's rehearse them together before we ship them both halfway around the world. And it was a good job we did. The gas turbine, which is just a big engine—a jet engine on the ground—was vibrating, wobbling above a certain speed, and we picked it up on their instruments.

" 'Ah, but it was the first time we made it.' And this with a Swedish-Swiss company!"

Nigel started to tell me about a piece of equipment that arrived with the wrong card in the computer control. "Simple to fix. Just . . . [he mimed taking one card out and slipping in another] If you happen to have the right card in the middle of the desert . . . "

"Desert?"

"But that was another project."

And he bounded to the blackboard with a sideways goat's leap to give me the basics on this refinery.

"Here's the schematic." He drew four boxes with a number in each.

"That's in millions?" I asked.

"Yes."

According to the diagram, five million was spent on a feasibility study. Caltex did that in-house. Then forty million (the second box) was spent on the Front End Engineering Design—the FEED—which Nigel worked on with a Texas engineering firm.

"This is where Al came in," Nigel informed me, tapping the FEED box.

"He was with me here." He taps it again on the word "here" and for him, for a moment, the two-dimensional box evokes a city, a room, or perhaps only a conference table during those weeks and months when he and Al struggled together over the drawings. Al gave Nigel full primacy. "He scouted the site back in 1988. The project was on hold a few years. When it was reactivated, Nigel began commuting from Dallas to Thailand. He made thirty trips in the year before he moved to the site."

"Here's where your bank money starts." Nigel chalks in arrows to set off the bottom two boxes—Engineering, and Procurement and Construction. Actually, Chase would have been participating from the start through those ongoing loans to Caltex for "corporate purposes" which underwrite feasibility studies and the expense of keeping people like Al and Nigel on staff.

Underneath all four boxes Nigel writes *$1093*.

"That's one point one billion?" I ask.

"Yes," he says erasing the number as soon as I copy it. "We don't want our Japanese friends to see that, because we got a pretty good price from them."

"Our Japanese friends" are The Japanese Gasoline Company (JGC), the Yokohama-based construction firm that won the primary contract to build the refinery.

"You know what Shell is spending for the same thing? You can just add half a billion."

Someone popped his head in at the door and Nigel left for a quick consultation. While he was gone, I leafed through the papers he'd left on the table. I probably shouldn't have copied from them, but they were standard progress reports. I just wanted the language.

Progress report #41 through April ———

. . . The construction site work force has leveled with 9,700 persons on-site, including JGC and sub-contractors staff. . . .

. . . The project has exceeded 25.5 million building hours since the last lost-time accident. Including 21.3 million man-hours by JGC and other sub-contractors . . . Project cost remains within budget through April. . . .

Within budget and on schedule! No wonder he left these things out for me to see. But what's this?

As of the end of April—99.5% of the cost for equipment and materials has been committed to the vendors. The engineering progress has reached 96.1%. Accordingly, the overall progress of the engineering contract has reached 88.7% against a planned 91.7%. The differential is still predominantly caused by the delays in delivery of air-fan coolers and high-pressure heat exchangers from X [company's name], Italy. Management changes in X prompted by lending bankers should now ensure that outstanding equipment will soon be finished and shipped.

I didn't copy the name of company X, even into my own notebook; this is not an exposé of Italian air-cooler suppliers. But what is this about the lending banks? Do banks follow their loans so closely that they step in to "prompt" changes in the management personnel of one of their borrowers' suppliers? And how can they?

Nigel explained the paragraph when he got back. He had paid for the coolers in advance from company X. But the company's director (I'll call him Y) had been taking money out of the business. It was Y's own lending banks, not Chase and the refinery syndicate, that required Y's company to "bounce him from the board." (That's Nigel's phrase.)

"Air coolers," Nigel responded to my question, "are the tubes on top of the structures. The hot oil goes through and you blow air across to cool it. Y makes beautiful tubes but he'd been skimming money to subsidize his other companies. We were worried that his banks would walk in and hold up their money, then the workers would walk out and there'd be a period of no work while the banks were deciding what to do. So we were getting ready to go in quickly, ourselves.

"I says to the guy over there, 'You go into the back, hide in the restroom overnight, and identify every piece that's ours and spray our name on it.'

"If they go bankrupt and they liquidate," Nigel explained, "you have to show that this is yours, paid for, built out of the materials you supplied.

"Fifteen years ago I faced a liquidation and I said 'This is mine; I paid eighty percent on it.' And they said 'How do you know your steel that you paid for went into this piece?' I didn't. It was several weeks before we got the stuff. Possession—physical possession—is nine-tenths. So this time I said 'Stand right there and say this is mine.'"

Eventually Nigel paid the Italian company's suppliers directly so that the company would have the materials to work on his coolers. The things an engineer has to think about.

———

Nigel had to consult with some people about the graphics for the computer-control system.

"You haven't seen the control room yet." He was rushed, but he wanted to give me a peek at what would be the heart of the refinery. It consisted of two computer work stations in a cozy nook.

"This will be the control room and it will run the whole thing. . . . No, not just monitor it," he answered my question. "Open and close the valves. Run it."

"How many people will work here?" I asked.

"Two inside, one outside. But you only need one to push the buttons."

"How many will be needed to run the whole refinery?"

"Four hundred and sixty will be the total SPRC personnel. [SPRC, The Star Petroleum Refining Corporation, is the entity that owns the refinery. It's 64 percent Caltex and 36 percent Petroleum Authority of Thailand (PTT). PTT seemed to be a silent partner.] But that four hundred and sixty," Nigel emphasized, " includes the CEO, the PR people, the accountants, all the people in that new permanent office building down the road. But on this site, the night crew, the people it takes to run the refinery—twenty-eight.

"Twenty-eight?!"

"That includes the lab people. They would be testing the oil twenty-four hours a day. And they will also be trained as firefighters and for other emergencies. The critical number for a plant like this is not how many you need to run it, but the backup number, the firemen."

Nigel seemed proud to have gotten it down to that low number, but he must have had reservations, too, because he went on to explain:

"SPRC is my client, even though it's part of Caltex. And SPRC is looking to keep the staff lean. After all, the cost of living is high here, and we can't lay people off because of the social problems—you're the big bad oil companies."

"But they surely know you're not going to keep needing the nine thousand seven hundred people you have out there now," I defended the big bad oil companies.

"Not the construction temps. The construction, everyone knows it's finished because they can see it finished. But for SPRC this refinery is designed to have a minimum permanent staff because it's a problem to fire them."

Nigel went out to consult about the computer graphics, and I read more exemplary project reports.

On shore construction reached 63.9% versus a planned 65.7%. ... Actual physical construction (not including temporary facilities) is now 48.8%. ...

"Is everything going as well as it seems?" I asked Jack Bradie of the "snoop team" when he passed. "The élan is real, I can feel that. But I couldn't tell anything from looking at the columns or the piping shop."

"No, you couldn't," Jack answered. "But it is."

Doctor Jack Bradie, of the defiant Scots accent and avuncular twinkle, had been borrowed from British Petroleum in Singapore to serve on the inspection or "confessional" team, as he called it. He had become my resource person when he wasn't too busy.

"If Nigel's instructions are to build it on time, on budget, of the right quality, then yes. It's happening. But this is not Nigel's refinery. The problem now is to transfer it to the people who'll be running it. Because, as you know, this thing starts with money and now we've got to close the loop. We've got to get it up and running so it generates the money to pay you back. If we don't close the loop, we can't build more refineries and I won't get to have all that fun."

Since the construction was going so well, the confessional team had apparently been focusing on the transfer. I wasn't privy to any of their criticism and self-criticism sessions but I suspect that they'd zeroed in on the danger that Nigel's project team, with its internal esprit de corps, had been developing a possessive attitude about the refinery that excluded the people who would soon take it over.

So Nigel must work on bringing them in. Or at least that's the theme Nigel emphasized, a bit stiffly, when he returned from his meeting on computer graphics.

"Basically it's just a matter of loading databases. But it's very important that the people who are going to take over the plant control the graphics selection. If they say 'we're going into yellow,' they have to know what that means." That was Nigel concentrating on the transfer.

But with 9,700 workers on the site, something could still go wrong in this phase. In fact, he heard that there was some kind of "us against them" feeling brewing, and that there was going to be what he called a "union meeting" in a restaurant near the plant. He had asked his driver and his secretary Sunee to keep their ears open during the day and see if it was something he should go to. Sunee advised Nigel to drop in, have a beer, and let the Thais raise the problems if they wanted to.

"Nothing serious," said Nigel when we dropped him off at the restaurant at 7:30 in the evening. "Just little things adding up. And I thought I was running a happy camp."

Nigel stayed at the meeting until 11:30 P.M. and was already at the refinery when I arrived at 8:00 the next morning to hear what happened.

"These guys [The permanent refinery staff] work for SPRC. They're doing a nine-to-five job. The Project buses [as opposed to SPRC transport] have been picking them up and brining them back, but we're on a seven-day schedule now. So often there's no ride. Well, they got used to it. So where's the bus?"

"Possible solutions: we could formally go to SPRC and say 'Your chaps need a ride. You have a bus, send it back to the site at 6:00.' Or Norio [JGC's personnel director] could do it with one of his vans and he could say 'I'll throw that in.' I don't want to see any bills."

Another problem was parking. The spots in the shade seemed to go inequitably to project people. Shade is an important perk in Thailand. "So yesterday I said, 'Okay, first come, first served.' But I could see there was something else lingering. Someone had been ill in a village some distance away, so we let him take a car. Well, as soon as we did it once, we could do it again. And if we can't, then it gets to be a problem of project versus permanent, Thais versus ex-pats. Thais are not complainers, but still it gets to them. All little things, like I said, but they add up."

This hadn't been a real union meeting, of course. (If it had been, alarm bells would have rung all the way up to Dallas.) And the workers involved were many layers above the migrants who camped out around the refinery.

Nigel was talking to permanent workers who wanted a shaded area to park their motorbikes. There were temporary laborers, as I learned from my next interview, who crawled under tractors at noon because it was the only shade they could find during their lunch break. Some of them may have grumbled together or perhaps even complained to a foreman. But it was so many layers away that Nigel would never hear their complaint and I would never get to interview them.

My Caltex hosts honored me instead by arranging an interview with the Japanese Gas Company's head man at Map Ta Phut. Before I saw him, I'd heard people refer to Shoji Morimoto as "The Comandante," after the prison-camp commander in *The Bridge on the River Kwai*. The real Japanese work camps had been in Thailand, and Morimoto was a stout-chested, detail-oriented Japanese man who commanded an international labor force in Thailand. I don't think the resemblance went any deeper. In fact, I think people felt free to call him The Comandante because they liked him enough that there could be no malice.

My first impression, jotted down as he strode into his office was, "very large, very earnest, very British Boy Scout."

I began by expressing admiration. It must be difficult to come someplace where there's no water, no buildings, and have to make things happen.

"This is our job, to go any place which our client requires to design and build."

"True," I acknowledged, "but when an ordinary contractor discovers he needs a typist he calls personnel. Here, there's no personnel and there's no phone."

"In my experience so far [Morimoto had worked for JGC for 25 years], this is best place. Men had already built here, there are facilities. The worst place is the desert, no green, no growing, no sea. If you have just one of them sea or growing, very much helps. If you have two, like here, it will be Okay."

I tried next to compliment him on JGC's extraordinary safety record. Zero fatalities and 20 million man-hours since the last lost-time accident.* "How do you do it?"

---

*It would eventually be a record 35 million man hours and finally one fatality on the complete job.

"The Thailand men are willing to work under safe conditions—wear hats, masks—but in many cases they don't know how, so I need to make courses."

"What sort of courses?"

"We call groups together and set safety subject depending on the job. For instance we have big . . . [he gropes for the word] ground tractors?"

"Bulldozers?" I suggest.

"Hai! At lunch time they just stop them. Many case the workers, after lunch, they are sleeping under the tractors."

"For the shade?"

"Hai. The driver he doesn't know." Morimoto-san mimes the innocent driver running over a man. "So we are teaching 'don't sleep under cars.' And to the drivers, 'Always check under cars.' Otherwise people are killed. I have heard about it in other plants in Thailand, and Singapore. Also we need to teach care of elevated people, why they need to wear safety belts and make scaffolding safe."

"Will the safety habits the men learn here gradually spread out to the rest of Thailand?" I ask, giving him one more chance to take credit for something.

"I don't think so. Safety depends on the mind"—Morimoto points to his temple—"of the management, not on people. Many times they try to save small money and make poor scaffolding." The Thai construction industry was notoriously dangerous. Statistics were unavailable but bodies seemed to fall from the sky every day in Bangkok.

"Depends on laws. For instance, US is very for safety, also Japan. If you kill any people you will get in big trouble."

He stopped and looked at me:

"Do you know what is the price of a Thai life?"

I shook my head.

"Some three hundred thousand baht, which is ten thousand US dollars. If you kill a construction worker all you need to compensate his family is ten thousand dollars—finished."

"And that makes the difference?"

"In places where the price is big, they are forced to make safety."

Morimoto-san left to check on something. (I don't know what, since he was called away in Japanese.)

His secretary brought me tea and I looked around. The office, smaller and neater than Nigel's, was "decorated" with the same progress charts—Piping Shop Fabrication, Concrete Pouring, Piping Erection—all with double columns: PLAN and ACTUAL. There were also two sets of framed pictures: one of the King and Queen of Thailand; the second, "The Erection of the Vacuum Column Jan 12," next to a photo of the same site a year earlier—empty space.

When he returned, Morimoto-san talked to me about the months of preparation and the hundreds and hundreds of design drawings and equipment specifications completed at JGC's home office in Yokohama before such a project got underway.

"Are there surprises anyway?" I asked.

"Yes, surprises. The way to minimize them is to find the surprises as early as possible so to do something. If you find a big surprise just before completion . . . " He trailed off.

"What kind of surprises are we talking about?"

"For example if we buy some equipment . . . [I pressed for a specific example] a compressor—he's supposed to fabricate it as per drawing. So we construct the foundation. Sometimes when it come actual dimensions different from drawing. How come? They have quality control inspectors. They are responsible, yes. But we have the problem." (Nigel says that really silly mistakes are growing more common. "The manufacturing is still good but they fired too many quality control people when they downsized.")

"If changes make big problem, we must plan to reallocate people. Have found few cases go exactly as planned, always ready to solve and people needs to change too. So from this job many people have ulcer, couldn't sleep well. But we are here for only two years and must keep healthy to work."

"So how do you do that?" I ask.

"Sunday golf."

"Golf?" I had heard that Morimoto dominated the golf course and that it was an honor to be asked to join his party.

"I have now my wife here but normally we work in Yokohama office. There work Monday to Friday. Here I'm working Monday to Saturday and sometimes Sunday. So can have only one holiday in the week. Because of one day must cover two days, Sunday very important.

"I have to do! I have to do!" (He shakes two tight fists to illustrate the pressure to "do.") "So I have to be efficient on Sunday. Cannot relax. If I have too much to drink on Saturday night [he cups his hands on the sides of his head imitating pain and regret] Sunday afternoon sleep. "What have I done Sunday?" I feel very much frustrated.

"So I am from Sunday morning seven o'clock golf, to lunch with people, fish in the afternoon, walk on the beach which cannot do on the weekday. If I miss the chance I am very much frustrated.

"I am here not on a holiday but a contract with a tight schedule. Twenty-nine months including design. Is the fastest I am doing so far. At end of April halfway with construction. From now on ten months to go. [Oh, no. It will take me longer to finish my book then it will take him to finish the whole refinery. And I know which one of us will bring it in on schedule and on budget.] I come home every day after seven. So my wife may join me here if she can be independent in the daytime but if she insist I go with her any day but Sunday, I cannot go."

I asked Morimoto about his children.

"I have two children. First daughter I met with her several months after her birth. Second one, two weeks after. So sometimes we miss the family and we bring the family when schools are better. But if the site is in a desert I cannot bring the family here."

———

Even before Morimoto-san arrived to start construction, JGC had sent its trim, delicate-featured personnel director, Norio Miyagawa, to figure out how to house and feed their workers. JGC would directly employ about 180 foreigners and 200 locals at Map Ta Phut. Their primary function was to coordinate and supervise some 40 sub-contractors, each of whom would hire and care for its own workers in turn.

It was important that everyone on-site—there were 9,700 when I arrived, and at the peak more than 11,000—come under the supervision or protection of some primary team or employer. But I, as an outsider, couldn't always distinguish between an acronymic entity and a real team.

Was there, for instance, a functioning Star Petroleum Refining Company (SPRC) that ran this Star refinery? If so, what was its relationship to Caltex

Services Thailand, Ltd., or to real Caltex—the one in Dallas? Not to mention its "parents," Chevron and Texaco.

And how was the Project Team headed by Nigel related to the Technical Advisory Group headed by Al? Both men thought of themselves as Caltex people. But what about the others on their teams? Where would they go when the refinery was finished?

What about all the Chases? The one in Bangkok was called Chase, Manhattan, NA. The one in Singapore is Chase, Singapore. And what about the Petroleum Authority of Thailand (PTT)? They were a 36 percent partner in the SPRC refinery. Did they hire anyone with my money? Such matters are deliberately obscure all over the world.

But in Thailand I found a firm rule for identifying the real protagonists. A true employer or venture in Thailand is one that erects and blesses its own spirit house.

Each Thai habitat or enterprise erects a miniature companion dwelling nearby. For a shop or family residence, it might be as small as a birdhouse. For a high-rise office building, it could be as large as a playhouse. The important thing is that the spirit house be sufficiently more elegant than the human house, to lure the spirits to settle there instead of wandering into the big house, where they'd inevitably engage in pranks or get even meaner. When a business expands or a family redecorates, they often redo the spirit house to make sure it remains proportionately more attractive.

So each independent employer or project at Map Ta Phut, even if housed in someone else's temporary building, had its own spirit house to protect its own people and endeavors.

If a Thai muckraker wanted to determine how many "partnerships" with local contractors are really partnerships with local politicians who earn their "contractor's fees" merely by arranging government permits, the investigator could check on how many of those "contractors" actually set up spirit houses. I don't think anyone would be cynical enough to set up a spirit house to bless a bankbook.

By the spirit-house standard, there were about 40 autonomous employers at the Map Ta Phut site, each in charge of housing, feeding, and protecting its own staff.

Norio took the responsibility for JGC's people, particularly for the mental and physical health of the ex-pats, very seriously. He provided food, shelter, bottled water, transportation to and from the site, and occasional transportation to Pattaya "for recreation or show. All gentlemen; we don't have any females."

At the time I was there, JGC's ex-pat staff included about 70 Filipinos, 63 Japanese, 32 from the United Kingdom, a few Chinese, Malaysians, Australians, and New Zealanders, and one Pole, who supervised piping installation.

To facilitate communication, JGC had prepared a half-dozen phrasebooks for the various engineering areas—civil, electrical, piping, et cetera. They contained thousands of useful phrases like "Make sure you blow the dust out of the pipe with an air compressor," "Take two pieces of three-inch flange to the lank area," "A scaffolding is necessary for this work," "Yes, but where do I get the materials?" "Don't move the plumb bob," and "Well, that's done. Let's have lunch," in transliterated Thai, Japanese, Chinese, and English. But the lingua francas on site were sign language and English.

When Norio had first arrived, he'd had the good luck to find an empty condominium near the coast on which construction had been halted. JGC rented 180 of its 250 apartments and set up a cafeteria in the basement for breakfasts and dinners catered by a Japanese restaurant in town. The condo was a wonderful find. The ex-pat staff could be lodged together, which made transportation easy, and yet they lived in apartments rather than a dorm.

"I wonder who they would have rented those apartments to if you hadn't shown up?" I asked Norio when we toured the building.

"Honestly they don't have any plan, the Thais. Just construct straight ahead. They have good luck, get money; no luck, no. See, still they're doing." Norio chuckled as he pointed to a man plastering in the lobby.

I'd heard many Westerners (I include Japanese in that) joke about Thai businessmen and their lack of planning. The Japanese also generalized about the lack of discipline among their European workers. Norio complained that if you give them home leave or days off it becomes an entitlement. When the project reaches the stage where it demands six days a week, ten hours a day, the Westerners, particularly the British (he didn't employ any Americans), still insist on what they feel entitled to.

But no one was scornful of Thai laborers. Indeed, Northeast Thai welders had an almost legendary aura, like Native American bridge spanners. Nigel told a John Henry tale when he took me around a welding shed.

"We have a new machine that can do the work of ten welders. But we have one welder—do you see that woman?" He pointed to a small, masked figure covered in gray cloth about the same color as the dust in the air. I only realized at that moment that she and many others of the welders were women. "She did as much as that machine one day and the machine only does simple welds. This is the first time JGC is using it."

I wonder what will happen to Thai women welders when the machine becomes standard. John Henry's was a Pyrrhic victory.

"Have you seen the sculptures they dug up in China?" Nigel continued. "They come from northern Thailand. Now look at those men over there. Their features are like that. [I couldn't even tell a man from a woman in the dust.] They are the top-class welders."

Another ethnic group about whom I heard generalizations was Shell.

When I toured the perimeters of the two adjoining refineries, I was invited to notice how messy things were at Shell. There were indeed stacks of parts lying around. The workers' huts and lean-tos looked more makeshift, and Shell seemed to permit a greater variety of local vendors, which may have been a plus.

On Malaysian construction sites, Indonesian migrants hung airy bird cages above the closed metal containers that they themselves lived in. In some Malaysian camps, women workers ran canteens out of one room of the long house so the single men could buy cheap dinners with a home flavor. Perhaps some workers liked the sloppy or laid-back Shell camps better than Caltex camps.

I was told that Shell had already had two fatalities. I heard that they started six months earlier yet would finish about the same time. It was said that they were always losing parts. One of JGC's strong points was organization. There were tens of thousands of pieces of pipe on the Caltex site, and every one of them had a metal tag or an embossed number on it. Morimoto was reputed to know where all these parts were at any moment. But at Shell, I was told, they put things down and couldn't find them. (I don't vouch for these things. I'm just passing them along to illustrate the competitive spirit.)

For all the team rivalry, there was basic cooperation. Shell was allowing Caltex to run a pipe under its property; Caltex agreed to let Shell use its sulfur pelletizing plant for three and a half million up front and an annual fee; the two refineries had chipped in to buy one million dollars' worth of Danish oil-spill equipment "in the unlikely event." And, according to Norio, the two companies had agreed not to compete over welders. Neither would hire a welder who had worked for the other company even if his contract had simply expired.

"Welders could go back and forth Shell to Caltex, no good for us," Norio explained, "so we have agreement Caltex and Shell. [He locked his knuckles together backward to illustrate tight accord.] We have agreement not to do that. They must to find other project."

So a welder with a six-month contract has to sign up again at the same refinery or leave. I wish I could have asked one of the welders what they thought about that. But whenever I suggested that I'd like to talk to a worker, my Caltex or JGC guide answered that these were not their workers but the workers of a subcontractor. It would violate some etiquette, it seemed, to just talk to one.

Actually they were all my workers, I figured. After all, these men and women were eating *now*, before the refinery they were working on produced any income, and the tools and material they were working with were paid for even though there was no oil money coming in yet. All this labor and material was mobilized through the power of capital. That's what control of capital means. You can pay people to do things for you with money that will buy them other people's goods and services. In this case the power to pay was based on borrowed capital, and I was supplying it.

If I were braver or more resourceful, I would have ignored the etiquette and interviewed my own workers. I'd have needed my own infrastructure—car, translators—the kinds of things my loans supplied for Shell and Caltex. It's always hard to interview workers in a company town. This would have been even more difficult.

But stealing back at night to talk to Caltex workers would have seemed rude, if not treacherous, to people who'd been so generous and made so many exceptions for me. So I walked through sheds and looked into the eyes (that's all that was visible) of the mysterious small welders. And I looked through car windows into the open-sided temporary shelters.

I particularly remember a bare-chested old man who sat up on a cot, scratched his shoulder blade, and turned until he stared through me with the deep, world-woe of a Rembrandt self-portrait. (Rembrandt was probably worrying about money, too.) The northeastern welder would remain mythic to me for the time being.

————

Nigel's secretary Sunee had a Chinese father. "That's why I'm so tall," she told me.

We got to talking when she asked me if it was true that many American women don't want to get married.

"I'm fifty-three and I just got married before I left on this trip," I said. "So . . . " I shrugged uncertainly.

"I'm thirty-eight," she said.

"Do you want to get married?"

Now she shrugged uncertainly.

"Does your mother want you to get married?" I asked.

"Well, if I married, the custom here is to go live with the husband's family and work in their home. My mother would not like that because she wants me to keep living with her."

I asked Sunee what her father did.

"He owned a tapioca factory. When he died we had to stop."

"Why?"

"The farmers who grew the tapioca were selling their land for these industrial uses and for the resorts. There used to be much rice growing here. Now, like the tapioca, it's gone with the wind."

When Sunee's father died, her mother sent her to an English school where they weren't supposed to speak Thai or look at a Thai book—even a dictionary—for three years. Now Sunee takes jobs with the foreign companies. She has a group of friends, including engineers and other professionals, who tell each other when new projects are hiring.

"Maybe when this is finished you can go back with some of the project people to Dallas!" I suggested. "They think very highly of you."

"They have plenty of people who speak English there."

"You could communicate with the Thais."

"They have their own Thais."

Sunee had already been to America, it turned out. She'd visited a friend in Simi Valley, California, and they'd gone to Las Vegas and Disneyland. She'd been to China five times to visit her grandmother. When Sunee's father was alive, they had brought his mother to Thailand from a small Chinese village. "It's a hard life there, but once she was here she was unhappy. She wanted to go home. We said, 'We have worked so hard to get you out of China.' That was some time ago, before it was opened up. But she went on strike. She wouldn't eat; her eyes were always water. So we took her back."

Sunee's also been to Switzerland. "To visit a friend, a man, he has a wife and children and a chalet. I saw the snow on the mountains, but I couldn't talk to the children because they spoke German."

My notion that a permanent job in Dallas would be Sunee's heart's desire was as chauvinistic as assuming that every secretary wants to marry the boss.

Sunee doesn't want the job or the boss. I wonder what she does want.

If this is where the children of the tapioca manufacturers wind up, I wonder where the children of the tapioca farmers went. I learned from the man who purchased the land for Caltex (about 500 acres) that almost all the parcels were in the hands of Bangkok people by the time the oil company was buying. Very few tapioca or rice farmers reaped the windfall. I guess that's the way it is everywhere—but more so in Thailand.

———

Nigel said he could spare his driver to take me back to Bangkok. "I have some chores for him there, anyway."

It came with a small thud. After only two days I had a circle of people whom I said "Good morning" to; I had a corner for my purse; I liked being on the Caltex team.

And everyone had been so open. A foreman even took my picture next to one of the tallest columns. A refinery is usually as restricted as a military base, so when I said I'd like a souvenir of me inspecting my investment, JGC had to issue a formal photographer's badge. But it was just a matter of signing a paper. I was beginning to realize what a special kind of access I'd lucked into.

But what about my next oil refinery? In Singapore, the Caltex facility occupied an island a half-mile off the coast, and the workers I wanted to talk to lived on a boat. How would I get to them?

I decided to try from this end, where my presence was already accepted. JGC was the primary contractor in Singapore also, so I explained to Norio that it would give my story an interesting global flavor if I could describe the difficulty of running kitchens that fed Muslims on one floor, Hindus on the next. I asked if he could think of a way I might meet someone in Singapore who ran or supplied the kitchens on this delightfully international boat.

It not only sounded innocent, it was true. I'm fascinated by food sociology. Besides, a subcontractor would bring me at least one step closer to what Norio called the "direct worker."

Right in front of me, Norio-san phoned his opposite number, JGC's head of personnel in Singapore. The conversation was in Japanese. I could only make out the words, "Barbara" and "journalist." He set down the phone before I even realized that goodbyes had been said.

"They are very sensitive in Singapore about lights."

"Lights?"

He wrote the words on paper for me: Human Rights.

"Mr. Aika must get the owners' approval or he cannot talk to you. So ask Mr. Sismondo [head of Caltex Singapore] to ask the other owners if you could talk to Mr. Aika."

"Ah, very good. Thank you very much."

Singapore? Am I crazy? They'd sent a convicted graffitiist back to the US with four stripes of a cane making his the most famous American backside since Marilyn Monroe's. They had just executed a Filipina maid, and the Philippine government had cautioned young women about going there. They had drug-sniffing dogs at the railroad stations. There were serious penalties for chewing gum on the subway. And I'm going to walk around a Singapore oil refinery asking to talk to migrant workers?

———

Oil project experts like Al, Nigel, and Jack Bradie formed a world within a world. They had crossed paths in the past, and when they met on the next project the roles of inspector and inspectee might be reversed. Before they left, the snoop team had a dinner with some of the project people. We filled a long table that ran down the center of an arbor-like restaurant open to a canal.

Nigel came late (he was still running a project) and sat down between me and Jack Bradie at just the moment that someone at the other end of the table used the word *reengineer.*

"I'm an engineer," he said. "I wish they would chose some other word, like just say 'we're going to fire you all.'"

"Or be like our Japanese friends," said Jack. "We say, 'You've got to get rid of two thousand of those four thousand people of yours.' They say 'Okay.' We come out the next day, we see the same four thousand people. We say 'I thought we told you you have to get rid of them.'

" 'We did.'

" 'Well, how come there's four thousand people out there?'

" 'Oh, they're not with JGC. They're with our subcontractor, ABC.'

"That's what companies used to do," Jack continued. "They got too big, they split off, start new companies to do something else. Now they get big they use the money to buy back their own stock. Shows a great lack of imagination, I'd say. Can't think of anything the world needs."

Buying back and retiring stock is, as Jack suggested, a way of making the remaining stock more valuable while essentially freezing or shrinking the size of the company. It's a form of self-M&A.

Jack was correct to interpret a buy-back as management's acknowledgment that they couldn't think of any more profitable way to use money than to pass it directly to their shareholders: *i.e.,* there was nothing profitable enough left to do in their own line of business. But I'm not so sure that the root of the problem was lack of imagination. In 1997, US companies had bought back 179 billion dollars' worth of their own shares while issuing only 100 billion dollars in new shares. And that was only one way of passing money directly to shareholders without using it. The trend was the same in all of the rich countries. Since the early 1970's, growth and real investment in the mature economies had slowed down. Unless you believed that a severe imagination-deficit disorder was sweeping the entire western world, there had to be another explanation.

As dinner proceeded there was a bit more bravado about Shell. This time I heard that they started a *year* earlier but would finish at the same time. Then someone (a man who would be staying to work at the refinery, I think) said, "Shell emerged as the biggest oil company in this decade; they must be doing something right."

"I'm glad," I said to Jack Bradie, "that I don't understand enough of what I'm seeing to spill any technical secrets if I talk to people from Shell. How do you manage to compartmentalize what you learn so it doesn't go back to British Petroleum?"

Jack assured me it was simple and that the competition is comradely anyway. "It's like you said about project people. They're the Green Berets. Well, your Green Beret may be patriotic to his own company, but when it comes down to it, the special forces of one army have more to say to the special forces of another army than to anyone in their own organizations."

As the Caltex men talked about people they'd worked with in different parts of the world and people they might work with again, Jack confessed that he was jealous. "There's a good spirit among these. They haven't been through the kind of re-engineering we've had at BP. I envy them."

I knew that Jack worked for British Petroleum in Singapore and that he had been borrowed for the week because of his expertise in refinery construction. But I didn't know exactly what he did in Singapore.

"I'm overseeing a refinery expansion for SRC."

(*Uh-oh, another TLA, three letter acronym,* I think to myself. *Wait a minute, SRC, Singapore Refinery Company is . . .*)

"You're building that refinery where they live on the boat?!"

"Don't mention that boat, it's my biggest headache."

"But you're BP?"

It took me a moment to untangle it. The refinery I would be visiting in Singapore was owned by British Petroleum, Caltex, and the Singapore Petroleum Company, together. But the joint venture was called the Singapore Refining Company—SRC. Through open bidding, BP (though one of the owners) had won the contract to oversee the construction of the new residual catalytic cracker (RCC). So in Singapore, Jack was Nigel.

"That's my refinery! The one I'm financing in Singapore!"

"Well, stop by and see me."

"Oh, I will," I said, unable to believe my luck.

I wasn't going to press Jack about the Love Boat just then.

But now the Caltex men were reminiscing about near disasters in Africa and people they hadn't worked with since Bahrain. It was beer-drinking-late-into-the-night kind of talk, but no one seemed to have had more than one bottle, and it was early. It may have been my presence (I was the only woman), but the conversation stayed on oil refining.

On the way out I noticed a few business cards tucked unobtrusively into the restaurant's matted wall. "Didn't he have an Indonesian wife?" someone asks. "I thought he was working in Nigeria." These cards—I'd noticed others around town—seemed to belong to engineers. "Too bad," says someone behind me. They are unemployed oil engineers, I now realized. Fallen comrades. You could almost feel people taking off their hats as we left.

Bangkok

On the ride back to Bangkok, I counted Caltex gas stations. We're ever so much more prominent than Shell. Nigel's driver dropped me off right at the house where I was staying, and as I unlocked the door, I was already calculating what it would cost to rent a car, hire a translator, and go straight back. I had to interview at least one northeastern construction worker. I couldn't imagine what one of those women welders would tell me.

Of course I'd have to trespass on oil-company property. What if I was stopped and taken to Morimoto's office? What a way to thank Al and Nigel.

It occurred to me that I might less guiltily and more easily trespass at the Shell refinery where, as Norio happily pointed out, the workers' camps were spread more sloppily around the perimeter.

I made a few phone calls to line up a translator. They wanted a lot of money to go out of town to Map Ta Phut. I began walking around Bangkok looking longingly at northeastern Thais who were *like* my workers.

Right next-door a young woman, a skinny older woman, and a three- or four-year-old girl were camping in the shell of a house whose floors and patio the women were cementing. Neighbors told me that they were northeasterners who would move into another half-finished building when this job was done. I spent hours watching them from my window. Every evening they neatly lined up three pairs of plastic thonged sandals. The child's were perfect miniatures. They were careful workers, and heartbreakingly tender parents.

I finally located a translator who was willing to go down to Map Ta Phut, but she declined when she heard that trespassing might be involved. Private guards in Thailand are less restrained than in America, she warned me. The plan was beginning to sound silly anyway. Not that that had ever stopped me before.

I drifted around interviewing people who didn't belong in my story. Was it the heat, was it the pollution, what was miring me in Bangkok? But by my good luck and their bad luck, almost everyone I interviewed that week would soon be profoundly affected by Chase loans.

I'm about to introduce you to a few of the people who didn't seem, at the time, to be directly on my money's path. You probably know what happened to the Thai economy in late 1997, and can probably guess what became of their hopes and plans. Eventually we'll find out what happened to these individuals in the crash and you may want to look at their stories again. But in the meantime try to hear them as I heard them. Take yourself back to a time when construction sites in Bangkok were as ubiquitous as Chinese restaurants in Manhattan, and the assumptions these people lived by were as reasonable as your assumption that your office will be there in the morning, your house will be there in the evening, your money will come out of the ATM when you push the button.

———

I described the two women with the child who were working in the house near me to a young sewing-machine operator who had also come to Bangkok from the northeast.

"They are sending money back to the farm," she assured me. "The farm is supposed to feed the family but in Thailand the whole family works to feed the farm."

Porngagagag...[?], nicknamed "Squirrel," was an 18-year-old with such intensity that she was compelling despite a drooping eyelid. She had come to Bangkok at 15 to work in a relative's garment shop.

"Normally the girls from my village are not sent to Bangkok until they are seventeen. But in the drought my family had to buy the rice to plant for the next year. If they had to feed us they would have had to borrow even more. So they sent me and my younger sister to the city.

"My father's cousin met us at the bus station and brought us to her house, which is also the shop where we worked. When we got there she opened the rice cooker and said we can have as much as we want.

"I remember how the women all smiled at us and laughed. I thought they were friendly. Later I realized they were laughing because two village girls thought it was a fine thing to have as much as you want of *plain rice*.

"One time when I went on an errand with the cousin I saw thousands of people coming out of a building. All these people, they all eat but not one of them grows rice. Who is growing all the rice for all these people? I did not understand it. On the paddy farm where we grow the rice we can go hungry, but in the city, no one is too poor for a bowl of rice with sauce."

By the time I met her, Squirrel had moved up from a house shop to a regular factory. I was interviewing her in a dormitory-like apartment house on her day off. I'd often heard that the cockroach capitalists who run shops out of their homes are more oppressive, more desperate perhaps, than the formal factories. So I asked about the hours in her cousin's place. Hard work wasn't Squirrel's complaint.

"I liked sewing. I was not bothered by the long hours. People who bend to transplant rice stalks with their feet in the water and leeches biting them do not think it's so bad to sit in front of a sewing machine.

"But when the cousin did not have enough work for us she would rent us out. [The translator stopped to confer with her.] Not a rented woman, nothing like that. She would send us to another woman to sew for her. But the cousin would keep the money. I knew that this was not right.

"I had got friendly with a woman who sold food at the end of our *soi* [lane]. She came from a village near mine. She told me about a woman from our district who had a sewing place a few streets away. Everything outside our soi was like a different city to me then, but one day I deliberately went all the way out and I passed by it. They had newer machines and a man working one of them. A woman who I thought was the owner smiled when I passed, even though she did not know me. I saw it was a better place to work.

"The next time the cousin wanted to lend us out I told her it was not right. We should get paid. She said she was feeding us and giving us a place to stay and fifty baht a day [the minimum wage was 135] and she was doing my father a favor because we were too young for the work.

"But I knew I was a good sewer. So I told my sister to get all her things. She was afraid but I told her I would go anyway so she came. My friend [the food vendor] took us to the other woman and she paid us ninety baht a day and also gave us a place to stay.

"The cousin came after two days and said we had to go back. She said she had trained us and we were her relatives and she was responsible for us and now the other woman had stolen us. She threatened to make trouble. The other woman gave her some money and she went away.

"My mother was very angry when we went home. She already knew that we had left the cousin and she said I had made bad relations in the family. But when she saw how much money my sister and I brought she took it. She never said I was right to leave. But since I had caused the bad relations, I'd better go back to the other lady next year.

"My father believed me. He knew his cousin was not a good person. He believed me about how bad she treated us. But he was afraid too because we had made bad relations in the family. He didn't want us to go back to Bangkok at all.

"But after the harvest I went back. The next year I worked for the lady who took us from my aunt. Then she became the supervisor in a factory and I went there too. Now I work in a factory; I have my own room; I do not sleep on the floor in anyone's house."

Squirrel shared her rented room with another young woman. Their cubicle contained two neatly made cots, a rice cooker, and two separate, well-organized stacks of personal possessions. They shared the bathrooms down the hall with the other women on the floor, all of whom seemed to be single factory women.

"I went home for Songkran to visit my family. I brought big gifts. But when they asked for money I said no. I will not throw my coins into the paddy water any more. I will only send money if someone wants to come to Bangkok.

"My father said the city is all right for you, but I am from here. If we lose the land how will I eat when I'm old and what will I pass to your brothers and sisters?"

"I said, 'I will take care of my brothers and sisters if they come to the city. I will give them a place to stay and I will help them find a job.' I told my father if he comes to Bangkok, even if he is old and cannot do any work, he will always have at least a bowl of rice and never just plain rice without something. I will always feed my father but I will never any more work to feed the farm."

Squirrel is not a typical Thai. My excellent translator, whose grace surely encouraged Squirrel's candor, was herself shocked. When people stay in the city, she told me, marital ties may loosen and money sent home may become less regular. But she had never encountered anyone who would announce to her parents, to a reporter, or to herself that she will no longer send money home. Squirrel's basic story—coming to the city to work for relatives, finding a better job and staying for longer periods—was common enough, but the farm and family (they were almost one) was the ultimate safety net for a working person. Even very wealthy Thais planned to retire to the "paddy farm" in some distant future. Renouncing all connection to the farm was as surprising, my translator felt, as Squirrel's way of expressing personal feelings, particularly the antipathy for her mother.

Unfortunately, the translator, who had come along for the afternoon, primarily out of curiosity, had to run to a regular job. As she was rushing away, Squirrel said that she'd like to take me on a short walk to see the street vendor who had become her friend. She was especially anxious that I meet her because the vendor's business was going well and it was possible that in a year or two the woman would be able to go from the street to a market stall. If she did, Squirrel would become her partner.

Squirrel spoke of the stall—the restaurant—with the same mix of contained joy and superstitious anxiety that other girls her age feel when they utter the name of a "certain" boy: a name that gives you pleasure to work into the conversation but that you dare not speak too often for fear of jinxing things.

We walked, translatorless but companionably, through narrow lanes, passing open-fronted shop houses where women sat at sewing machines, most working diligently, a few staring out for a moment. One, perhaps that hunched girl there, may have been rented out for the day by a relative. How would I ever know?

At the corner of a midsized office building, a woman with a glass-encased pushcart sold chicken and green papaya salad. She was hearty, perhaps 40, and greeted Squirrel with a smile that revealed great warmth and many missing teeth. I don't know how Squirrel described me, but the vendor responded with respectful pressed palms and bowed head. Poor people sometimes act grateful when I take down their stories, as if it were an honor or a favor. But when did my writing ever make their world better?

Embarrassed and helpless without a translator, I gestured my admiration for the lovely food and ordered a portion of green papaya salad *mai pet* (not hot).

The two women laughed.

Wielding her knife with blurred speed, the vendor chopped unripe papaya into long thin shreds, and set about mixing my special mai pet sauce. She squeezed a small lime, whisked a butter-pat-sized blob of yellowish sugar paste (palm sugar, I learned later) into the lime juice, and added a trickle, perhaps half a teaspoon, of fish sauce (it's a light clear liquid, I was surprised to see). Then she slowly and dramatically raised the pepper bottle—I watched apprehensively—and comically tapped in one tiny drop. "Enough!" I gestured. The women laughed again. The vendor folded the sauce into the papaya and garnished it with chopped peanuts, cilantro, and tiny sweet tomatoes.

It was cole slaw! Delicious papaya cole slaw with no oil. At that time I was afraid to eat meat from street vendors, something I regret when I look back on my trip to Thailand. But I was glad, then, that I didn't order the chicken, because there was no way I could have gotten Squirrel's friend to accept payment for anything.

The vendor seemed to be a good-hearted and competent person. (I suppose I'd like anyone who served me such fresh food.) She appeared less embarrassed, less self-effacing than many Thais I'd talked to, but not nearly so declarative as the forthright Squirrel, at whom she beamed like a proud parent.

I finished my salad, mimed my great compliments, said my *sawdee khas* (polite hello and good-bye salutations), and walked away, sad that I would never learn the vendor's story. How long had she been in Bangkok? How did she get started in the food business? Had someone helped her the way she had helped Squirrel?

Street vendors were the true heroines of Thailand's ten-year boom. Talk about production on demand. Wherever a new project or a new factory goes up, fresh food appears in the quantity, at the prices, and to the taste that suits the crew. As the labor force ebbs and flows, the food supply automatically adjusts. Feeding an army is one of the most difficult feats of military logistics, but Thai vendors fed the industrial army handily.

Food and justice are the two things I love most in the world. Bangkok was making me schizophrenic. Ordinary people ate the best food and swallowed the worst injustice I'd ever encountered.

I went to an outdoor rock concert where the popular 1960's group Caravan sang in support of raising the minimum wage. It was very poorly attended. Someone kindly took me over to a Burmese political refugee because Burmese intellectuals often speak English. (Thais tell you proudly that they don't speak foreign languages because "We were never colonized.")

The Burmese refugee was an earnest, soft-spoken man who spent his time trying to publicize the case histories that he collected from Burmese villagers who fled over the border into Thailand. He pulled out the testimony of a farmer who had witnessed the killing of his village head man. The head man had been ordered to round up a certain number of young men to work on a road which the government had agreed to construct for an oil company [Not mine!]. The village men, forewarned, had all run away. When the head man returned with no workers, he was shot in the head. (The eyewitness said he had been hiding in the bushes.)

The human-rights activist agreed to introduce me to an ordinary, illegal Burmese pipe fitter. We arranged to meet at the Burger King across from the office building that he was working on. That way he could join us on his lunch break.

I spotted him (or someone I hoped was him) by his bouncing walk. He looked so solidly un-Thai. Couldn't everyone in the Burger King recognize him as Burmese? Weren't all Burmese workers illegal?

B—— had lived illegally in Thailand for five years and had recently married a Thai woman. Like most construction laborers, he worked by the day, but he was employed fairly steadily by one contractor. On the current project he supervised a team of four other pipe fitters and earned 230 baht a day.

"A Thai in the same position gets two-sixty," he said.

"And the women?" I asked.

"Thai women get one hundred and Burmese women, seventy-five."

"Do they know that there's a minimum wage?"

"The women workers often get less than the hundred and thirty baht a day."

One hundred and thirty baht is what I heard and what I wrote in my notebook. But since I knew that the minimum at that time was 135, I put a light line through 130 and wrote [135?] in brackets.

As I did that, B—— stopped in mid-sentence and did a classic double take.

"Look, she understands Burmese!"

Apparently I had drawn my line through "130" at the exact moment that B—— was correcting himself, saying "Not one-thirty, I mean one-thirty-five." So it had appeared to him that I had responded without waiting for the translation. That means as he spoke, B—— was also reading numbers, upside-down, off my steno pad.

Now, this is the kind of man I'd love to talk to directly. If only I could punch through that glass wall of translation. But I couldn't.

"Were you a pipe fitter in Burma?"

"No. What I did in Burma is repair car engines. I tried to do that in Thailand but I cannot. The private shops, too many police come to repair their cars. If I do that job, police will meet me and the owner will have a lot of problems."

"Are there other Burmese on the building site you're at now?"

"There are two or three Burmese, he think. But if he know someone is Burmese he cannot go introduce himself because he is afraid of the police."

"But you're married to a Thai. Doesn't that make you legal?"

'No, it makes the marriage illegal."

"Do you get along with the Thai workers?"

"The Thai worker has a jealousy toward the Burmese worker. The Thai says the Burmese are working too hard. It makes my mind very . . . [The translator gropes for a word. B——'s gesture suggests conflicting forces pushing out of his skull from opposite directions.] . . . tired," the translator finally comes up with. "It makes his mind tired because he is trying to good control his group to do what the *tow kae* [Chinese boss] wants, but he must also to have very friendly relations with Thai workers. So he is afraid to give an order to the Thai worker because he can go to a policeman and tell him he is Burmese. Just one person can do that and Thais are jealous."

"Are there any agents that bring Burmese illegals in as a group?" I asked.

"Yes." ["You can go to the border at Raynong to see that," the translator informs me on his own.] "And these agents," B—— continues, "if they take the Burmese workers from the border line straight to a factory, sometimes they don't pay them for two or three months. And on some construction sites a very bad agent, before he gives the salary, he will give to the police the message that the illegals are there."

"You know that for a fact?"

"One time, when I worked out near the international airport the contractor did just that. In fact, I went to jail with them."

"You were in jail?"

"I was working on the same building but with a different contractor. I was doing drain work; the Burmese from the border were doing general labor. They lived in a dormitory and had gotten some advance money for food but they had not been paid for two months and they were almost finished with their work.

"One day I was working out in the back, the police came and surrounded the building. Then they closed it off and checked everyone's papers. I'm illegal too so I was arrested."

"How can you be sure the contractor brought the police?"

"Some people saw him outside with the police, pointing out people." ["Whomsoever I shall kiss . . . "]

"So what happened? How did you get back?"

"They put us in jail for three months. . . . The jail is outside Bangkok; it's called Khow Ho. After that they took us out and put us over the border and I came back."

"What did the other workers do?" I asked. "How many were there?"

"There were thirty-seven; fifteen were women. Some of these workers, they are afraid of Thailand, so they go back to Burma and stay."

"I'd be afraid, too."

"But in his case," the translator explains, "he have Thai friends so he can come back to Bangkok and he can get another job easily because he speaks the Thai language. Some of them they know nothing."

"Can a Burmese go to a Thai union with a problem?" I asked. "Like if you don't get paid?"

"No," said the translator without bothering to translate. "Ask him anyway," I said. B——'s response was a laugh.

The translator, a Burmese trade unionist, volunteered his own information. "In the workplace if the Burmese get the accident, like he breaks an arm or a leg, he cannot go to the hospital because he is illegal. But the company still take out life guarantee coverage three percent from the Burmese worker's salary. The Burmese union is thinking to talk to the Thai union about this. But there are eight Thai labor federations and they don't like each other, so the question is difficult."

"By the way, was that building ever finished?" I asked.

"Yes." Said B——. "It was a hospital."

"A hospital! [Why was I surprised that hospital contractors could be crooked?] Where is it? What's it called?"

"I can't pronounce these Thai names but...[He gestured toward my purse.] Let me see your map."

"It's on the road out to the airport," he said as he scanned the map. "Here."

"Have you noticed," I asked, "that Thais don't read maps?"

They both nodded.

"They don't get a British education," this illegal manual laborer explained sympathetically. "But they all read and write."

"Last night," B—— said introducing a new topic, "I saw on the TV a program that says there are two million illegal workers in Malaysia. After the news I told my wife, 'I want to go work illegally in Malaysia.' The pay is high but she is afraid. Maybe she could go legally to Singapore and I could come after."

"Take my card," I said, "in case you make it all the way to illegal in America."

"I'll try," he laughed. He pocketed the card and excused himself to get back to work.

What a buoyant soul. I hope he rings my bell someday. He'd make a terrific New Yorker.

I finally broke the Bangkok malaise and boarded the train to Malaysia. In Penang I was to see P'ng Lai Heng of the Hai Hong Marine Products Trading Company. He'd shipped about $50,000 worth of whitefish that year to JC Seafoods. Then I would take the train the rest of the way down the peninsula (do get out your maps), stop in Johor Bahru to see a shrimp farm that sent tons of frozen black tiger prawns to JC each year, and finally cross the causeway (the opposite direction to Al's suggested itinerary) into Singapore. Thailand and Singapore were oil explorations; Malaysia would be a seafood hiatus.

My image of a shrimp farm was a submerged, shimmering enclosure (I was vague about its borders—nets? Wires? Rocky jetties?) tended by bubbling Jacques Cousteau-like gardeners—a productive, peacable underwater kingdom where drifting tides of blue-green algae were converted into tons of delicious pink protein. Of course any farming had to change the balance of nature, but prawn's were bound to be less controversial than oil.

To be honest, I already knew better, or should have, for I'd been confronted by the detritus of shrimp farms back in Thailand. But it had been such a weird encounter that I hadn't processed the information there.

At the Thai refinery in Map Ta Phut, one of the Caltex engineers had asked me if I could see the shrimp ponds from my hotel window. "It's black tigers you're importing, isn't it?" I got a kick out of the way they treated me as the big investor—building refineries, importing black tigers.

I had seen them, of course. When I stepped out on my balcony to breathe the sea air, on that first disappointing exhalation I looked down at six ugly oblong pits. From up high they looked like excavations for giant swimming pools.

Once I found out that they were shrimp ponds I elevatored down to the second floor for a better view. From there the pits looked as large as building foundations, but shallower. Their crude dirt bottoms were dry except for a few mud spots. I was leaning over the railing, craning to see the whole layout, when a voice behind me said "No good."

"No good?" I turned and saw a smiling bellboy. He pointed directly down to the shrimp ponds and said, "No good. Bad."

"Bad? What do you mean, bad?"

But he didn't understand English that well. I strained for the little Thai I knew and finally came up with *udang* [shrimp].

"Udang?" I asked pointing down.

"Yes." He nodded.

"Udang bad?" I asked, pretending to taste a bad shrimp and pull back from it.

"No," he responded, *"ikan."*

"Ikan?" I made the motion of a fish in the water.

"Yes," he nodded.

"Ikan?" I pointed down to the ponds.

"No, udang." He confirmed that they were shrimp ponds. "Ikan gone."

"Ikan gone?" I asked "Fish gone?"

"Yes," he responded with simple sorrow. "Ikan gone."

Several strange things were going on here. First of all, I was speaking Malay. I've noticed that when I try to speak French I can sometimes dredge up a few words of the Spanish I studied for three years in high school. Now, trying to speak, Thai, I came up with the Malay words for fish and shrimp. I'm bad at languages, but food words impress themselves on my memory. ("Belimbi"—star fruit—is my favorite Malay word.)

More amazing than my own culinary glossolalia was this trilingual bellboy rummaging frantically through his mind to fling up English, Thai, and Malay scraps which he interspersed between apoplectic gestures and sweet apologetic smiles. Looking closely, I realized that the "boy" was in his thirties or perhaps forties. He was neither dangerous nor crazy, I'm fairly certain, just desperate to communicate the evil of shrimp ponds.

From what I eventually made out, he was a fisherman. He had come to fish with an uncle or other relative because all the fish in his own part of the ocean were gone. But so were the fish here, because of shrimp ponds. Now he was working in the hotel in order to buy a big boat with his uncle. Or else he already had a boat, but it was gone because of the udang. I think there may have been two boats, a big one and a little one. Somehow learning English was also part of the plan. I wouldn't swear that I got any of this right. There were only two points he made absolutely clear:

Udang [shrimp] bad : ikan [fish] gone.

When another hotel employee got off the elevator, the bellboy *waiyed* [folded his hands together and bowed his head] politely, backed off, and slipped away.

I spotted the bellboy, again, across the lobby when I was standing next to the Indonesian wife of a German tourist. But as soon as he saw me he took off, apparently frightened that I was pointing him out.

The woman said he was a Malay from southern Thailand. "They're Muslims, but very gentle people."

That's all I learned about him, and even that fact isn't certain.

Back in Bangkok, I spoke to the environmental reporter for an English-language daily, who told me about Thai shrimp farms.

They don't produce poison shrimp. But their wastes, discharged back into the ocean, create algae blooms and other problems that kill or drive off the coastal fish. Seepage from shrimp farms also salts nearby agricultural land. Aside from ruining the surrounding land and water, the Thai farms are so intensive and poorly managed that they pollute themselves with their own sewage. So, after two or three hugely profitable years, the owners generally abandon the pits and move up the coast, leaving unfarmable land, unfishable water, and big ugly holes in the ground. Enough of Asia's coasts were used up, even then, that these operations were moving on to South America and Africa.

As it happens, there are laws in Thailand that make some parts of the coast off-limits to shrimp farms. But government officials seemed less likely to enforce these laws than to drive local farmers and fishermen off their own land at gunpoint to make way for new ponds.

In the US, we are familiar with the kind of civil disobedience in which brave people break a law they disagree with and wait peacefully to take the consequences. In Thailand, there's a brave form of civil *obedience*. Heroic individuals stand in the open obeying a law that runs counter to the interest of some wealthy individual, and wait calmly to be shot by his thugs.

Such martyrs had made the practice of shrimp farming on protected land public knowledge, but it didn't seem to make any practical difference. Thailand was the world's largest exporter of frozen shrimp at the time of my visit, and it looked like the shrimp farmers would stop expanding only when they'd used up the entire Thai coastline. (In defense of shrimp farms, my informant suggested that the enormous Thai fishing trawlers that practically vacuumed all the fish out of the sea would have wrecked the coastal fishing anyway.)

But I was leaving Thailand and heading for mellow Malaysia.

———

After Bangkok, Penang seemed like paradise. Even now, I remember it as one of the most restful places I've ever visited. It may have been especially restful because I treated myself to the E & O. The same Armenian hoteliers who built the famous Raffles in Singapore had opened the Eastern and Oriental in Penang two years earlier, in 1875. But while the cheapest room at Raffles was S$400 [400 Singapore dollars] a night, I could still get a room at the E & O for $60. True, my room looked out over the Esso station, but I could sit on the terrace where Maugham and Kipling took tiffin and drank "stingahs." I could loll at the pool under coconut palms and frangipani, and I could gaze out over the Indian Ocean from just that turn on the island where the mountains of Kedah mysteriously appear and disappear.

Kampong Madrasah

From the E & O's entrance, I could board a tour bus with stops at the Snake Temple, the Butterfly Farm, and an "authentic" Malay fishing village, or *kampong*. If my shrimp farms really drove out coastal fishermen, then an authentic village belonged in my story somewhere. I decided to find one without a gift shop.

I located my authentic village through an ascetic-looking Indian doctor who put me in touch with a Malay community group called Yayasan Bina Ilma (Foundation for the Upliftment of Knowledge) that, among other things, helps fishermen get bank loans. A young man from the organization agreed to take me round in the late afternoon when the fishermen came in for the day.

The approach to my village was through a housing project and across a tire-strewn vacant lot. The one street was a wooden walkway leading past the same picturesque stilt houses I'd seen in the tourist brochure. Naturally, I peered in. The brochure didn't show cracked oilcloth, rusting Coke coolers, and old women sleeping with their feet sticking out of the doorways. But they may have been there too.

The walkway opened into a wharf where a single fisherman was cleaning his catch—one small snapper and a huge pulsing flatfish. The white, uneyed side of the flatfish arched itself across the rowboat seat, so vibrant in the sun that the flesh seemed not just naked but inside-out.

"Yes, catches were better years ago," the man acknowledged as he cut into the live fish and dumped its guts into the water. But he expected a good price at the market for this one [the flatfish], which is why he came in a little early.

Another fisherman was repairing an outboard motor. He hadn't gone out that day.

Neither fisherman was anxious to talk, so I waited around until a few others came in. At one time there had been close to 200 fishermen in Kampong Madrasah. Now about ten went out regularly.

After a while, two more boats tied up and we were joined by a couple of men who'd already bathed and changed into their sarongs. The group, now sitting or squatting on the floor, agreed that catches were much smaller now than 15 years ago. They also agreed on the reason: pollution from hotel sewage.

"How can you be sure what the pollution is?" I asked.

"You go out to the ends of their pipelines and you know it's human waste; we smell it."

The men claimed that it started 15 to 20 years ago. By ten years ago the waters were visibly polluted with the waste, which poisoned the fish.

The fisherman's chronology coincides with official history. In the late 17th and early 18th centuries the British established three colonies in the straits of Malacca: Penang, Malacca, and Singapore. The oldest of these straits settlements was on the fishing island of Penang. But Penang, "Pearl of the Orient," fell behind once the publicity-savvy British colonial administrator Thomas Raffles arrived in Singapore in 1819, and it stayed behind for 150 years. That left Penang with the least modern development, the oldest colonial architecture, the clearest water, and the most secluded beaches. These features made it the perfect hangout for early '70's hippies, who were followed by Australian and Japanese tourists, then by hotels and condos.

The resort development called Batu Ferrenghi (Foreigner's Rock) is named after the rock where the foreign hippies liked to smoke pot, it's said. *The Rough Guide* for Malaysia, Singapore, and Brunei reminisces about Batu Ferrenghi in "the early seventies when the island's waters really were jewel-like." The hip authors console today's latecomers by saying "since every major hotel has a pool, with luck you'll never have to swim in the sea."

So the fish swam away from the tourist excrement and the tourists swim in the pools. Why, then, do these men keep fishing?

"I don't like working in the factory."

"I have my own boat; I'm my own boss." The men now go about 16 miles out in rowboats with outboard motors.

"If you work in an office you only get paid once a week. If you work on the boat you get money every day."

"In case of emergency you don't apply for a leave, you just stop fishing." This man had worked for the Penang Park Commission for 400 ringgets a month. [The Malaysian ringget, or dollar, was worth half a US dollar at the time.] "No matter how many weeks, months, years you come on time, one time you come later they are angry. Then I see my friend he work twenty days he make nine hundred."

"But that's the biggest catch in a long time," someone else objects.

"You work with the government you get four hundred a month. Here you work hard, you get more."

They talk about the good days and the great catches: the week one man made 400 ringgets; the single fish that sold for 40.

"Some fisherman are lazy," a younger man comments. "If they caught a lot today, they don't go out tomorrow. But I think different. If we catch a lot today we go out tomorrow, catch more."

Another man differs politely.

"You're free to do what you want. You can go out three days a week or twenty days a month. *You stop when you have enough.*"

I didn't underline that sentence at the time. It took me the rest of the voyage to understand that it was the most subversive sentiment I would hear in all my travels. The one thing that my money could not do was stop.

Everyone agreed that the fish around Penang were getting smaller.

"In Norway, fish they catch are bigger than our boat, thirty feet."

"I once caught one fish, I got 40 ringgets," a man repeats.

Despite the fish stories, many of the men are only part-time fishermen. One works in a store but goes out when he can. Another fishes three days a week. A third has begun to take sport fishermen out from Penang Bridge for ten ringgets. This presents him with a painful sight. "Some people like to struggle with the fish. They catch it and let it go. Me, nah, never." It hurts this man to see a valuable fish swim away but "I make more money taking the man fishing than from selling that fish."

A younger man says he goes out at least two days a week. He's here now waiting for his father to come in.

That reminded me to ask people what their parents did. Everyone who answered said that his father and grandfather had been fishermen.

A grizzled man who had been rubbing his leg muttered something to the others.

"He was stung by a jellyfish," someone explained.

"Does it hurt badly?" I asked.

"We're used to it."

The grizzled man pointed first in one direction than in another.

"He's telling them where they are so they can be careful."

I wondered how you describe a point in the ocean. You can't name the street and cross-street.

"We don't have echo sounders, we don't use charts," someone explained. "We know where is west. You look from this spot to the yellow cross." He points, making a vector with one arm. "Then from that spot to the roof." Using the other arm as a second vector he makes an angle. "We know how far is . . ."

From the fisherman's gestures he seemed to be explaining triangulation or something like the parallax location systems used by the ancient Greeks.

My classics professor said it was advanced geometry that allowed the ancients to venture all the way across the Mediterranean. The professor cited it as an example of the high achievement of pre-Hellenic civilization.

It shouldn't have taken parallax navigation to remind me that there was something worth preserving in the culture of kampong fishermen. Besides, a man doesn't need an anthropological justification if he'd rather fish three days a week than work in an electronics factor for five. Isn't that the choice I've made in life?

But did it make economic sense for Yayasan Bina Ilmu, [The Upliftment Foundation] to try to keep these fishermen in business with small loans? The boat loans, typically between 1,000 and 3,000 ringgets, were made by major Malaysian banks to the individual fishermen, but the foundation backed the loan with its own credit because the fishermen had no assets that a bank could foreclose on. As it happens, the foundation has no assets either. But it could fund-raise, primarily among well-off Malays, if it was necessary to pay a man's loan for a while. So the banks were safe.

But there was a larger economic question. If the hotels had driven the fish beyond the reach of the traditional boat, could fishing with a new outboard motor garner enough extra fish to cover the old living expenses plus the new costs of fuel and interest on the loan?

I asked Doctor Jayabalin, the Indian MD who put me in touch with the Upliftment Foundation and who volunteers his professional services to seemingly every help and self-help endeavor on the island, about the loans.

"We have not had much problem of repayment," said Dr. Jaya, as he's called. "Just, circumstances might make a payment late."

Circumstances for a fisherman could mean an illness or losing one of the part-time jobs that he or other family members held to cover expenses.

"The fishermen all told me about big catches," I said.

"Traditional Malays are optimistic people. They talk about successes and don't dwell on their failures."

"But can a fisherman earn enough from fishing to support himself and pay his loan?"

"The price of the fish is up. So whenever they land a good catch, they can get a good price from their middleman. It is possible to earn a hundred and twenty ringgets on such a day. But the water is polluted, the fishes are depleted. Mostly when I go, I see the people come in with nothing or a small catch."

"So why does the foundation encourage a man to take out a boat loan?"

"Fishing helps preserve the social structure of the village. It preserves his way of life."

"That's nice for me," I said. "I get to tour a truly authentic kampong. But how does it improve the fishermen's life if he has to work at regular jobs in order to pay the boat loan in order to work as a fisherman?"

"Compared to the other jobs—construction work, office work, assembly work—fishing is what he does best. Besides, there is the lure of a big catch."

"Oh, Doctor, I've met people who tell me that they earn their living at the race track. They believe that because they only remember their winnings. The truth is they're probably living off a small inheritance. But these fishermen don't have inheritances."

"He has learned many things from his father and grandfather."

"So you think he should gamble on the big catch?"

"Fishing is a handed-down tradition. . . . He wants to be close to the sea. . . ."

I thought about friends who want to be writers; who *are* writers, except at tax time when they realize that their main income is from word processing.

". . . Two thousand ringgets in five years is a very small repayment. So even doing odd jobs . . . "

The movie sale is the writer's big fish.

". . . The Malays are romantic people."

The doctor and I argued on amorphously about preserving lifestyles.

Kampong Madrasah was only 50 to 100 years old, he told me. There may have been fishermen on that spot before the British came, but its present residents are a distinct caste of Malays who married Indians. These South Indians (including Dr. Jaya's ancestors) had been brought to Malaysia by the British to work on rubber plantations and in the civil service. The name Madrasah means Little Mosque, or shrine, and Dr. Jaya estimates the kampong's age from its oldest artifact, an eighty-year-old printing press that was used to print Moslem tracts.

There were already a lot of lifestyle shifts in that brief history. As it happens, Dr. Jaya and I both had ancestors who were forced to make painful changes because of economic "development." One result was that we both spoke English. That may have involved shame and struggle for our grandparents but we both felt grateful to speak the language of Shakespeare and world commerce. And I felt grateful that I could talk to the doctor without a translator. I wish I knew enough Malay to understand the grizzled old fishermen as the romantics that Dr. Jaya knew.

I asked the doctor how Kampong Madrasah differed from the "authentic" village in the hotel brochure. He said they looked about the same. I might even spot the rusting-Coke-cooler furniture on the tour. The main difference was that in my village, people's day jobs were at electronics plants or construction sites. In an authentic village, the young people would probably work at the nearby hotels. "So you might say the older people hold down the job of being authentic as part of a two-generation scheme to bring cash in through the hotels."

"Well, then," I chuckled, "we can count on hotels to keep the last few fishing villages going,"

"Until they need that space," the doctor retorted.

I pictured Penang island completely walled with condos, the only public opening to the sea, a wooden walkway through the last fishing village. "By the time they want the last space on the coast," I said, "the island will be so jammed that tourism will be on the decline. So the system is self-regulating."

But I couldn't tell him whether it would self-regulate before or *after* the last fish and the last fishing village were gone.

The muted argument meandered on.

Yes, things are always changing: there had been a small population of fishermen on Penang when the British arrived and began clearing the island with fire, often shot from cannons. (The British say there were about 100 fishing families then.) Surely those people didn't welcome that change. Now there were a million people on Penang. Most of them don't want change either. But they accept the changes that brought them to this point.

And yes, change hurts: we're familiar with the heart attacks and increased mortality among people who merely lose their jobs. What do you suppose happens to people who lose their profession, their income, and their home all at once? Dr. Jaya knows these fishermen intimately—he knows their blood pressures.

It was easy for me to be philosophical about change when I didn't have to do the changing. It was easy for the doctor to be romantic about preserving traditional occupations when he was a physician among fishermen and lived in the most comfortable island I could imagine.

In truth, Dr. Jaya believed much of what I said and I believed much of what he said. And the fishermen were so marginal that the banks didn't care one way or the other. Loan officers weren't scouring the island for fishermen customers, but each bank could afford to make a few boat loans because, like Community Reinvestment Loans at Chase, they were underwritten by various do-good agencies and ultimately, if push comes to shove, by the government.

The same was also true about some much larger loans that Chase was making in Malaysia through Malaysian banks—not to fishermen. Those debts too would be covered by a government if push came to shove, which it did before this story ends. But neither I nor the fishermen knew anything about those loans at the time. Oddly enough, it was those big loans that they never signed for that the fishermen would eventually be pressed to pay back.

The Tower Mall in downtown Penang

I went with an Indian women to see a Malay love story at the movie theatre in the downtown mall. I'd seen the poster for *Selembu* everywhere, even on the wall of a construction-site "long house" used by illegal Indonesian workers.

Somehow the movie line got mixed into a line of young women who were filling out job applications. An electronics assembly plant located in one of the industrial parks on the island had set up a recruiting table at the mall. (When there's an eight percent growth rate, employers go where the workers congregate.)

My companion recognized a young Malay who grew up in one of the kampongs. We asked what she was doing.

"Applying for a job."

"I was talking to some fishermen at Kampong Madrasah," I said, taking advantage of the free translator. "They don't seem to catch much fish anymore but they don't want to quit fishing and work in the electronics plants."

"Neither does my father," she said. "Neither do I."

"Why is that?"

"When my father is fishing he looks up at the sun after only a little while and the whole day has gone. When I'm at the electronics factory I look up at the clock after an hour and it's only two minutes later."

"Why are you applying for the job, then?"

"My sister and I must give my mother some money soon for an eye operation and my husband and I want to buy a bed. I will do it for only nine or ten months. It will go fast."

Meeting Mr. P'ng

Bumi Putra, "Prince of the Earth" is the heroic epithet for the ethnic Malays who make up about 60 percent of the Malaysian population. Bumi Putra is also the name of a policy of preferences in business, finance, and education that were put in place after anti-Chinese riots at the beginning of the 1970's.

Under the Bumi Putra policy, large employers were required to hire a percentage of Malays. Since only Bumi Putras had the right to buy land, a business that needed to purchase property had to have a genuine Prince of the Earth partner. Universities were required to assign places to Malays, Chinese, and Indians in proportion to their numbers in the population which is roughly 60 percent Malay, 30 percent Chinese, and 10 percent Indian. The government also provided scholarships and enrichment opportunities, like travel abroad, for Malays.

The policy, a kind of affirmative action for the majority, succeeded in educating many Malays who wouldn't have gone to college or even high school before. But since the majority of Chinese youth would normally seek higher education, the 30-percent quota didn't provide enough places. Chinese college students frequently went abroad, many to the University of Singapore.

The group that probably suffered the most from the educational preferences were Indians. Language and other factors made them disproportionately likely to go to college, but they were far less likely than the Chinese to come from families that could afford to send them abroad. It also became difficult for Indians to advance in their traditional sphere, the civil service.

Bumi Putra was intended to create a class of Malays who would learn the ways of commerce from their Chinese partners. Some did, I suppose. But in many Chinese enterprises the Malay partner was regarded more like an ethnic payroll tax, an annoying but calculable extra cost of doing business. The effect for the nation was to place a slight handicap on their most efficient firms. It didn't seem to have dampened productivity as much as it should have.

I noticed a typically Malaysian wrinkle to the policy at a suburban housing development in the capital, Kuala Lumpur. Bumi Putra regulations required the developers to sell the new subsidized houses according to the 60/30/10 formula. As a result, Chinese with the money to buy recruited Malays to make the original purchases and then immediately resell to them at a markup. Nobody seemed to care that this ruse fulfilled neither the goal of distributing housing proportionally nor of creating integrated neighborhoods. That would have been nice, but it was good enough that the policy simply siphoned some cash from Chinese to Malay bank accounts. For the Chinese, the two-step purchase process was yet another redistributive tax. An efficient one, I suppose, since the money never passed through any government bureaucracy.

As a form of redistribution, Bumi Putra worked. According to *The Economist*, "In 1971, when the government introduced the new economic policies...60 percent of Malaysians were reckoned to be living below the poverty line: this had dropped to 14 percent by 1993." By the time I visited poverty, at least in mainland (or Peninsula) Malaysia, was so low that poor Malay fishermen of Penang could be looked upon as quaint relics, their future discussed in terms of cultural desiderata.

Free-market fundamentalists would try to attribute the prosperity entirely to rapid growth, but economic growth doesn't always raise all boats. Thailand, with 8 percent growth, still had the vast majority living in abject poverty while income inequalities grew. The result was a meanness you felt a dozen times a day. Malaysia's ten-year growth rate, though high, had been somewhat lower than Thailand's. But the new wealth was sufficiently more evenly distributed that to me, as an outsider, it felt like a kinder, gentler society.

But Bumi Putra isn't just an economic policy, it's a racial policy. It may have been a mixture of class and race resentments that galvanized the riots, but it was to the racial component that the government responded with its unique kind of income redistribution. And it was racial fear that impelled wealthy Chinese to accept the new handicaps quiescently. (When else do the wealthy allow themselves to be equalized nonviolently?)

Substitute Jew for Chinese, substitute Aryan Controller for Bumi Putra partner, and the policy starts to sound different.

There had been anti-Chinese riots even on the very Chinese and peaceful island of Penang. I must remember when I speak to my seafood contact P'ng Lai Heng, that he had lived through something like *Kristallnacht*.

Mr. P'ng called for me at the end of an auspicious day. "We have joint ventures in Myanmar, Thailand, Indonesia, and as of today," he told me, "Vietnam."

P'ng had scouted Vietnam six years earlier but had decided that it was too difficult to do business there.

"Maybe because I met the wrong people. They say they have a certain number of workers, I go, I see fewer. 'That's because I got a big quantity in my storeroom now,' he says. I visited the storeroom, nothing there. But everything is 'Okay.' 'No problem.' Six years later government policies change. Also I meet different people. I have confidence now."

So Vietnam will soon have a modern jellyfish processing plant. It tickled my fancy to think that my money, in the form of a JC Seafoods letter of credit, had helped P'ng explore Vietnam before the US embargo had been lifted. There are times I don't mind being part of a global capital flow that defies national sovereignty.

Currently P'ng sends dehydrated jellyfish from factories in northern and southern Thailand, Burma, Malaysia, and Indonesia to his big markets Japan, Korea, and Taiwan. A few hundred bags even find their way onto grocery shelves in North America. At the same time he sends frozen whitefish from Thailand to the US and South America.

"The Thai fish comes from Vietnam, India, Bangladesh—it's hard to know. Thai trawlers are very, very big, and they process on the boat. Twenty boats will go out around a mother vessel and all will transfer fish to that mother, and that will bring it back to Thailand. So that is how we say 'Thai-origin fish.' But it is not."

P'ng also buys mackerel from Norway to sell in Thailand, "because there is not enough fish left in Thailand. Every year the catching becomes less and less."

And he imports cuttlefish from Vietnam and India to be processed in Thailand.

P'ng's fish, mollusks, and coelenterates seem almost as mobile as my dollars. And since it's fungible, my money flows through every rill and rivulet of the P'ng family business—or businesses, I should say. Mr. P'ng's gold, red, and black business card lists three Malaysian seafood and two Malaysian "development" companies, plus two Thai seafood associates, and what the card describes as "factories and associates also available in Sarawak, Sabah, Indonesia, and Myanmar."

P'ng's father got into jellyfish as the employee of a Japanese company. "He married a Thai woman. That's why we have a base in Thailand." His brother, whose desk I passed as we entered the Penang office, seems to handle their real estate. Mr. P'ng manages the international trade. In fact, it was he who brought the family from processing into trading.

"Do you have one of those Bumi Putra partners?" I asked, looking around the three-desk, two-file-cabinet office.

"We're too small!" He literally brushed the annoying subject away.

"Our family is in the jellyfish business since 1971; dehydrating and now exporting. Not many people do it. We are known internationally for our quality control."

"What exactly is involved in drying jellyfish?" I asked.

"It is *dehydrated*, not dried. We buy the raw material from the fisherman, we own no boats, and we always process in the country of origin."

At first, Mr. P'ng doubted that I could be interested in jellyfish, but he was happy to describe the procedure when I probed.

"For the processing we use salt, alum, and sodium bicarbonate. We need fourteen days in at least four stages. The first stage lasts one day and one night in the chemicals, the second stage, three days in the same chemicals. The third stage, five days in a different mixture of the same chemicals. The fourth stage is one week. In that stage it's only salt."

Though the formula sounded straightforward, it was very hard to get people to do it just right. "I have to travel a lot. I follow my jellyfish." That meant December to May in southern Thailand, April to June in Burma, June to August in northern Thailand, and September to November in Indonesia. Now Vietnam would be added to the itinerary.

"The first season in a new place is always very hard. In the first two years we cannot make any profit at all."

At the time, wages in his jellyfish countries were $6 a day in Malaysia, $5 a day in Thailand, $4 a day in Burma, and $3 a day in Vietnam. But the reason for expanding internationally was not to tap the low wages (they just didn't make enough difference) but to be near rich new sources of jellyfish.

In their southern Thai plants, the P'ngs had many older workers who came back season after season. This made me think about my bellboy/fisherman.

I asked if some workers might have been fishermen before or if perhaps they fish between seasons now. P'ng thought not. They were factory hands, more likely to work in other seafood-processing plants.

"They are not highly motivated," he volunteered. "The motivation is, if you are not working you cannot get money. Sometimes our payment is every week, sometimes every ten days. After the payroll day, many of the workers will disappear for one or two days. They finish using their money and they come back."

I asked if that problem was apt to be worse in the countries where people were less used to industrial work.

Mr. P'ng thought it was about the same in each country. "Same in Indonesia, same in Burma, I predict it will be the same in Vietnam. I think if they are very hard workers they wouldn't be daily workers very long."

The lack of motivation made it just that much more difficult to get a good product.

"What is a good dried ... I mean dehydrated jellyfish?" I asked.

"Crisp on the outside but soft enough to stretch your finger through—chewy."

"I'm going to have to try jellyfish," I said.

"I export about two, three thousand metric tons a year of already finished product. If we talk about two thousand tons that would be [he does a quick calculation] six million US dollars a year."

"And jellyfish is not like oil!" I said with admiration. "Oil in the ground is equivalent to dollars. It can be bought and sold twenty times while in transit. But jellyfish are only good to the people who want to take delivery." In this I was echoing Jim at JC, who had said to me, "Fish is still a hunted item, unpredictable. It doesn't lend itself to a futures market. The last thing someone in Bear Stearns wants to do is take physical delivery of a forty-thousand-pound container of fish. But it's the only thing anyone in the fish business wants. Fish people are not interested in paper, they're interested in fish."

"You can't speculate in jellyfish," I said.

"Oh, yes you can," P'ng replied.

"How?"

"It is impossible to predict before the season whether it will be a good catch or a poor catch. It's not based on weather; it's not based on last year's catch. Some years the jellyfish disappear. But we know" he grew confidential, "the jellyfish start the life as eggs on the . . . [he groped for the word, and I made the motion of tentacles in the water.] "Yes, the legs. But you can only tell at the beginning of the season when you hear there are a lot of eggs on the legs. I know almost all the jellyfish people in the world.

"If it's going to be a small season, we buy first. The price may be a little high but a month later it will be higher. If it's going to be a big season, we sell first, even though we have not caught any fish yet, because we know they will get cheaper. This is how we make a market."

I couldn't help thinking about the Rothschilds, who made a fortune trading francs against pounds because they got the outcome of Napoleon's battles ahead of everyone else via carrier pigeon.

When I suggested that there was no speculation in jellyfish, I'd meant to praise Mr. P'ng as a man who dealt with something realer than money, a man who delivered a crispy yet chewy coelenterate to people who knew the difference. It's harder, it seems to me, to get a product to its consumers in the quantity, quality, and the time required than to buy and sell futures of the same product. But Mr. P'ng was almost insulted that his commodity should be considered below the level of speculation. And he's right. After all, speculation is a skill of its own, regardless of its economic value.

P'ng packs a good jellyfish. But he's also an all-around businessman. I looked up from my notebook and noticed that the stubby hand across the desk from me had a long, manicured pinkie nail. That reminded me that I should be open to appreciate this man in all his aspects, financial as well as industrial.

Jimmy Domino in Brooklyn found his way into world commerce by hard work, of course. But what he brought to the table was the hinterland of moneyed seafood lovers that he had access to as an American distributor. The P'ng family of Penang had inserted itself into a business in which they had no financial advantages either as producers or buyers. And since the international fish trade was in dollars, they also had to hedge currencies.

It's amazing that capable people like P'ng Lai Heng are willing to slog away in what my bankers call the "real sector." The material world of spoiled fish and unmotivated workers must be frustrating compared to the frictionless realm of finance. I think we're lucky that people like P'ng don't move over entirely from production and trade into speculation.

The same Commercial Fish of India chart that I'd seen in Brooklyn hung on P'ng's wall. It brought me back to my trail. I asked what activities and what expenditures were set in motion by an order from JC. He launched into a list:

"We get an order from JC; we buy the raw material—cod," he used as a for-instance. "We hire labor to wash it, cut it, and freeze it in our plant, BSA, in Thailand. Then we pack it in poly bags and paper cartons. Then we keep it in a cold room. We've got to rent cold-room space. Then before we contact a shipper . . . "

"Like TSK?" I interrupted, pointing to the wall. P'ng had a different shipping line calendar than Domino and Ravidran.

"Yes." He nodded. "We order labels, we pay fish farmer, we pay for cold-room or storage charges, poly bags, printing [P'ng makes labels for the wholesalers whose brand names go on the bags], paper boxes, plastic strips for packing. Then there's freight charges. The containers will come by truck to our factories. . . . Yes, the refrigerated ship container comes on a truck. We fill it."

"More day labor?" I asked.

"Usually the same cold-room laborers will stuff. Before that, Lloyd's of London. We pay them to make a report. That's usually required by the LC [letter of credit]. It's called a Lloyd's Survey Report. . . .No, no insurance. Our terms with JC are CFR [cost plus freight.] If the terms were CIF [cost insurance and freight], then we'd buy insurance."

So the arrival of a Chase letter of credit sets secretaries, trawler captains, fish cleaners, label printers, errand boys, truck drivers, stuffers, guards, and

Lloyd's of London inspectors to work. All these people (and many more) buy food, clothing, toothpaste, and movie tickets while their employers order office supplies and pay phone and fuel bills. Through these purchases, I could follow my money from Malaysia to just about anywhere in the world. (Though it's sad to think what a tiny trickle reaches Africa.)

But the most dynamic thing about P'ng's operation is where he sends the profits: Indonesia, Burma, and now Vietnam—that undiscovered country from whose bourne no capital thus far returns. Though the US had dropped its embargo and there was enthusiastic talk about this latest Emerging Market, Vietnam was itself hesitant, too divided or perhaps just too bureaucratic to encourage foreign investment. At the time I was writing, thousands of representatives were hanging around bars in Hanoi and Ho Chi Minh City waiting for permits to start new enterprises. Meanwhile, fewer than 20 state enterprises had been privatized. I wondered if Chinese/Vietnamese associates or relatives had helped guide P'ng around these outer reaches of capitalism. But it would have been too sensitive to ask if his joint venture partners were Chinese.

Mr. P'ng asked what I'd like to eat for dinner.

"Jellyfish," I answered, of course.

The level of taste in Penang wasn't up to that, he told me. He sold no jellyfish there. As a matter of fact, P'ng had no factories and did no business at all in Penang. His offices were there because that's where he was raised. He seemed proud to gain his livelihood out in the global fray while providing a sheltered home for his family on this Arcadian isle. "Though it may be getting overpriced," he commented, as we drove past new condos and hotels. As we headed toward a fish restaurant (my second choice), we passed a row of extraordinary mansions set apart against the sea.

"What are these buildings?" I asked.

"Just houses."

"Individual houses?!"

Mr. P'ng all but sighed. His grandfather had wanted to buy one but his grandmother said no. "My mother always says that if *her* mother hadn't thought it was too big to clean, you could be rich now."

"Oh, sure," I quipped. "If I'd only kept that sixty-five-dollar-a-month apartment in Greenwich Village; if my mother hadn't thrown away my comic book collection. We all could have been rich."

"But they're landmarked," he lamented.

Seaside terrace of the Eden Gardens Restaurant—quickly deepening twilight
The seafood restaurant was magical. Its front entrance was a wall of tanks with shimmering fish and exotic crustacea, including the largest prawns I'd ever seen (one to a ten-gallon tank) propelling themselves forcefully, heads down. The dining room, a la wharf, had the first breeze I'd felt in Asia.

Without any menu Mr. P'ng ordered crabs, prawns (not the monsters), and a whole red snapper.

"You must be tired speaking English to me for so long," I said, when the waitress left his beer and my *jus belimbi* (star fruit juice).

"No. I speak it all day with my Korean customers, my Japanese customers."

When P'ng started school, children had to choose between a Chinese or English education. English was the more useful language but the family felt that the Chinese schools were superior. Since his native dialect is Hokkien, the Chinese education meant learning Mandarin. He forced himself to learn English later when he went to school with the students who had chosen the English education. [For a brief period much later, Malaysia's Bumi Putra language policies required elementary school to be conducted in Malay. "It was like being forced to learn Afrikaans," an Indian-Malaysian New Yorker lamented to me.] Mr. P'ng now speaks English, Hokkien, Hakka (another Chinese dialect), Mandarin, and Thai.

"Are we going to meet someone here?" I asked, because of the way P'ng raised himself off his chair and scanned all the tables.

"Just counting the crowd," he answered. "They do a good business."

I had been hoping that his wife and children would join us. There were several parties with children in the restaurant. The adults spoke Chinese among themselves, but many, both parents and grandparents, used English to correct the children. No one near us seemed to be speaking Malay.

Mr. P'ng made a call on his cell phone, which reminded me how much time he was devoting to me on the momentous day when his Vietnamese partners had been in town.

The crabs arrived with their shells already cracked and a hint of black bean, the prawns were curled and sweet, and the snapper shimmered with an almost imperceptible glaze.

This must have been a very expensive restaurant, I now realize. When I suggested fish I thought of it as the local fare. Perhaps I should have taken the hint when P'ng pointed out the hawker stalls that "many local people enjoy."

A vine-ripened New Jersey tomato is more expensive in New Jersey, even at the height of the season, than a California tomato picked by machine and ripened by gasses. A Thai mango is more expensive in Thailand than a Coca-Cola. And a fresh fish is more expensive on this fishing island than the extruded noodles and fish pastes used in fish-ball soup. The food "products" that my loans help manufacture are becoming the world's true local cuisine. I wonder when anyone in the fishing village last ate a whole red snapper like the one in front of me.

Mr. P'ng had spent a lot of time and, I now feared, money, entertaining someone who would never place an order. I didn't want him to count these hours as a total waste. (And poor Mr. P'ng could not help but count.) So I promised that when I got back to New York I'd buy several bags of dehydrated jellyfish and experiment cooking them. Perhaps, I told him, I could open the Caucasian market for jellyfish by publishing a recipe in my book. [See Appendix: Jellyfish Recipe, page 331.]

"By the way," I asked before he dropped me off, "is there a book I can read about jellyfish?"

Mr. P'ng laughed for the first time. "By now you are the world's expert on jellyfish."

"World's second expert," I deferred.

"No, third. My father, then me, then you."

Trade Vs. Speculation

You can tell that I admire Mr. P'ng's expertise and energy. He's a useful person distributing a useful product.

But suppose he wasn't a manufacturer. Suppose he didn't supply the equipment, train the staff, supervise production, and build the factory— that's typically his half of the investment in a jellyfish joint venture. Supposing Mr. P'ng merely located supplies of jellyfish (or cod or mackerel), then took possession and paid to get them to the port where they were needed. Suppose, that is, he was primarily a trader, like Jimmy Domino. Would I then regard him as a parasitic middleman? I've been rather harsh on speculators, after all.

There's an important difference between trade and speculation: trade brings new wealth into the world.

Let me give a semi-fictional example.

Suppose one of Mr. P'ng's ancestors came to Penang when the British first "opened" this fishing island. (Though it's much more likely that they came at the turn of the 20th century.) Let's say this earlier Mr. P'ng brought with him a stock of ceramic jugs and basins. He shows them to the Malay fisherman and their wives, who immediately think of dozens of ways they could make their lives easier with these vessels. And they're so beautiful, too. Mr. P'ng looks at the fat snappers they're hauling from the boat and says he'll trade his merchandise for fish.

Until then, these fishermen had stayed out until they had enough to eat. Now they have an indirect use for fish, so they catch a few extra. (In those days there was literal truth to the saying, "There are plenty more fish in the sea.")

P'ng sells this new surplus to the British colonists for cash. He also figures out how to dry some of the small fish that the fishermen usually toss back. He takes the dried fish back to China and sells them there. Using British sterling and the dry-fish money as capital, he orders many more jugs and basins.

With P'ng's dried fish in the pantry, entire Chinese families can spend more time filling P'ng's porcelain orders. And the Malaysian fisherman may save so many trips for fresh water that they can catch extra for Mr. P'ng and still have as much free time as before. Most historians believe, however, that people like Malay fishermen usually work considerably longer once they're drawn into the pound or dollar net. But whether folks are working fewer or more hours, they are definitely producing more porcelain basins and catching more fish. Human wealth has been increased through trade.

The present Mr. P'ng does the same when he opens markets in Burma and Vietnam. Though the same individuals often shift from trade to speculation, these are two different economic functions. Traders catalyze the creation of new wealth; speculators keep buying and selling the same, not a different, kettle of fish.

Another endearing thing about Mr. P'ng's business is its size. Two hundred companies produce and/or sell a third of the world's goods and services. Hai Hong Marine Products is one of the hundreds of thousands of midsized companies that share what's left with unnumbered millions of enterprises as tiny as Thai street vendors.

Despite his skill, experience, and healthy balance between financial caution and experimentation, Mr. P'ng wasn't likely to lead his family firm into the top tier. That's partly, I believe, because he doesn't feel secure dealing with capital sources or partners beyond his circle of Chinese associates. Why should he? The P'ng family had inaugurated their jellyfish business during what turned out to be a year of anti-Chinese riots in Malaysia. They probably have relatives, certainly acquaintances, who were expelled from nearby Burma merely for being Chinese. Like many Jews in prewar Europe, the P'ngs created an enterprise whose material assets, the books and contact lists, could be transported out of the country in one or two suitcases. The most valuable asset, their expertise, was in their heads. I wish I had felt free to talk to Mr. P'ng about these matters, but a distrust of outsiders like me was one of the obvious and reasonable effects of being a Chinese businessman in Malaysia.

I started with only one appointment in Penang and I'd managed to stretch my stay to over a week. But everyone has to leave paradise eventually, so it was onward and down the Malay Peninsula.

Singapore's Colonial District; the American Club—late afternoon

Somewhere between a quarter and a third of the shrimp sold in the world are farm raised. That's a million tons, or about fifteen billion dollars' worth a year. JC Seafood used their three-and-a-half-million-dollar Chase line of credit to bring in an enormous tonnage of frozen black tiger prawns. A great quantity were contracted through Mr. Ravidran of Asia Pacific Seafoods, who traded by fax and phone from a Singapore office that looked very much like Jimmy Domino's in Brooklyn.

But Ravi was not only an importer/distributor/trader/broker; he was also, like Mr. P'ng, a producer. Or at least he was partners, in some way I couldn't quite pin down, with the government of Johor Bahru, the southernmost state in Malaysia, in the largest, most modern, and longest-surviving shrimp farm on the peninsula.

Since Ravi was exceedingly busy, he suggested that I speak to Randall Angst, who managed or co-owned (again it was hard to pin down) their model shrimp farm.

Things were hectic the day of the scheduled visit. Two Angst children had recently arrived from Florida for the school holidays, and Randall and his wife had to be in Singapore on business. Could I possibly interview them at the American Club in Singapore? (I wanted very much to see the shrimp farm in person but what could I do?)

At a private club in Singapore's manicured colonial district, a disheveled New Yorker and a raw Floridian with wife in cut-offs and a protesting child had no trouble spotting each other. For the Angsts, it was the end of a long day with errands in two countries, dragging along an eight-year-old, perhaps promised an outing, while the older boys were waiting back over the causeway in Malaysia.

I felt guilty taking their family time but when the kid squirmed away, the Angsts gave me their attention. They had no idea what being interviewed might involve (would it take ten minutes or two hours?), and we made a few awkward starts.

But once I asked Randall Angst about shrimp culture, we were midstream (midpond?) before I could click my ballpoint.

"... water parameters you have pH (if you get a lot of rain the pH is less), temperature, dissolved oxygen, and salinity—you have to check them daily. Every time you harvest you should flush with water then let it dry. Then, depending on the amount of sludge from the prawn wastes, you ... "

"Wait—what would I see if I went there?"

"Okay, I'll back up a little. It's called East Johor Marine Farms."

Mr. Angst drew a diagram of squares extending in rows from either side of a double line he labeled Water Main Channel. "That goes right down the middle." Water from the sea was pumped into the main channel, then into smaller channels that flowed between the squares, and finally into the ponds. A completely separate outlet channel carried the waste away from each pond to a river that went back into the sea several miles downstream from the farm.

"It's got a hundred and twelve ponds of one point five hectares each ... "

"*Averaging* one point five?" I asked, remembering the crude pits along the Thai coast.

"No, exactly. A hundred and twelve square ponds, one point five hectares each."

"How much shrimp do you get from that?"

"A hundred and twelve ponds, two turnovers a year makes it two hundred and twenty-four ponds a year times four thousand kilos makes it eight hundred and ninety-six thousand kilos."

"Does that mean shrimp will get cheaper, like salmon?" I asked gluttonously.

"It should stay good for another few years because there's a big problem with disease."

"Huh?" [Sick shrimp is good?]

"Viruses," Randall explained. "Black tigers get *P monadan*. Various viruses—white spot, yellow head. So prices can't drop because of oversupply."

"Ah."

"Why Salmon got so cheap, they grow in cold water. There's not as much disease. Shrimp should stay good for another ten years."

"Gotcha." [It took me a while to stop thinking like a consumer.]

I knew Randall Angst was connected with prawn farms in India as well as in Malaysia. He also maintained what his business card called a "liaison office" here in Singapore, where *his* company, Monotech, had a staff of ten. But he wasn't a trader like Domino or a trader-processor like P'ng. "What exactly do you do?" I asked. "Do you own farms? Do you manage them?"

"I call myself a 'motivator.' There's certain things you have to do, actions you have to take at an exact certain time. I teach people how to do it. I'm Technical Director of all the farms and hatcheries."

"Hatcheries?"

"You need the hatcheries before you have the farm. We breed our own. We don't have to go out to the sea and catch big females with eggs. We're totally closed, totally independent from the wild source."

It's almost sweet, I thought, how profoundly men long to create life independently from women. In a less balanced man I suppose it could be termed the Dr. Frankenstein complex. But Angst's declaration of independence, I realized later, was meant to clear himself from the charge that shrimp farmers raid the sea for pregnant prawns, thus depleting the wild shrimp catch.

"You raise them in the hatchery for thirty days—average length is fifteen millimeters—then you put them in the pond. Then the worker must spread out the food evenly for the first forty days. In the beginning the job is canoeing through the pond at night adding fertilizer nutrients for the algae to bloom."

Canoeing through ponds in the Malaysian moonlight. I hadn't grasped how big these prawn ponds were.

"The feeders must move at a certain pace; they must feed them at night. After the first forty days you can feed from the sides of the ponds because the prawns are big enough to swim to the food. But if you don't spread the food evenly the first forty days, then some will get more and some will get less. So people must listen and do exactly what you tell them. But it's outdoors, it's hot, it's night, you can't keep your eye on them. So you must motivate them to do exactly what's right for the prawns at each stage. This is the most important thing I do."

"Will these prawns be a uniform size, then?" I asked.

"There will be three categories. Ten percent small, sixty percent medium, thirty percent large."

"Ten-sixty-thirty in each pond? It's that predictable?"

"It's not as predictable as farming vegetables, but even vegetables vary. If the worker feeds them properly they won't vary much."

"Your large prawns" I asked, "could they have been the giants I saw swimming head-down in a Penang sea food restaurant?"

"Eden Gardens?"

"Yes, with the wooden patio and tanks of live seafood up front."

"Their distributor comes to the farm, they buy from us. But the big ones you saw, twelve inches, three to a pound, they're not ours. They were the mother prawns, the breeders. Those are wild."

Randall believes that his medium prawns (26 to 31 to a pound) are tastier than his large prawns, and not so tough or chewy as free-range shrimp.

"Wild shrimp, what you get when they trawl and they pull up squid and

fish, these animals are under stress. When you're raising prawns you're raising lazy prawns. They don't have to compete."

I may have tasted Angst's lazy 26 to 31's either in Singapore or Penang,
where P'ng wisely ordered mediums, not mothers. Almost all the shrimp I'd
eaten in the US had been frozen. If the prawns I ate in Asia were Randall's,
they were sweet yet springy-fleshed for animals that had lived such a soft life.

Mr. Angst began his professional relationship with prawns at the Ralston
Purina Company, which started a research lab to develop feed. The basic in-
gredients of pelletized prawn feed are corn, wheat, squid meal, fish meal,
flour, lecithin, and binders, I learned from Angst. "CP, that's a Thai company. [Chareon Pokaphand Co., Ltd.] is now the biggest producer in the
world of prawn culture [and a major promoter of intensive aquaculture]."

"In Thailand they say that prawn farms have to shut down after about
three years. Is that true?" I asked.

"It's a matter of management. The problem in Thailand, everybody owns
a pond or two and they dig wherever they want. There's no plan. They bring
the water from the sea and discharge it right back into the sea. That's a disease problem will contaminate everybody.

"In India they tried to plan at least a certain amount of distance between
prawn farms, but in India not many people will put in a seawater line, it's too
costly. I don't have one in J. B. [Johor Bahru] but you don't need one here.
Texas had three farms that got wiped out by disease. But I been running one
farm ten years in Johor. Our water goes eight or nine kilometers, then into
the river and it's not released near other pond farms. "In India we built a jetty
and pump the water on top."

"On top, like a Roman aqueduct?"

Randall nodded yes. "We spent nearly a million dollars for one of those
prawn farms in India.

"First thing, the site selection must be good. The criteria are good-quality
sea water—mixed, brackish but unpolluted. And the soil conditions; you
need a certain percent like twenty percent clay in the soil. The big criteria of
site selection is not being so close to one another. You should have at least
four, five miles between farms.

"In Thailand, Malaysia, India I'd recommend an area with no prawn
farms around and no industrial waste coming from any factories. Your dis-

charge water should always run north of you so your discharge never comes back. You should treat your water before it goes out, so you really need sedimentation ponds, which would take more land. It's a matter of management."

And capital, too, I thought, with some pride. With solid orders backed by my letters of credit, East Johor Marine Farms could borrow enough to do things right.

"To manage a large farm is difficult, it's a big investment: four, five, six million US. And people must listen and do exactly what you tell them."

Randall excused himself to look for his wife, who had gone off to find their son. While they were gone I tried to convert those 896,000 kilos to tons. *Let's see: multiply by two point two . . . one million, nine hundred seventy-one thousand and two hundred tons of black tiger shrimp a year!? That can't be. Wait, that's pounds. For tons divide by two thousand. Or wait, maybe . . .* However you do it, it's a lot of seafood.

"How many people does it take to harvest all those shrimp?" I asked, when the Angsts returned alone. (Their son was neither in the pool nor in the play room.)

"Four to eight per two ponds. We contract out the harvesting. You don't want them around all the time. We harvest twenty or thirty ponds a month and we need the workers about twenty days out of the month but only six or seven hours, not a whole day." Half the men of Malaysia were once fishermen. Now a few score of illegal Indonesians, working part-time, were harvesting more seafood than all of them had. "They may have to come for a few hours then go home and come back."

"Split shifts," I muttered.

"They're mostly Indonesian, I think, but they're managed by a Malaysian."

It was getting to be time to drive back across the causeway. As Mr. and Mrs. Angst came and went, more actively seeking their son, I picked up bits of their personal story from one or the other or both.

Randall and Debbie met in Florida when they became next-door neighbors. "In 1965, was it?" "Were we seven or eight?"

They went though elementary school and high school together and then . . .

"You separated to go to college?" I guessed.

"No," replied Randall, "I never went to college."

"You went into the army?"

"No."

"You must have separated." [The boy and girl next-door had to separate in order to fall in love, right?]

"Our longest separation has been recently because the children have to stay in one school. The older boys needed to go to high school in the States to get ready for college," said Randall.

"So the only one I can take with me now is ... " Debbie pointed with her chin toward the offstage child. "He was born in Malaysia in 1987."

Mrs. Angst had just brought all three children from Florida to Malaysia for summer vacation. "So the family is together. But he just went to India, left us here."

"India in the heat wave?" I exclaimed as Randall reentered. "How was it?"

"Terrible. The project's going well."

If so, it was one of the few prawn farms going well in India, where diseases were ravaging the East Coast.

The Angsts had earlier lived in Singapore for nine years. "Now we're based in Florida," Debbie said. "North of Tampa."

"Yeah, we have a house there," Randall modified her description. The problem of making it more than a "house" or a "base" was on both parents' minds.

"Trouble is, the father has two weeks—" Randall said when we were once again alone "—the father and these days the mother too. So it's like you don't get to know your family except on vacation. Even then . . . when I was a kid and we went away, I played with my cousins, not my parents." A profoundly self-made man, I thought. Not just financially.

Debbie thought she had it worked out so she could spend more than just school vacations with her husband. Both sets of grandparents lived near the house in Tampa and could alternate moving in with the boys. "If I didn't have the third, I'd be free and clear now—two grownups."

"Why do you keep the Singapore office?" I asked Randall.

"I do nothing here and I'm registered in the Virgin Islands where I do no business and pay no taxes. I'm an offshore company!" Angst declared, with seeming surprise at his own status. "I'm in Singapore because my Indian

clients can fax me or phone me or come to Singapore easily. We have an office in J. B., but they can't always get through from India or Thailand."

So it's the physical infrastructure.

When the children were younger, Singapore had also been a good Asian
base, they explained, because there were appropriate English schools for all
three ages. (And the social infrastructure—education.) "But it costs like for
college," Debbie let me know.

Furthermore, the Singapore label on seafood could get it through a US inspection more quickly, Angst suggested, "but don't write that down."

I appreciated what he meant when I visited one of my Singapore contacts
and found a basement full of Indonesian day laborers peeling foreign cartons from frozen fish and putting the product into boxes labeled "Singapore." (So the regulatory infrastructure makes Singapore convenient too.)
Few US business organizations recognize strict government regulation as an
asset that makes your product valuable around the world, but Singapore recognizes it. In fact, I'm leaving that Singapore-based shrimp source out of the
book because Singapore officials would probably get right after him if I described his operation more fully—though why he deserves my protection I
don't know.

"Did someone order a Coke?"

A Coke arrived on a silver platter carried by a serving maid wearing a lace
cap.

"Must be my son," said Debbie, slipping a gold card into the leather bill-
presenter. "We have a problem. He thinks he's the boss."

The effervescing glass flushed out the eight-year-old, who emerged to
drink his Coke through a straw.

There was one more question I wanted to ask before we parted. I hoped it
wouldn't sound like an accusation.

"Does shrimp farming kill off the fish around the coast?"

"The water we discharge is not toxic waste," Randall reminded me.
"Shrimp waste will oxidize as the air hits it. The bloom will die out. It doesn't
affect local fish. They just go farther out."

I took this as a relatively honest answer from a man who doesn't feel accused because he isn't aware of Malay fishermen. Angst might feel ecological guilt for dumping wastes too near other shrimp farms, but he could

barely imagine fishermen with boats so small that they couldn't follow the fish farther out. Nor could he imagine nearby subsistence farmers whose rice crop was ruined by salt seeping into their soil.

Randall Angst summed up prawn farming with a couple of predictions. "Taiwan used to be the biggest farm producers of black tigers. Now they're lucky if they produce twenty thousand tons a year. Then China was big. It got hit with diseases. Now they import prawns. [And still sell some too—mostly wild.] Now Thailand is the biggest producer. They must have more than twenty thousand farms. It may be thirty thousand by now. India will be next.* "The shrimp business is good for at least another ten years. I'm going to retire in four."

———

I suddenly realized how happy I was to be back in the real sector. Oil and fish just smell better than money. I admired Angst and P'ng for many of the same reasons that I liked Al and Nigel and Jack Bradie. People in the real sector are proud of what they do and like to talk about it. They're Odyssean problem solvers whose minds are directed to problems with empirically testable solutions. But since the sphere they solve in is the physical world, anything that they do on a large scale is bound to alter the environment.

Another mental trait may redeem that, however. These engineering minds, so direct and directed, are also redirectable. Al, Nigel, and Jack would happily apply themselves to the problem of minimizing the damage from burning oil if that factor were put into the equation. And knowing Randall Angst, he could probably come up with a dozen uses for shrimp waste if he was prohibited from dumping it in the ocean. He already uses sediment tanks and sea lines where conditions or governments require it.

As I write, some shrimp farmers are digging their pits inland and retaining the coastal mangroves to filter the waste naturally. To avoid salinating surrounding farmland, this method should entail limiting the density of their crop. Unfortunately, many Thais who have abandoned their intensive and now diseased ponds on the coast are rushing to locate similarly intensive inland ponds in rice-growing areas, with results just beginning to be known.

*Before that prediction had a chance to come true, several Indian states banned shrimp farms altogether. The bans were struck down as of this writing.

Who can force them to slow down before they do to the rice land what they've done to the coast?

The right salinity and density for shrimp farms in each area is something Randall Angst might become the expert on in his "retirement," if someone would pay him to think in that direction.

But no one firm can burden itself with the expense of innovations and limitations unless others do too. That means international regulation. Easy enough to suggest, but who will bell the cat?

I was aware, before I went to Asia, that burning fossil fuel harms the atmosphere. There were innumerable books and articles on the subject. But there was little public discussion of shrimp farming when I left. So I had to find out more when I got home. If the reader doesn't mind a little discontinuity, we'll flash forward briefly, before we explore Singapore.

New York: The UN and Greenwich Village—one year later

Back in the US, I heard about Mangrove Action Project, an organization devoted to preserving the coastal mangrove forests where so many sea creatures spawn. Shrimp farming had already ripped out about a quarter of the world's mangroves, so it had to be an issue for the group. I was a bit leery about calling, however, because many people concerned with endangered species have an antipathy to the species I'm especially partial to. But this group had found reasons to ally itself with humans.

The coastal fishermen I met in Penang were economically marginal, and most could, at that time at least, have found work in a factory or a hotel. But there are places where coastal fisherman still provide most of the protein anyone gets; places where there are few other sources of income besides the fishing and mixed farming that are both threatened by shrimp ponds. Mangrove Action Project works with NGOs (Non-Governmental Organizations) from regions where sea turtles and humans are both endangered when their ecological niches are wiped out.

I hadn't visited places like these on my money tour because they're the outlands that my money barely trickles to. In rapidly developing Thailand, my bank deposit led me to the capital and to an industrial park. But over 70 percent of the Thai population is rural. If the smaller of my loans produced hundreds of tons of prawns but left these people hungrier, while my large loan reached them only as the money spent locally by returned migrant oil workers, then these places and people, though far from the dollar flow, were still affected by my Chase deposit.

So I was excited, after a year of receiving literature (accompanied by modest bills for photocopying), when mangrove activist Alfredo Quarto called to say that community organizers from Thailand, India, Bangladesh, Sri Lanka, Ecuador, Honduras, Indonesia, Mexico, Papua New Guinea, and other countries were coming to New York for a United Nations Shrimp Tribunal. There would be UN sessions in which his side would appear along with pro-prawn Chamber of Commerce speakers. They'd also use the occasion for strategy meetings with their international allies. I was welcome to attend all the events with them and, oh, could a couple of people stay at my house?

Of course. Why not? Hadn't Caltex put me up? What goes around comes around; to each according to his needs, etc., etc.

The mangrove crowd was a piebald mix of young, intense, sometimes brash ecology folks from the Western countries, with motherly women and delightfully giggling older men, from the Third World countries. The former brought statistics and journalists, the latter brought pictures and testimonies. One of the Indian NGOs had stopped local shrimp farms through mass demonstrations, and several groups had organized substantial reclamation and alternative aquaculture projects. Despite their very different situations and tactics, there seemed to be a lot of respect and accord among them.

They differed, however, on how to respond to a group of new loans that the World Bank was offering to start shrimp farms. Because of the stir made by the people in that very room, the World Bank was offering small supplemental loans to provincial governments to study the environmental effects of the World Bank–financed shrimp farms in their jurisdictions, and to compensate people for possible damage to surrounding land.

Some welcomed this as an official recognition that shrimp farming had its costs. The studies could create an opening, they hoped, to push for regulatory standards. But one of the Mexicans reminded us that some governmental units were either too corrupt or too bumbling to make useful studies. (Collectively, the two to three dozen people in the room had an impressive personal knowledge of the government agencies and bank officials involved.)

Another objection to the linked loans was that they were both just loans. The research money would have to be paid back out of the national treasury. Why should private, profit-making businesses be allowed to do damage that would be righted (if possible) by the nation through its taxes? Why shouldn't private investors be responsible for the research and for the damage they do?

The arguments were interesting and balanced, but no matter what policy the group settled on, it would be difficult, they all agreed, to stop any World Bank shrimp-farm loans.

When I asked, naïvely, why the World Bank, a quasi-aid organization, would push loans that were unwelcome or controversial, I was reminded that "the World Bank is a bank. Selling loans is its business." "It also has the job," someone said, "of creating the conditions in which private banks can make profitable loans."

Since no bank could collect interest from subsistence fishermen (they *stop when they have enough*), some in the group felt that all World Bank loans were ultimately aimed at opening new loan markets by destabilizing what was left in the world of self-sufficient communities and turning their inhabitants into dependent individuals. In other words, self-sufficient people were deliberately pushed off the land to make way for borrowing, interest-paying investors. If those people happened to starve before enough investors materialized to provide them with cash income, than they died of unexploitability.

Those who reasoned that way should, following the same logic, oppose all shrimp-farm loans and, in fact, most World Bank loans. But they didn't. They just wanted to find a safe, sustainable way to raise seafood commercially and a mechanism to get the less-destructive methods adopted worldwide even if they weren't as profitable. And they wanted to do that before all the mangroves and fishermen were destroyed. Ambitious goals. But considering who they were (nobody), they'd gotten surprisingly far already.

The individuals who stayed at my house were the intense Alfredo Quarto from Port Angeles, Washington, and the soft-voiced, smiling-eyed Pisit Chansnoh. Kuhn (Mr.) Pisit represented Yadfon (Raindrop), an NGO from Trang Province, southern Thailand. Working in 17 small fishing villages, Raindrop helped start penned aquaculture and small-scale animal rearing for cash income; had created a co-op to buy fishing equipment and gasoline at a discount; and had organized people to replant 587 *rai** of mangrove forest. As a result, catfish, threadfins, mullet, several species of crab, squid, and shrimp, plus turtles, dugongs, and dolphins have returned to their waters. According to their brochure, incomes of the 500 families in their target area were up about 200 percent and the fish catch was raised by 40 percent in five years. Now they're petitioning the local government to enforce existing laws against destructive fishing and aquaculture techniques. (In Thailand? Good luck.)

After two days of meetings, Alfredo, Pisit, and I walked around Greenwich Village (my neighborhood), where Alfredo shopped for biscotti to send to his mother while Pisit marveled that Washington Square was like a permanent festival.

Many Malays live on the southern Thai coast where Raindrop works, so I told Kuhn Pisit about the fishermen/bellboy I'd met near Map Ta Phut. He wasn't sure what to make of it.

I asked whether his organization encourages boat loans of the kind that the Upliftment Foundation sponsored in Malaysia. No, Yadfon did not encourage such loans. Things might be different in Malaysia, but where he was, "The middleman to the fisherman is like the World Bank. When he sees you can't pay the loan, you must do what he tells you."

I asked him to elaborate and this is what I copied down on the classic café napkin.

"For example, you loan me money to buy the material for a crab basket. But once the crab population is dropped down, my payment is dropped down. So the middleman may say, 'Why don't you purchase another trap to collect squid?' I may not be skilled in squid, but I have to. Then when I cannot pay the two loans he says, 'I want you to come work for me on my boat.' Or they give the fisherman the money to buy a motor for his boat. When he cannot pay, the middleman takes the boat and the fisherman works for him.

"But it may happen that the fisherman hears about a job in another town, maybe working in the palm oil [plantation]. Or maybe a hotel like the man you met. But the middleman does not allow him to go. Maybe it was the middleman's idea that he buy the motor or a bigger boat, but now, he cannot leave his boat even if he hears of a better job.

---

*1 rai = 0.4 of an acre.

"So the middleman controls the direction of economic development of the village in the same way the World Bank controls the direction of development in a nation that is indebted to it, even though the World Bank suggested the original loan which cannot be paid back."

"Is it possible," I wondered, "that my Map Ta Phut bellboy had run away from a loan?"

It was *possible*, Kuhn Pisit conceded, but most fishermen in his area wouldn't know how to get a job so far away.

"But there was the uncle," I reminded him.

"Perhaps," he said not liking to contradict.

"But would a local fisherman [I now reversed my own argument] be able to pinpoint shrimp ponds as the thing that drove off the fish? I mean, assuming there was no organization like yours in his village to help him develop this consciousness."

"The effect of the shrimp farms is undeniable," Pisit replied. "The fisherman recognizes it before the NGO."

"So it could be!" I grew excited. "The bellboy I met near the oil refinery might very well have been a fisherman from a Southern Thai village. A man who lost his livelihood, his boat, his tradition, his identity. And then [I grew more excited as I added a new piece] and then he became entangled in a web of debt. Maybe he came to Map Ta Phut to escape the debt. That's what made him so scared."

This time Kuhn Pisit contradicted flatly. "The hopelessly indebted commit suicide before they run away. I've seen it all too often."

So I still don't know who the bellboy was. But as we walked through Greenwich Village I had a gradual revelation about who the mangrove people were; the excitable woman from Ecuador, the birdlike storyteller from Papua New Guinea, the semicompulsive Alfredo and the quiet gentle Pisit. These are Sylvia Ostry's "transformational coalitions." [See page 50.] These are the infinitely subversive groups who, according to Ms. Ostry, are not just asking for a piece of the pie, but are abrogating to themselves (in the name of some economically marginal fishermen) the right to determine *how it should be baked.*

Ms. Ostry had been brought to the Waldorf conference by AT&T, Citibank, and Dow Jones. But here are these people with nobody's permission, nobody's sponsorship, and just about nobody's money, turning down the World Bank and replanting mangroves. That's literally transforming the land. Who are they to decide what should be done with the world's resources and labor? That's the privilege usually reserved for Sylvia's sponsors. No wonder she's irate.

But I'm pleased. Chase multiplied my money many times when they extended a line of credit to import shrimp. But that's nothing compared to the way this antishrimp farm coalition leveraged a one-night loan of my apartment. Perhaps if I looked carefully I'd find that each of my high-level global investments generated a balancing global response from below.

Singapore and Malaysia were both colonized by Britain in the 19th century, both occupied by Japan during World War II, and both granted independence after the war. As a matter of fact, they were briefly a single independent nation. Geographically, Singapore is just another of the many steamy islands that straddle the equator between the Indian Ocean and the Pacific. Ethnically, it's composed of the same mix of Malays, Chinese, and Indians as Malaysia and the surrounding Indonesian islands, except that in Singapore the Chinese predominate.

I was in the country to look at a catalytic cracker, a sophisticated oil-processing unit that Caltex was adding to its Singapore refinery with the help of a Chase loan. This time I meant to interview one of the migrant construction workers on the project—no matter what. But I couldn't help asking, as I went about my business, how this particular tropical island had become the wealthy city-state of Singapore.

My own tentative explanation for Singapore's prosperity was "no corruption." When I asked Singaporeans or foreigners who lived there for any length of time, their answer was unhesitatingly "Lee Kuan Yew."

Lee Kuan Yew, Singapore's first prime minister, had led the colony to independence in 1959. The former socialist immediately jailed a few of his trade-union allies and instituted a system of regulated capitalism that borrowed economically from Sweden and morally from Confucius, but had its own unique political twists. Verbally Lee espoused a kind of social Darwinism: inequality; let the smart get rich. Yet community and business life were regulated in ways that made it hard for an individual to fall into the gutter. It sounded like rugged individualism but felt like a welfare state.

To tourists, the paved and landscaped island can seem like one giant, hygienic shopping mall. But to foreigners who have worked there for a while, especially if they've also worked in the more picturesque surrounding countries, the rigid lack of corruption was itself almost exotic. For instance:

When I visited Jack Bradie at the Singapore refinery, where he was the head of the expansion project that I was financing, he was consulting with a young woman whom he'd brought from Britain to help solve the sulfur problem. Sulfur is an impurity in crude oil that corrodes machinery, fouls up catalysts, causes acid rain, and smells like rotten eggs. Singapore had just toughened its standards for sulfur in the air, and all the refineries had to find new ways to get rid of it.

" 'You're right,' I told them." Jack was recounting his conversation with Singapore officials. " 'We breathe here too. But the equipment to process it cleanly will cost thirty million dollars. What do you say?' They say, 'Hard luck.' "

"Now, if we produced in a country with no environmental requirements, we could make you thirty million more." Jack got a kick out of addressing me as the visiting financier.

"Then why are we in Singapore?" I asked. Caltex was in Thailand to refine oil for that booming country's population of 70 million. But Singapore's population was only three and a half million. "They don't use oil, they don't produce oil, they have tough environmental standards, and there's no one to pay off."

"That's exactly why we're here," Jack responded.

Apparently other oil companies agreed, because Singapore had seven offshore islands set aside for the multinational oil companies that chose Singapore as a place to process oil that they sold in other countries. And the refinery islands were so crowded that the government was expanding them through a landfill-and-causeway project.

One reason the companies don't move out when environmental regulations become more demanding is that Singapore's rules are reasonable. Or at least, they're about sulfur, not about setting up a tollgate that your company has to contribute its way through.

Another reason that the oil companies refine in Singapore is the excellent infrastructure. The Singapore government had built a four-foot-in-diameter pipeline to carry oil from out where big tankers could anchor, over to those refinery islands that didn't have deep enough harbors. The use-fee was five and a half cents a barrel. That's not cheap. But no one would ask for another penny. No one from Caltex Singapore would have to sit in a bureaucrat's waiting room for three months wondering what other oil companies offered for a permit to deepen the harbor, as happened during the course of refinery construction in Thailand. The Singapore pipeline was soundly built (not by someone's brother-in-law), and the costs were equitable for all the companies and could be calculated in advance. It's important for business costs to be predictable.

Engineers like those who planned the Singapore pipeline could be hired by other governments in the region. But the discipline to choose the best, regardless of self-interest, and to administer the facility for the common good was uniquely Singaporean. I asked Jack how he accounted for the quality of civil service.

"What happened in Singapore is Lee Kuan Yew," he answered without hesitation. "If they see any corruption they come down on it hard. It's not a cultural thing; it's a national decision that comes from the top! I feel lucky to work here."

How to Make a Refinery Go Whole Hog

You can think of petroleum refining like hog butchering. They hack the ribs off for chops, the belly for bacon, the thighs for ham, the guts for chitterlings, and grind the bones into fertilizer. Crude oil is a mixture of thousands of different compounds. Refining is a distilling process that separates the mixture into salable "cuts" (that's the term in the industry) like kerosene, naphtha, gasoline, and diesel fuel. The cutting is done with heat.

The crude oil is heated in huge processing vessels until its components boil off as vapor. Butane will vaporize at less than 90 degrees Fahrenheit, gasoline between 90 and 220 degrees, various heating oils and diesel fuels between 450 and 800 degrees. Eventually we're left with residues so thick and heavy that they're used to pave roads.

But there's an important difference between meat and oil: through the process of catalytic cracking, some petroleum cuts can be changed into others. Using chemical catalysts at temperatures above 900 degrees, our new catalytic cracker would transform cheap, heavy residues into high-grade gasoline.

"Pigs feet into pork chops?!" I squeaked to Jack Bradie.

"Straw into gold, I'd say."

"So I've made a good loan."

"That depends on the price of gold."

Building a new refinery from scratch is, as we learned in Thailand, unusual. But refinery upgrades are constant. Caltex Singapore had borrowed over 300 million dollars to pay for its part of the catalytic cracker under construction at the refinery that Caltex shared with British Petroleum and the Singapore Petroleum Company.

Jack Bradie, that crusty/soft Scot I'd met in Thailand, was director of the team building the cat cracker. His office was at the construction site on Pulau Merlimau, the island which housed the joint refinery called the Singapore Refining Company (SRC). But before I visited Jack on the island, I took the official tour.

The Guided Tour

Peter Foo, retired from the Caltex Singapore treasury department, was called back to guide me for the day. He was a tiny, lively man whose age was suggested only by his bowed legs and old-fogy opinions. Example:

"How you like Singapore subway?" he asked me.

Now, the Singapore subway is the eighth wonder of the world, so why not admit it? "It's glorious, Mr. Foo. Quiet, clean, perfectly air-conditioned."

"Not like New York subway."

"Well they're older, of course, but ... "

"Very dirty I'm sorry to say. But you have your human lights."

He enumerated the right to litter, the right to chew gum, and the right to draw graffiti. That last right was the most controversial at the time, since Singapore had recently caned the backside of an American student convicted of recidivist graffitiism.

"Many Americans agree with Singapore on that," Mr. Foo assured me. "Want discipline." My noncommittal shrug evoked a Socratic dialogue on discipline that lasted throughout our drive across the island.

"You hear they say we hang someone too quick?" Foo asked. "Same thing, you know, human lights."

He referred to foreign protests still swirling around the execution of the Filipina maid, Flor Concepcion, for a murder that her defenders suggested was committed by her Singapore employer.

"I'm sorry, I didn't follow the case."

"Also, you know Tiananmen Square?"

"Oh, yes. I did follow that."

"Students say they have human lights. Anyone can do anything. That your human lights?"

Funny, this sympathy for the government of China. Foo's economic philosophy was hardly leftist. Here's a sample:

"Cars are expensive here. Where all these people get money to buy them? CPF [Central Provident Fund] not working."

Every Singapore worker is required to put 20 percent of his salary into his Central Provident Fund, to be matched by his employer. So at least 40 percent of all wages are saved for retirement. Under Lee Kuan Yew, the government had borrowed that money (the funds were individual but invested by state banks) to build the Housing Development Board estates in which most Singaporeans lived.

"The CPF-forced saving is supposed to be antiinflationary," Foo complained, "but banks have so much money they make loans to buy cars."

"Can you take money from your retirement fund to buy a car?" I asked. I knew Singaporeans could borrow from their funds to buy an apartment or to pay for education.

"No," Foo explained, "but the banks have so much money that now they want to make installment loans, and if the house is paid for out of CPF loan and the college, then you don't need the money each week so you buy a car.

That defeats antiinflationary purpose. As the prime minister—senior minister," he corrected himself, "Lee says . . . " Lee Kuan Yew had retired to the position of senior minister.

We reached the pier from which we caught the SRC ferry. At 9:45 A.M. there were about 40 men in short-sleeved white shirts on the boat. I made a note to come back here by myself at 6:30 some morning to watch the migrant construction workers going over. But it turned out that they used separate piers less accessible to me.

On the short ferry ride Mr. Foo pointed out an electric power station and two islands: "Here SRC, next-door Esso, the big boy."

"And what's that?" I asked, knowing that the pinkish hulk moored off our island had to be "the Love Boat," as it was called when it was used to house troops during the Gulf war. Now it was rented as a dormitory for some of the migrants working on the catalytic cracker. There were eight official nationalities housed on the ship, and separate mess halls that served Philippine, Burmese, Bangladeshi, Indian, Malaysian, Indonesian, and two kinds of Chinese food.

"That the floating hotel," Foo answered.

"Do you supposed I could visit it?"

"Hotel is not part of tour. After this project it's going to Thailand."

So in Singapore, the workers I wanted to interview were not only off-limits, but offshore. In fact doubly offshore, for they lived off the shore of the offshore island where they worked.

I surrendered my camera—I had no cell phone or cigarette lighter—when we landed, and Mr. Foo helped me fill out my visitor's pass. "Here you write passport number; here I write Caltex [as the sponsor of my visit]."

Near the turnstile where employees swipe their ID cards, a warning sign said *"Tempat Larangan"* ("This Is a Protected Area"). It was also written in two Asian scripts and illustrated by the silhouette of a man firing a rifle into the head of another man with the shot man falling backwards.

"Singapore security is very proactive," said a fellow with a walrus mustache and eyes he could roll like the comedian Jerry Colonna. "During the Gulf War a hundred soldiers were stationed on the island. It was a regular armed camp." We were joined by SRC's theatrical public relations man, Joe

Fernandez. Mr. Fernandez, "born and bred in Singapore," as he told me, was an East Indian. His Portuguese name probably came from Goa or Malacca.

"If you notice, there are four flags flying now: SPC, Caltex, BP, and the fourth SRC. [The Singapore Refinery Company flag had a blue triangle with a yellow oil drop.] During the war the government said 'Please take down the flags.' Reason: 'We don't want to tell any infiltrator we got British or American investment here. After the war, okay, you can fly your flags again. Very proactive."

Even in peacetime, the photo I asked for—me next to the catalytic cracker—would require permission from all three shareholders. "And Peter Foo would have to be rehired to come with you another day," Fernandez discouraged me. But the refinery's photographer would be happy to take my picture out here by the ferry. "Smile."

I'm so dumb that I actually thanked the man and gave him my address without realizing that he was there to take security photos, not souvenirs.

Formalities over, F&F [Foo and Fernandez] rushed me into an over-air-conditioned conference room where Fernandez bombarded me with slides and statistics.

"SRC has fourteen to fifteen million Sing dollars a month operating expenses, to be recovered in different proportions from the three shareholders. Last year we paid Sing dollars three-point-three-five-eight million interest cost."

"Mr. Fernandez . . . "

". . . Electricity twenty-four, twenty-five million; pipeline fee, five and a half cents a barrel . . . "

". . . I'm not actually here about . . . "

"Ferry two-point-five million each; water is supplied by Esso."

The word "water" seemed to arouse Foo. "As our prime minister, excuse me, senior minister says, 'if you feel sick from drinking our potable water, you let us know, we give you medical care free.' Ha, ha."

"Okay [back to Fernandez], "this is what the head count is like: two hundred and thirty-seven execs, three hundred and ninety-three non-execs, for the RCC [my Residual Catalytic Cracker] we got twenty-two."

"Twenty-two? What about that boat out there?"

"Laborers," he dismissed them. "The contract went to JGC [The Japanese Gas Company]. They got forty-two hundred workers at the peak of the project, fourteen hundred stay on the *Habiba*. It belongs to a shipyard. JGC leased it."

"These four thousand workers are not allowed to go onto the mainland," Peter Foo said.

"People with work permits can be shuttled every day." Fernandez seemed to be contradicting Foo about the rules for migrants, but he smoothed it over. "It's all done by JGC. SRC doesn't want to know anything."

There we are again: "Not our workers."

"Mr. Fernandez, did anyone tell you I'm writing a book about the way my own money moves around the world? My bank happened to lend Caltex the money for the catalytic cracker. What I'm really interested in is . . . "

"Okay, I'm going to show you a video now, 'Cracking the Crude!' I'm sorry if I disappoint anyone," he said taking the tape out of its box with a theatrical leer. "It's only blue on the outside."

He shoved in the tape.

"I don't think I need to see a videotape. Please, I don't do that kind of journalism."

But F&F were out the door before I could stop them. The music rose; it was the same heroic theme as "Raising the Column at Map Ta Phut." Twenty minutes of petroleum chemistry in a freezing room.

As it ended, they returned bringing soft drinks, and Fernandez flashed a slide of shift schedules for the coming year. "In Singapore we have eleven public holidays . . . "

"Mr. Fernandez! I'm in Singapore for the residual catalytic cracker. I've come halfway around the world to see it."

"Presently there are seventy-seven tanks on the island. The RCC will add another nineteen. [Ah.] "The RCC will cost one-point-four billion—original estimate one-point-three billion. [I guess that's not bad. But my Thai refinery is coming in exactly on budget.] It will add thirty-three thousand barrels per day and the accounting will become even *more interesting*."

He was right. Accounting between the rival petroleum companies was indeed interesting. Each of the three companies owns different shares of the various facilities on the island. Caltex might own 41 percent of the crude distilling unit, British Petroleum 38 percent, and Singapore Petroleum Company the rest. They would own different shares of the completed catalytic cracker, too. Each of the three companies also sources its own oil. Caltex was the first American company to buy crude from Vietnam after the end of the Vietnam War (which in Southeast Asia I heard called the American War). The Singapore Petroleum Company had been buying oil from China since early in that country's opening to capitalism. British Petroleum got a lot of its oil in the North Sea. And of course, each of the three competitors sold to its own customers.

As for Fernandez's direct employer, "SRC doesn't buy or sell any oil. Our three shareholders buy and sell and they come to us and say 'SRC, will you refine this for us?' "

Some weeks British Petroleum may want a lot of naphtha and the Singapore Petroleum Company may want a lot of diesel fuel. Caltex may own 60 percent of the naphtha-producing facility while the Singapore Petroleum Company may have bought some crude which contains a lot of naphtha. The oil, meanwhile, flows continuously. Who owes whom what?

"We've got a section called the oil-accounting section, which keeps track of the borrowing and lending. There's so many committees. There's ten meeting rooms in just this building alone. You'll like the 'demurrage' committee." Fernandez used his eyes to put quotation marks around the word "demurrage." He knew I collected industry lingo.

"Demurrage," he explained, "is the money you pay for the idle time of a tanker. If we [SRC] say to Caltex, 'Okay, you can come at eleven and load asphalt,' but at eleven o'clock we are not ready, we pay demurrage. If a Caltex tanker comes in and a BP tanker is still occupying the berth, BP has to pay Caltex. There's plenty of cases of demurrage between the three shareholders, and we got a demurrage subcommittee."

These days computers make settling up easier. But like the bookkeeping between rival banks that lend each other hundreds of millions overnight with no security, electronic accounting between the oil companies replicates systems of trust and cooperation that go back long before computers. I was amazed at how these international competitors cooperate at the top.

There was cooperative bookkeeping among oil employees at lower levels, too. Demurrage, keeping a tanker waiting, usually involved a miscalculation on someone's part. "If I owe you eight million in demurrage at the end of the month and you owe me six million," a not-to-be-named Asian engineer explained to me, "that's two million changing hands and a lot of waste to report to home offices. But if I owe you three million and you owe me one million, that's the same two million, but we each look better." So they modify the numbers proportionally. It's nice to see international cooperation among workers too.

Unfortunately, it seemed to stop at that level. When I visited the three top officials of the United Workers of the Petroleum Industry, Salehan, Subramaniam, and Song, they made it clear that they represent only Singaporeans. That triple-S leadership team, as well-integrated as the precinct squad on a US TV cop show (except no women), was a testimonial to Singapore's resolve to contain ethnic hostility. The governments of neighboring Malaysia and Indonesia had been rightly accused of exacerbating ethnic tensions, at times, to firm up their power.

The well-integrated and well-tamed union leaders described their employers' economic problems sympathetically, then they approvingly explained the tax system that requires Singapore employers to pay the government a monthly levy per foreign worker. In some cases the levy is as high as the foreign worker's salary.

"But that's a hundred per cent tax on a very poor fellow worker." I said.

"But if it went to *him*, the money would go out of Singapore and wouldn't be part of *our* GDP," said one of the union leaders. The important thing, as the three labored to make me understand, was that the wage and levy *together* be high enough that employers couldn't use foreigners to undermine the Singapore wage. But what part of the money the migrant worker got paid was not a union concern.

None of these men had been a union leader before Lee Kuan Yew's tenure. That generation of trade unionists had been dispersed or jailed. That made it easier to offer Singapore as a low-wage haven in the early years of economic development. Those years coincided with the period in the early 1970's when Western manufacturing was moving abroad. In other words, it was the opening of what many called the global era. A World Bank publication called "The East Asian Miracle" described the process, saying "Japan, Korea, Singapore, Taiwan, *restructured* [emphasis mine] unions to insure political stability."

At a later stage of development, Lee Kuan Yew decided that low wages were subsidizing inefficient businesses and allowing Singapore firms to keep going without automating. To increase productivity at that stage, the government began to regulate for higher wages. That was the policy still in effect when I visited. These cooperative union leaders had never personally experienced a government push to lower wages.

––––––

Did I ever get to see my catalytic cracker on the tour? I'm not certain. We eventually drove around the refinery. If I assume that any construction in progress was connected with the catalytic cracker, then yes, some of the tanks and pipes that I drove past must have been constructed with the Chase loan. But they didn't make much of an impression.

I did get a closer look at the Love Boat. From the ferry it had seemed pearly pink in the morning, but when we drove past at around noon it was a flat gunmetal gray. I didn't see any people on deck in the middle of the day, but I did see two shirts hung out to dry.

From this medium distance I could imaging life aboard as anything from prisonlike to a World War II troop ship with Frank Sinatra, Gene Kelly, and Jules Munshin set to come bounding off for shore leave.

"Tour over."

––––––

That's as close as I would have gotten to a refinery worker if it hadn't been for Jack Bradie. When I visited him in the director's office, Jack obligingly introduced me to the JGC personnel man. JGC was the primary contractor that hired the subcontractors that employed the manual workers who were raising the catalytic cracker. This interview should have brought me one step closer. But though the personnel man answered all my questions, I didn't learn a thing. Migrant labor is a sensitive subject in Singapore.

"Those questions," Jack said, "if you asked any subcontractor they'd be suspicious." He could think of one possible exception, "a capable lady" who ran a shipping and construction firm that was doing some specialized piping on the cracker.

"Edna Ko is smart, and charming, and no bigger than you."

I called Ms. Ko from Jack's office and we made an appointment for the day after next. (This wasn't the first time sizeism had worked in my favor.)

A large open office in a mixed business/light industrial mall—employees, in the background, work at drafting tables and computer screens

Ms. Ko was as charming and smart as reported, and straightforward besides. "Our contract on the RCC is for seventeen million dollars," she said as she led me from the reception area to her own small office. She made me comfortable and excused herself to take a phone call. Here's her end.

"Hello, Steve.... This is to give you a verbal confirmation. The broker's on leave but I'm quite sure we do not require an extension.... You want that written?... Maybe letter?... Local ... Okay ... okay ... okay ... okay ... can I get back to you Tuesday because Monday is a holiday in Hong Kong.... No, it's a matter of the value of the vessels.... Everything.... Thank you, Steve, Bye-bye."

Vessels? Brokers? Hong Kong office closed Monday?

"Ms. Ko, how did you get into such a specialized business?" I asked. It sounded embarrassingly close to "What's a pretty little gal like you doing with ships and oil pipes?"

"My father started the business—my late father. Our company basically does a certain portion of the job, engineering and piping, both fabrication and installation. My brother runs the Hong Kong office."

I mentioned that I had toured the refinery that Caltex was building in Thailand. "Did your company work on that?"

"We were invited to bid by Caltex, and Shell, too, but we passed. We couldn't get the manpower at rates that the local contractors could. For that we'd need a Thai partner."

"It must be difficult to find labor here in Singapore," I said, approaching what I thought would be the sensitive area.

"We relied on Malaysian before," Ms. Ko answered matter-of-factly. "But because of that labor supply becoming depleted or more difficult to source or more ... [she searched momentarily for the word] ... more expensive, we can say, we have to go to nontraditional sources—Philippines, Bangladesh, Mainland China ... "

"You actually go to China?"

"Let me get my chap who's the expert on that." She spoke into the intercom in Chinese.

A man with a crew cut, short-sleeved shirt, chinos with bulging pockets, and rubber-soled shoes appeared almost immediately. (Ms. Ko, by the way, had smooth bobbed hair, wore a fashionable unfitted suit jacket, a slightly flared skirt, and flat heels, and had a Prada purse.) She explained to Mr. Goh that I came through the people at Pulau Merlimau and would like to understand the special problems of recruiting labor in Singapore.

Given the O.K., Mr. Goh was off and enumerating faster than I could copy it down. "Quota, levy, security, testing . . . "

I gradually made sense out of a ream of regulations designed to control migrants and make sure they don't stay in Singapore, and administered (at least currently) to insure that foreign labor doesn't undercut Singapore wages.

Every request for migrant workers had to be approved by a government agency that examined Ms. Ko's contract with the oil company, checking the duration and value of the job. Each industry is allowed so many foreigners per Singaporean employee. Mr. Goh's quota at the time was five to one, or, "One Singaporean is worth five foreign labor," as he put it. The workers may come from only specified source countries. "In present labor market," Goh explained, "we must go to NTSes [nontraditional sources], which means Thailand, Philippines, Burma, Sri Lanka, India, Bangladesh, and seventh China is a separate category." (Workers from neighboring Malaysia, the "traditional source," can come and go more freely.)

In addition to salary, employers pay the levy, then $440 a month (in Singapore dollars) for unskilled workers, S$200 for skilled. (Making unskilled workers as expensive as skilled workers was part of the policy of increasing productivity.)

Mr. Goh has his skilled workers pretested in the country of origin to make sure that they can pass the exams they'll be given in Singapore. For most jobs the tests would take half a day, but because of security and safety concerns at refineries, it might be 14 days before a pipefitter received the photo ID that allowed him onto the island. Goh would try to find off-site tasks until then, but he couldn't become a labor contractor renting his workers out.

The company also puts up a security deposit of S$5,000 per migrant, to be returned when the individual goes home.

"How much does this all cost you, Mr. Goh?"

"Unskilled the pay might be four hundred and fifty a month and the levy now four hundred and forty, meal allowance two hundred and fifty, plus air ticket, insurance, accommodation, and utilities in the accommodation..."

Ms. Ko took up some paperwork while Goh continued. "... For skilled worker the levy is two hundred, pay in the region of nine hundred. Plus the same two hundred and fifty for meal allowance, accommodation, insurance, testing ... Yes, we pay for the testing."

"So all together, the monthly cost of a foreign worker?"

"Every job is different but a foreign welder costs about two thousand five hundred a month."

"And how much would a Singapore welder cost?"

"Salary fifteen hundred, CPF ... [Central Providential Fund]" Mr. Goh did a quick calculation and came up with the same number, 2,500 Singapore dollars a month.

"I would like to use Singaporeans if I could find them but there is pros and cons. They are choosy." I was struck by that use of "choosy" because I'd just seen the word used the same way in a speech by Lee Kuan Yew scolding Singaporeans for refusing night-shift jobs. "They can just go off the job in a day, unlike ... [Mr. Goh took a few photo IDs from his pocket] These people have no choice."

I picked up the ID of sad-eyed, mustachioed F. Pellegrino from the Philippines.

"Their passport is retained by us; their contract is for two years." I wondered why Pellegrino's ID was at hand, but I didn't ask.

"If a Singaporean says 'I'm not coming anymore,'" Goh explains, "he will have to pay one month salary minus what's owed to him or I go after him in small-claims court. But if a Filipino wants to go home he will have to repay his air fare and buy his ticket home and pay the company for two months if he worked six. If he frustrates his contract he will be held in detention till he is repatriated. But disadvantage, I must keep paying his food, accommodations, utilities at accommodations, even if work stops." It's the old debate: wage labor versus slave labor.

Mr. Goh gave me capsule descriptions of some of the migrant groups that he could choose from at the moment.

"The Banglas are obedient. They feel committed because of the money they paid to come." Goh pays a local agent to find and screen workers, but workers also pay agents themselves. In Bangladesh it can cost a few thousand dollars to arrange job, transportation, and permits. Many rural people sell their land or go deeply into debt to send one family member abroad this way.

"The Bangladeshis are well behaved," Mr. Goh volunteered, "but some have very low I.Q.s. They are peasants. Our Bangladeshis are all unskilled; no test required. They may not know how to read. I will talk to them in English and I will gauge whether he understands the language. I will look into the well build of the person."

"Hmmm?"

"Whether he's strong, well-built, twenty-five to thirty-three is what I take. Just visually, if the guy is wearing glasses, I don't take people with glasses. The funny thing about the Banglas, they don't wear glasses. Either their eyes are very good or they can't afford glasses."

"And these Filipinos?" I was still holding Pellegrino's ID.

"The Filipinos are one of the best in terms of skills, ability to interpret the job, and they can speak English because the Americans have trained them up in Subic Bay [the former military base.]. This man," Mr. Goh referred to the card in my hand, "has been with us six years. I am getting him a permanent pass. But I must cancel his temporary permit." So that's why it's out.

I turned the card idly. Mr. Goh must have thought I was examining it. "The traditional source [a Malaysian] has same card but different bar code."

Bar code? Now I did examine it. There was nothing to see. With a scanner, however, authorities could tell the legitimate bearer's nationality, work sites he was entitled to enter, et cetera. I was starting to realize how carefully the Singapore government categorizes and keeps track.

"Indians, I only have six now. I'll see how they work out."

"And the Thais?" I asked.

"No Thais!" Ms. Ko breaks in, looking up from her work. "They're rigid and not so cheap."

"I heard they were good welders," I suggested tentatively.

"We had forty-five for the Mobil job two years ago—welders, fitters, and riggers," she explains. "When we wanted to split the group up they want to be together, all forty-five."

"They're very fearful outside Thailand," I defended the unknown migrants. "And there was that sleeping death scare, a couple of years back."

"But they were willing to be split up for more money," Ms. Ko replies.

"Ah-ha" said I, "so they were negotiating."

"I don't know if you'd call it negotiating or demanding. We were in the middle of a critical phase, and they're so smart. They could see it." Ms. Ko was re-seeing it herself now, in her mind's eye. "They put down their tools. They are capable to form a mutiny. So we repatriated them."

"Sent them back?"

"The same morning."

"The same morning?!"

"Not so much problem," Mr. Goh explained, perhaps misinterpreting my amazement. "There's direct buses out of Singapore. You only have to ensure that he has boarded the transport and surrendered the work permit and do final exit permit in full. Your five thousand security is jeopardized if the exit pass is not signed with proof he went directly to his country of origin."

Should any of his workers fail to leave the country as scheduled, the employer would have to come up with the S$5,000 security money in cash and forfeit it. By making the employer responsible financially, the government made as certain as possible that migrant workers would go back home. And as we've seen, they also made the use of migrants as expensive as the use of Singapore workers. Singapore was serious both about controlling population flows and about making sure that illegal workers didn't undermine local wages.

I was used to the US, where lowering wages had been bipartisan government policy as long as I could remember. So despite periodic campaigns against illegal aliens, no US administration seriously troubled the employers who hired them, and several government programs supplied low-paid legal immigrant gangs to employers like chicken processors and sugar-cane growers. Of course in Singapore, if Lee Kuan Yew should decide at some point that it was in the national interest to lower wages, he could do so openly with little opposition.

"Do you normally have to see each worker out individually?" I asked.

"We have to physically hold his hand and say bye-bye." Ms. Ko exaggerated only slightly.

The Thai mutiny was an abrasion she could still feel. "We tried to talk to them. One of them spoke a little English. We had a contract we had to comply with, we were already on a forty-four-hour basis, but if we have to go round the clock [she is talking to the Thais now] we can give you this much more. No . . . yes . . . no. The agent flew down from Bangkok. He is talking to them; we don't understand. We talked until four o'clock in the morning but he failed to reach an agreement."

"You were there, Ms. Ko? Right in that room?"

"No, my agent. I was on the phone seeing what it would cost to get replacements by the next day. It was a hard decision."

Mr. Goh told me about a new labor source that promised more predictability.

"In China we have recently made contact with a company that operates the same type of projects as ours. They have a hundred thousand workers broken into divisions just like the army.

"We tell them we want one hundred to two hundred people, we give them the breakdown of the trades, we negotiate the salary we will pay. We give the company the mobilization fee of two hundred dollars per worker and they'll bring them in a group, a complete work team with a project manager that comes in from China as foreman and their own middle managers and supervisors. Their team is like a sub-sub-subcontractor. But we will pay the worker directly by his own check and he will sign a contract with us." Hiring and paying each worker individually is a Singapore government requirement.

"Will the Chinese be coming soon?" I asked.

"They are already with us. Two hundred Chinese already work on the RCC."

"You mean I'm already paying them? What kind of people are they, Mr. Goh?"

"We have welders, pipefitters. A Chinese welder I pay seven hundred. But the other costs, ticket, accommodations . . . "

"But what are they like?"

"They are from two different divisions. In that country each division has thirty thousand men."

"But is it an army? Are they . . . " free labor, I was thinking.

"The uniqueness is that they kept their families with them. There's a province set up by this company in China and the family lives together and has their schools, their culture."

"Did you see any of the women? Did you see any schools?"

"We were seeing a lot of Chinese women welders but we could not get approval from the Singapore government for women welders."

"Ah," I said.

"At one time we thought the Chinese would be cheaper," Ms. Ko interjected, "but they are aware of the rates now and if they work in Singapore they know what the local worker is getting."

"Ah, I see."

At the time there were said to be fewer than 100,000 Chinese laborers sending home remittances. (There were half a million Thais abroad in construction work alone.) So my 200 Mainlanders were truly a part of a vanguard. Remittance money had been a crucial source of foreign currency for kick-starting Korean industrialization. Now my bank deposit, lent by Chase to Caltex and paid as wages to Ms. Ko's welders, was helping to build the new capitalist China. Should I be proud?

The interview was coming to an end but my mind kept going back to one matter.

"I keep wondering what I would have decided about those Thais," I said to Ms. Ko. "I'm not the kind of person to say on principle 'You can't tell me what to do.' I'd want to know what it was going to cost me either way. Now, I could calculate what it would cost to replace them, but the problem you had was . . ."

"Exactly," Ko nodded in grateful agreement.

"Once you've got this indiscipline . . ."

"Exactly!" She jumped in. "Once you've got this indiscipline on the site you don't know what other delays they'll cause or what other people will demand later. We needed to get them out because we were afraid they would set the rest of our workers asking for the same things. It was a hard decision."

I probably would have done the same thing, I concluded. Predictability is the sine qua non for fulfilling a contract. Still, employers, even those as poised and rational as Ms. Ko, can act irrationally when balked by workers.

I asked Ms. Ko if labor was her main cost.

"No, our main cost is equipment—cranes, et cetera."

I wonder if a demand to renegotiate an equipment lease would evoke the same raw feeling as had the Thai "mutiny."

I was more determined than ever to interview one of my own migrants. The Thais still seemed the most exotic. (What had those mutineers really wanted?) But I couldn't talk to them at work, couldn't hang around their separate pier or ride in the vans that took them to their dormitories. So I hired a Thai translator and went down to the only seedy mall in Singapore.

When you ask Singaporeans for directions to the maids' mall, they nod and even smile. "Straight up Orchard road. You'll hear the chirp-chirp from outside." Despite Flor Concepcion's execution, no one seemed frightened of the thousands of Filipinas who alight at a particular downtown mall every Sunday. Nor did people seem to mind the hundreds of slim South Indian men who stood talking in the parking lot at the entrance of the Indian quarter. But when I asked directions to the Golden Mile, people said "The Thai mall? That's not really Singapore," or "Maybe you don't want to go there alone."

Construction workers are generally free only on Sunday, so I'd cased the Golden Mile the Sunday before, ostensibly to buy green papaya for a salad. Young men flanked the entrance ramp, oddly silent. Inside it was run down and there was rock music on the loudspeakers. A few men drank beer at tables. Many more squatted or sat in circles on the floors, joking and eating peanuts. They tore up cartons for the cardboard to sit on. Groups that had been there earlier had left spectral circles of cardboards and peanut shells. In Singapore litter is shocking.

But nobody had bothered me as I crossed the ground floor, escalated to the supermarket, and picked out a papaya. Still, it was creepy to move among so many men, none of whom spoke English. I was relieved to chatter to the checkout clerk about how you shred a green papaya. (*Are we the only women here?* I wondered.)

Now, back in the same supermarket with a translator, I noticed a young man engaged in intense conversation with an older woman. She was skinny and had to be almost 40. *Look at the way they lean in toward each other.* I thought.

"What are they talking about?" I directed the translator to the couple with my eyes.

"The health of someone from their village. She had to be brought to

Bangkok to find a doctor. Either this one's his relative or the one they're talking about."

"Oh."

––––––

In an upstairs remittance shop, a sinewy old man thumbed through a sheaf
of receipts. "I've sent home almost half a million baht and the wife says
there's no money."

"How come?" I asked, already embroidering a drama of infidelity with a
homecoming like Agamemnon's.

The man explained that he'd been a welder in Singapore for 11 years,
never missed a day's work. His company—*Ferrenghis* (Western foreigners)
who build shopping plazas—gave him a big bonus after ten years, about
80,000 baht. His wife had been buying land with his earnings and built a
house on one of the plots. "We paid two hundred thousand, now it's worth
four hundred thousand. But there's never any money."

The drama got less classical. Still, half a million of anything is a lot, even
if it's only baht. And 11 years is more than half of Odysseus' voyage. The last
time the man had been home was three years earlier.

"Does your wife ever visit you in Singapore?"

"The wife says she wants to but I don't allow it. Letting her come to
Bangkok is enough already. If she came here there'd be no one to look after
the children."

A second old man gave a supplementary explanation. "It's troublesome to
get a passport for a woman. They say you want to be a prostitute. If a woman
comes back from Japan they take her to a room in the airport, they say 'How
much did you spend?! What did you do?! Who gave you that?!'"

My translator confirmed this. "The last time I flew to Bangkok I saw a line
of women outside that room."

Another old man wandered in to check the plastic boxes. Once you've registered with a remittance shop, you can use it as a mail drop. The boxes here
were labeled alphabetically; another shop arranged theirs by village. The new
man flipped through the mail to see who else was in Singapore. This seemed
to be the old-timers' hangout.

Over in the electronics store, young men watched a kung fu movie,
dubbed in Thai, on a large-screen TV. A magic warrior somersaulted up and

backwards. The area of the floor where the men were allowed to sit was filled but not packed.

———

Downstairs I bought a few *pudsa*, (they look like tiny apples) from a man at a card table. He was originally from northeast Thailand, he told me, but he was now based in Had-yai to make this trip from the border every week. He'd gotten up at 4:30 that morning to peel 80 kilos of sour mangoes. "That's my sister." He pointed to a woman cooking fish balls in a large wok on the floor of a cosmetics booth which they sublet on Sundays. "We have a regular Singapore sales permit. Business is pretty good."

There were also sit-down restaurants. On weekdays, the Golden Mile is a regular though slightly shabby mall where many Singaporeans come for Thai food. But the migrants seemed to make do with fruit, beer, fish balls, and peanuts.

The place was getting to feel almost homey. At first I thought of remittance shops as akin to the pool halls and credit jewelers around US army bases. But I gradually began to see the Golden Mile as a useful, if not stimulating, community center.

A lively group of about eight men just finishing their business at a remittance shop invited us to sit outside with them in the alley. They bought bottled water from an old lady who ran after us with newspaper when she saw that I was going to sit down too.

"There are benches across the way," I said, pointing into a housing estate. They indicated politely that perhaps they'd better not. "Singaporeans don't like to see us on the street," one said. I couldn't tell how much that bothered them. They were here "for the money." They each gave the same answer. Their stories were the same as a dozen and a half others I'd collected that day. Registered with an agent in town, paid 40,000 to 50,000 baht. Their jobs in Singapore: "Do cement." "Build flats." "Work in the shipyard." Everyone I asked was married. The money was sent back to wife and children.

"Are *you* married?" one man asked me flirtatiously.

"I have a daughter twenty-seven!" I said with mock indignation.

"Is *she* married?"

Everyone laughed.

I found on this trip that any indication of my age turned unwanted interest into chivalrous solicitude.

"I'm thinking of finding a Singapore wife," said the flirtatious one.

"Wouldn't it cost money to have a wife here?"

"Yes, I'd send less home than I'm sending now."

"I can tell *you're* not thinking that way," I said to a fellow I remembered later as round-faced with sandy-red hair and freckles. (Impossible of course, but he was so visibly a country kid.)

"No, I've got two children. My wife is working in the paddy fields now with hired help. [At 60 or 70 baht a day.] I'm not looking for a second wife." This was his second stint abroad.

Another had left his farm for the first time. "My wife will work it with the children and she'll hire people. This is the first time I've missed a harvest. It makes me feel very funny to think someone else is clearing the paddy." It was the farm that his parents and grandparents had worked.

"And your children?"

"I want them to go to school and work in government offices. I'll hire people to do the harvest when I'm old."

They had plenty of questions to ask me.

"What do construction workers get in America? How much did you pay for your ticket here? What about between Singapore and Thailand?"

My experience there was almost relevant, since I'd traveled the peninsula by train and discount Bangladeshi airline. One of the men asked me to repeat the name of the student travel agency I'd used.

Others had useful information too.

"A couple of people from my village went to Israel. They take care of your food and lodging better than Singapore from what I hear."

"When you go to Taiwan they will check whether you have worms in your stomach. Here they only check for fitness but not worms."

"In Kuwait the pay is better and you save it all: there's no place to go. You finish work and you sit in your air-conditioned room. They don't like Thais there." I've heard Indonesian women give similar reviews to Saudi Arabia. The reputation for having abusive or disdainful employers undoubtedly jacks up wages in those two countries.

"What about working in Thailand?" I asked.

"Plenty of jobs, but low wages." "Even in Bangkok, the language and the low cost of living don't balance the high pay in Singapore." "But in Bangkok"—a plaintive young face—"when you miss your family it's reachable. In Singapore, you cannot just leave."

"What do *you* do?" the man who wants a second wife asked the translator. "Sell insurance."

He processed that, alert for any associations. And why shouldn't he be? Isn't travel supposed to broaden? I only met one Thai at the mall whom I'd call a hustler.

———

He was handing out fliers for a new remittance shop. "The only remittance shop owned by a Thai," was his spiel. "Drop your remittance number into the glass bowl and win a thousand baht."

"Hello. You US?" It was the first English I'd heard at the Golden Mile. He wore slim-legged black pants and pointy-toed boots with stacked heels. His family still had a paddy farm in the north but "Farming in Thailand is old-fashioned and the reward for the money is no good." Years ago he'd been a trishaw driver. "I had a GI friend, Larry. I very much like Americans."

When I looked more closely I saw that this slight, black-haired man could be in his late forties.

On his first trip to Singapore, Larry's friend had paid an agent the usual 40,000 baht. Now he was back on a tourist visa, picking up whatever work he could on his own. He was currently a building guard and also painted rooms for an interior decorator.

"And you do this, too," I indicated the leafleting.

"I'm just doing that for my friend. Friends do things for each other. If you do good, you get good. That's what they say in my family."

Till that moment, I hadn't connected the Southeast Asia I was visiting with the Southeast Asia of American GIs on R&R during the Vietnam War. What happened to the hanger-on types when times changed? They're still here now, of course. Just as the decent and self-respecting were always there then.

———

It was toward the end of the day when we sat down with three young men drinking beer (one bottle each) and looking bored or sad at a table against the wall. Two were classically handsome Thais in T-shirts. The third had chipped front teeth, a plaid shirt, and a goofy center part that made him look like Alfalfa in *Our Gang*.

All three had been brought from Nong Khai by their Thai agent and now lived on the premises of their Singapore contractor in corrugated metal containers, five people per container.

"I have a container with air con [air conditioning], refrigerator and TV in the common space," said Alfalfa. "You cook outside. Most of them have a window."

The shyest of the young men—"He doesn't talk to us either," the second-shyest explained—did unskilled construction work on new apartment buildings. The other two were pipefitters sent out to different oil refineries.

"Oh, which refineries?" I tried to sound casual.

Alfalfa fanned out a set of plastic IDs. Mobil, Esso . . . and there, with its blue triangle and yellow oil drop, was the card he swipes to get onto Pulau Merlimau.

This man works for me!

I asked, as open-endedly as I could, if there was anything he particularly disliked or liked about the refinery jobs.

"Sometimes I have to go to the factory to construct the piece [of pipe] that they need. Then I bring the piece back to the refinery and even though I did it according to the drawing and everything was correct, when I bring it back, sometimes it doesn't fit. This makes me fed up because I thought I could finish but now the job is not finished. I have to take it back and redo it."

"Will the foreman be angry at you?"

"No, he knows it's not my fault. Something is always different in the reality than when they drew the plan."

"Some people would think it a nice break, then," I suggested, "to go back over instead of working in the sun."

"But I don't like to have to redo what I did. You feel stupid even if it's the fault of the drawing. You feel so good when everything's right."

"Is there a part of the job you particularly like?"

"He likes it when the pipe has to fit with a forty-five degree angle," said the translator. "He doesn't like the ninety degrees."

"What makes the forty-five degrees more interesting?"

"You have to think harder for the forty-five degrees. Here, I can draw it for you." He took my pen and sketched two figures in my notebook. "If it's ninety degrees they tell you this length." He made an arrow. "It's straight-forward. But if it's forty-five degrees they only tell you this side. So I have to do some calculation. I have the ability to find out what is the other length. He marked the unknown with an X. "There is a formula," he added modestly.

"And you yourself do the figuring and the cutting and fitting?" I said appreciatively.

A warmth I could just about feel flooded his face.

"That is my ability," he said, looking down. "Yes."

All three of the young men came from a small city in northern Thailand near the Laotian boarder and expected to go back there. None of them currently lived on a farm, though other family members did.

Here in Singapore they woke at about 6:00 A.M. "The boss [they used the phrase *tow kae*, Chinese boss] will come at about seven-fifteen. There's a little excitement waiting for the foreman because we don't know to which place we'll be sent."

Because he'd had asthma attacks in Singapore, Alfalfa hoped he'd get to work outside where the dust is less. "Also to see the real thing is more interesting than just the drawing."

"Do you ever ask to be sent on one job and not another because of dust, say, or because you'd like to stay together with other Thais?"

"No," Alfalfa answered, "because you must respect the feeling of the foreman and what he needs to get the work finished." These were certainly not my Thai mutineers.

"Everyday is routine work," said the quieter pipefitter. "Only some days you wake up and think 'I am so far from home!' When you're sick in Thailand other people will do for you—your family, your wife. But here you have to get water yourself if you're sick. Your friends cannot help you because they have their own work."

All agreed that they missed family at home. Alfalfa's wife was a school-teacher. "And we have a nine-year-old."

"But you look so young."

"I'm twenty-eight."

"You said that in English!" I had already written it down when I realized.

"I'm twenty-eight," he repeated.

"He also speaks a little Hokkien on the job, he says," says the translator. But he was embarrassed and would not attempt to say anything else in English.

Alfalfa had been in Singapore for a year, and planned to stay only one more. The original contract was for four years but it was renegotiable after two. "Now that I have the money, I want to continue studying in Thailand."

Would it be helpful or discouraging, I wondered, to suggest how poor so much Thai education was, particularly outside of Bangkok? Indeed, Alfalfa had already taken courses that earned him an electrician's credentials. "But there are a lot of people in Thailand with those qualifications and the pay is too low."

"Will you stay in the construction field?"

"No, I don't think so."

Thai migrants who make it to Singapore tend to be the best-educated people in their region. The remittances they and other migrants send home constitute over 50 percent of the income in some provinces. You can tell a village with good migration connections not only by the TV antennas on bamboo houses that journalists find so ironic, but by pickup trucks, fish ponds, and irrigation and other agricultural improvements. But few of the returning workers will contribute the methods they learned abroad to the Thai construction industry. You can't blame them for trying to get out of construction work, especially Alfalfa with his asthma. But the sorry state of Thai education and economic planning meant that more courses wouldn't necessarily prepare him for a better job at home. I couldn't bring myself to say that.

"By the way, you know that boat off the SRC island?" They all knew the Love Boat. "Do you suppose it makes people seasick to live there?" I fished.

Alfalfa actually knew someone who had lived on the boat. "He never complained about the rolling or anything." No, he couldn't introduce me to his friend. "He's gone from Singapore a month already."

I knew it was pushing to ask about another worker. And it's possible that Alfalfa was being politely evasive. But it's more likely that his Love Boat acquaintance was indeed gone from Singapore. Migrant life is migratory. The people you meet get transferred or go home.

The Maids' Mall, Luck Plaza, Orchard Road, Singapore

The following Sunday I went to the maids' mall, but without a translator. I was not lucky enough to run into a Filipina who just happened to work for a Caltex executive. But I had a nice chat with four friends who asked me to snap their picture together, first in front of the Kmart, then outside on Orchard Road. Though they had been neighbors on a small island and had signed with the same agent to go abroad, this meeting of all four in Singapore had been difficult to arrange because maids only get one Sunday off each month.

Three of the women worked for Singaporeans. "*My* Mister is an American," said the fourth. Everyone agreed that she had the best deal.

All four had left their own children and come to Singapore "for the money." Their families had decided that this was a good investment and pooled their savings to pay the agent's fee. One woman's family had borrowed the money. She was aware that they risked a crippling debt if for any reason she didn't finish her contract.

As part of their investment, family members, including husbands in three cases, had agreed to take care of the children. The one single woman was worried, however, because her sister, the chief caregiver, was getting remarried. She feared that her 14-year-old son and his new uncle would get in each other's way, and that her sister, with a new husband on the scene, couldn't give the younger children enough attention.

I asked lamely if the women missed their children. "Yes, very much," they all said. They couldn't seem to express it any better.

"I miss my children but I also take care of children here," said the woman with the teenage son. "The little boy I take care of was always frightened and crying when I first came. His mother says, 'If you not good the policeman will come!' or 'Auntie broke her leg because *you* spit.' "

Guilt evocation must be popular with Singapore parents, because the other women chimed in quickly with their own examples: "The lights went out because *you* were crying." "The train is not coming because the train man knows, *you* are standing in front of the yellow line."

"I think the little boy is not so frightened now," said the woman who was worried about her own son.

"Then you must be a very good nanny."

"Thank you." She smiled unhappily. "But I will be glad when I can go home because here I am doing it just for the money."

These women can only enter the cash economy if they have a product that can be exchanged for money. But child-caring for cash seems stranger to them (and to me too) than pipe fitting for cash. In fact, it seems almost illicit. In the noncash economy they came from—that is to say, in the family—caring is provided for individuals one is presumed to love. Telling a woman that she does it well for strangers is not as welcome a compliment as telling Alfalfa he pipe-fits well for many different oil companies.

A product, whether it be pipe fitting or child care, is not the same thing as the money it's exchanged for. Bankers often talk as though they create things through their loans, when in fact they merely turn money into more money. Their vanity in taking credit for the product had sometimes annoyed me, but the opposite humble error disturbed me more. When a woman who takes care of children says that all she's doing is making money, I think, "What if that was true?" Could a child survive if his caregiver wasn't doing many, many things beyond her contractual job?

"It's too bad you have to come all the way to Singapore," I said. "There must be houses to clean and children to take care of in the Philippines."

"Our own," said one.

"But the money is in Singapore," said the second.

"It is like the nurses," said the woman with the teenage son. "People from home study to be nurses and they will go to New York. But there are lots of sick people on our island."

"Yes, but the money is in New York," her friend reminded us.

Right, I thought, *some of it is mine.* But how does that determine whose children get minded and which sick get nursed? Sometimes I understand this money trail, and other times I lose the thread and the results make no sense at all.

———

Migration routes, I was beginning to realize, don't run from nation to nation. They go from three towns in a rural district to three or four blocks in a distant metropolis, or from a particular island in the Philippines to a particular mall in Singapore. Legal or illegal, skilled or unskilled, migrant workers don't swarm over borders on speculation. They travel on marked paths to specific jobs. While I was in Asia, the indomitable Mr. Goh, using money that went from Chase to Caltex to Ms. Ko's company, was opening just such a pathway between Singapore and a province in southern China. But the path won't look like his blueprint for long. The migrants will modify it.

Chinese workers may be *drawn* to Singapore by my money, but they don't stream along like iron fillings in magnetic lines of force. After all, the mainlander can speak to a Singaporean in his own dialect, he can also read the *Straits Times,* the *Asian Wall Street Journal,* or a San Francisco comic book. He soon knows as Ms. Ko pointed out, "what the local worker is getting."

That mainland welder will report home not only on Singapore salaries, but on how he was treated, where to get a good bowl of noodles, on new welding techniques, and on matters that I can't begin to imagine. Ants, and even iron fillings, modify the paths they move along. Human beings make changes that are unpredictable before they happen but have a way of seeming obvious and even traditional as soon as they're in place.

My money, loaned through Chase, attracted rural Indonesians to Malaysia where they built and tended shrimp farms, and it attracted northeastern Thais to refineries in an industrial park south of Bangkok and in the city of Singapore. The migrants will take many things home besides money from these places. And despite all of Lee Kuan Yew's precautions, they'll leave more behind than the structures they were hired to build.

Styles of Corruption

Petty corruption slows down the flow of business and adds cost and grief to daily life. Corruption at higher levels causes a great amount of capital—which also means labor, material, and land—to be diverted from one use to another. It undermines both national and individual planning. Corruption is one reason that people can work very hard and still be very poor.

Before I left Asia, I learned how Caltex got the permit for its refinery in Thailand. The story involved both Thai-style and US-style corruption. It would have been handled somewhat differently in Malaysia or Indonesia. It wouldn't have happened at all in Singapore.

Thailand has no oil of its own. Oil companies import crude oil into Thailand and refine it there for the domestic market. Before the new Shell and Caltex refineries went up, the country had three oil refineries. In response to the booming economy, the Thai National Energy Policy Committee decided to issue a permit for a fourth refinery, and Shell won the bidding with its plan for a refinery at Map Ta Phut. But as we saw, Nigel Carlin had been scouting the same area for Caltex. In fact, Caltex had already acquired all the land it needed while Shell was still shopping.

But the Thai National Energy Policy Committee, seconded by the World Bank, was adamant in its decision that the country needed only four refineries. A fifth would destroy fishing and farmland for no good reason. As a kind of booby prize, the Thais ordered Shell to offer Caltex a 15 percent share in the new fourth refinery. That wasn't acceptable to either oil company.

Then suddenly the Thai government reversed itself and offered Caltex a permit for a fifth refinery without even opening bids. That seemed strange, since people knew that the Kuwait Petroleum Corporation was still contending for a permit. If a fifth refinery was now desirable, why not let everyone bid?

According to the *Far Eastern Economic Review*:

The decision was taken by Chatachi [then the Thai prime minister] and a small group of senior ministers, following US lobbying efforts which featured the US ambassador as well as senior Caltex executives. ["Over a Barrel: Thai Government in About Face on Oil Policy," *Far Eastern Economic Review*, March 8, 1990]

To justify their reversal, Thai government officials said that awarding the permit to Caltex was a tradeoff to get the US to accept more Thai textile imports, and to ease US pressure on Thailand to open its markets to foreign cigarettes and to protect intellectual property rights. In other words, in exchange for a fifth refinery permit there would be more textile jobs, fewer imported cigarettes, and cheaper pirated videotapes in Bangkok. The officials tried to present their switch as part of the give-and-take of ongoing trade talks.

Ignoring that explanation, Bangkok reporters jumped on the fact that one of the senior ministers involved in the policy change had a son-in-law who worked for Caltex. At the risk of sounding naïve, I honestly don't know how much or even if, the son-in-law affected the permit negotiations.

While no Thai official justified the fifth refinery in terms of sound energy policy, it's still possible that the permit was based on other Thai national in-terests. It's harder to imagine the public interest that induced a US adminis-tration to have its ambassador bargain away American textile jobs, cigarette sales, and entertainment royalties in exchange for one company's right to build a refinery overseas.

Based on traditional styles of corruption, Thais assumed that the decision was made, on their side, for the sake of personal enrichment, while I, as an American, assumed that my representatives were moved to action by cam-paign contributions. Perhaps the main sense in which Caltex and its parent companies, Chevron and Texaco, are *American* multinationals is that they make their ongoing contributions to American politicians.

It's also possible that global-era politicians so honestly believe that what's good for *their* multinationals abroad is good for the country that they would send in the ambassador with or without specific linked contributions. That may be more insidious.

Whatever factor tipped the permit decision in Caltex's favor, some of my bank deposit went into a Thai minister's son-in-law's salary, and some went into US political-campaign funds.

This is not to say that Caltex uses my money to spread corruption. Many kinds of corruption, particularly those most common in poor countries, are an impediment to day-to-day business operations. Companies like Caltex of-ten help to clean up corruption on those levels.

Julius Tahija, an Indonesian who was the head of Caltex Pacific Indone-sia for ten years, feels that "the promoting of an ethical business culture" is the most important benefit that a transnational like Caltex brings to his country. In a *Harvard Business Review* article called "Swapping Business Skills for Oil,"* Tahija says:

> A stranger once approached me at Jakarta's airport, introduced himself as a businessman, and said, "Something is wrong at Caltex.... Your accounting de-partment is delaying payment to people to whom the company owes money. Unless people pay bribes, they do not get what's due to them."

HBR, September–October, 1993.

I knew that this kind of extortion happened in some government offices. Even schoolteachers may have to pay bribes in order to get their salaries, but such a thing at Caltex was inconceivable to me.

Tahija investigated and discovered that it was true.

After taking severe disciplinary measures, I distributed notices to our suppliers and contractors that anyone not paid in two weeks should call me directly at home. The problem disappeared.

"Honesty and dishonesty do not mean different things in different countries," Tahija says flatly. Furthermore, "ethical conduct is in a transnational's best interest."

What would happen if government officials and the public began to believe that a company such as Caltex made payoffs? Or that Caltex responded favorably to bribes? Or that the company kept two sets of books to hide income from local taxation?

Every story of a payoff would stimulate requests for more. . . . The government would continually renegotiate contracts in an attempt to get its share of hidden income.

As for "contributions" whether directly or subtly requested:

Such contributions will win only temporary friends. When your payments stop, everyone's door slams shut. Once you buy a politician . . . the demands only grow.

Tahija insists that Caltex did not make payoffs, and I believe him. But he certainly understood the temptation.

A common rationalization at all levels of corporate responsibility runs like this: it's ethical to pay government officials to do things they would normally do to discharge their duties but it's unethical to pay someone to break the law. By this standard, paying a customs official to pass illegal goods is unethical, but paying that same official to expedite your shipment is all right. . . . Such rationalization is tempting when your request for a building permit is at the bottom of the stack.

Caltex often needed building permits. In Thailand, Joe Bartlett, the open-faced American who helped buy the land for the refinery at Map Ta Phut, also had the job of getting building permits from local officials. I asked him how you do that.

"You go to an office and say 'I'm trying to build a refinery.' They keep you waiting. There's no one to see. You just keep coming back till finally someone says 'Send us the paperwork.' What paperwork, what information? What do they want to know?!"

"Maybe you were supposed to pay someone off," I suggested.

"We didn't."

"So what did you do?"

"I came back and sat in that office for about three months. I asked other companies what information they sent to get permits. Some officials are afraid to sign. One man told me, 'If I sign that [a pier permit] now, twenty years later when I retire to my paddy farm and a boat crashes into the pier, they'll come to my farm and arrest me and put me in jail.' "

But "Caltex did not pay off," Joe insisted. I believe both Bartlett and Tahija about what happened at their levels.

But when Caltex found the perfect spot for a refinery, and then lined up the land and the money to build that refinery, they did not let someone just hang around an office waiting. And they did not accept a "no" based on the country's energy policy. They got the policy reversed through the highest officials to whom they had access. Some of that access, both in Thailand and the US, was bought with my money.

An unnecessary refinery uses up productive land and increases pollution, both at the site and by encouraging more oil and gasoline consumption in the rest of the country. But at least the Caltex refinery was built soundly. For good or ill, it functioned well. And its construction didn't exacerbate the kind of low-level corruption that Caltex Indonesia, under Tahija, tried to eradicate.

Julius Tahija mentioned the Indonesian practice of making schoolteachers pay bribes in order to get their salaries. In some third-world countries, Egypt for one, teachers' salaries are minimal but the teachers routinely extract tips or tutoring fees to teach students what they'll need to pass their exams. Families that can't afford the tutoring would only waste time and money sending their children to the public schools, so the low-level government job becomes a license to demand bribes from people one step lower.

In Indonesia, local officials were known to set up roadblocks to collect tariffs on public highways. I heard a story about such a toll in front of a hospital. Poor families with sick infants had to turn back in sight of the medical help they needed.

But honesty and dishonesty, as Tahija says, don't mean different things in different countries, at least not totally different things. Customs may differ, but this kind of corruption, even when you're used to it, must engender economic waste and human resentment. It also undercuts what little there is of public infrastructure, education, and health care.

One thing that makes bribery cost-effective for the givers is that recipients take private millions to misdirect public billions. But that makes it terribly expensive for the public. Widespread corruption also makes it difficult to plan for the common good.

Of course, free-market fundamentalists would say that Thailand had no business having a restrictive energy policy in the first place. If Shell, Caltex, and the Kuwaiti Petroleum Corporation are all willing to build new refineries at the same time, in the same place, let them. Their corporate profit motive will prove the best guide to how much refining capacity Thailand needs.

By that reasoning, Caltex wasn't subverting the common good, it was merely circumventing the rigid notions of some bureaucratic planner. At the time I had little way of knowing whether the four-refinery limit was sound policy (the plan was to slightly undersupply oil demand) or an annoying impediment to profit and development.

As it happened, the fifth refinery turned out to be a terrible mistake, even for Caltex. Within two years, oil demand dropped so precipitously that the Caltex and Shell refineries were forced to merge. But that was due to an economic crash that no one could reasonably have foreseen, except in the general sense that unpredictable downturns are predictable.

————

It's hard for me to imagine three adjoining countries more diverse than ancient, sophisticated Thailand; mellow, Islamic Malaysia; and modern, competitive Singapore.

In comparing themselves with their two neighbors, many Malaysians are proud of being moderate—even moderately corrupt. A left-wing Malaysian of Christian Indian background who distributes medicine, AIDS information, condoms, and other practical assistance among illegal Indonesians told me this story of Malaysian moderation.

"Yesterday at the entrance to a construction site I saw a group of Indonesians crying. The police is saying 'Passport, passport.' The man is crying 'Manager holds papers.' The policeman says, 'How much money you got?' The man says, 'Twenty dollars.' The police says 'Okay, give me ten. The other ten you can keep.' And they let him go into town.

"In Thailand they would take all his money. In Singapore they would take him to immigration, check documents. Even if he is legal, you lose a day's work that way. But here, the policeman took some money for himself and left him enough to buy a meal in town."

So Malaysia is the happy medium. Well, I must admit that as a traveler of moderate means, I found it the most pleasant of the three places. And if I were an illegal migrant I suppose I'd rather lose half my pocket money in Malaysia than work for nothing for three months in Thailand [see page 98] or be expelled from Singapore. But if I were a poor Southeast Asian, I think I'd rather live in rigid Singapore, because there I probably wouldn't be poor.

Stopping illegal migration and charging high taxes to bring in legal migrant workers was part of Lee Kuan Yew's policy to raise productivity and, incidentally, wages. This policy was administered flexibly enough to accommodate any vital industry that couldn't afford to pay a high wage. But the policy would have been meaningless if profitable enterprises could use the power of their profits to get the restrictions eased for themselves.

The same logic applies to protective tariffs. A nation can, indeed, foster an infant industry by keeping competitors out for a while. All of the rich industrial nations did just that at one time. The catch is that once an industry becomes profitable enough not to need the protection, indeed at just the stage at which protection makes a company too secure to make improvements, the firm is big and rich enough to influence regulators and legislators in its favor. It's a rare government that can help its weak companies to grow powerful and then ignore their well-financed demands. It's primarily because of its rigid morality that the Singapore government can implement flexible economic plans.

But how did one particular small island achieve this almost miraculous state of noncorruption? My tendency is to ascribe it to a myriad of historical and geographic factors that happened to coalesce at one time and place. The Singaporeans I met insist upon attributing that unlikely coming-together to Lee Kuan Yew.

———

Despite amazing cultural differences as you moved down the Southeast Asian peninsula, and despite their profoundly different styles and levels of corruption, Thailand, Malaysia, and Singapore were all growing at at least twice the rate of any of the rich Western economies or Japan.

In Thailand, that growth meant that a buoyant illegal Burmese in Bangkok could find construction work almost continuously. It meant that Squirrel didn't have to stand with her feet in water crawling with slugs. She had the option of coming to the city, and once there she had the further option of quitting her job in a relative's sweatshop and moving up to a regular factory. It might even be possible to save with her friend, the street vendor, and open a market stall. Economic growth meant that the Thai tapioca farmers who sold or lost their land when an industrial park was developed could reasonably expect some member of their family to make up most of the farm's income by working at one of the new oil refineries. It meant that Alfalfa could save four years' wages in two years by living away from his family, while Nigel's secretary, Sunee, could decide not to move away from her mother when the Caltex job ended.

In Malaysia, eight-percent growth meant that millions of illegal migrants from Indonesia would be tolerated to do work like spreading food over ponds that produced tons of prawns for the restaurant chains that Jimmy Domino supplied. It meant that Mr. P'ng had enough profit from his trade with JC Seafoods and other importers to open a jellyfish factory in Vietnam. And that probably meant that somebody farther up the Southeast Asian peninsula was getting his feet out of muddy water. It also meant that a Penang fisherman's daughter could work in an electronics factory she hated, to give her father the option of believing that he was still earning the family living in a traditional way.

In Singapore, the government-channeled flow of money meant that "choosy" workers could reject night shifts and still live in modern apartments with electricity and running water, and that entrepreneurs could get rich by importing maids and building malls that catered to the poorest Thai migrants.

Of course, in all three countries, there were ecological damage, physical injury, and some people who couldn't take advantage of the new choices. They must have felt, and in many cases actually were poorer than ever. But that was mostly in the hinterlands. Wherever my money flowed there were new choices and opportunities. When I left Asia, they were playing musical chairs with more chairs than people.

The Investment

Asia was still on a high simmer when I got home. But the next installment of the book advance had arrived, and I began to look for a US mutual fund where my money would presumably stimulate domestic business.

At the time, more than 40 percent of Americans had some money in the stock market, if only through their company or union pension plans, and there were more than 7,000 mutual funds. All I had to do was choose one.

But this would be the first stock-market investment of my life, and I was superstitiously convinced that my tiny pebble, tossed onto that mountain of money, would precipitate the "correction" that financial experts were talking about. I didn't want to write about a stock-market crash. I wanted to explore the norm. Besides, I didn't want to lose my money.

I spent weeks, which turned into months, researching. I told myself that I simply wanted to find the most representative fund. But in truth, my indecision had grown paralyzing. Then one day I got a phone call thanking me for my valuable investment advice. And I knew at once what to do.

Mrs. Pearls

I'd met "Mrs. Pearls" at a Chase shareholders' meeting before I left for Asia. I'd gone when I was still looking for my big loan. It certainly wasn't the right place. In fact, the annual shareholders' meeting had been such a circus that

I'd constructed a Dramatis Personae in my notebook in an attempt to give the event some order.

Time: A weekday morning

Place: The Auditorium at Chase Manhattan Plaza

CAST OF CHARACTERS

Thomas G. Labrecque	*Chairman and CEO, tall, thin, bland (deceptively?), beset*
Mr. Sitkah ⎫ Mrs. Davis ⎬ Mr. Brown ⎭	*The Shareholders interest clique, comical rustics*
Michael Price	*The Challenger (in black)*
Briefcase-on-the-left ⎫ Briefcase-on-the-right ⎬	*Henchmen who enter and exit with Mr. Price: silent*
Sister Kathryn Rinn ⎫ Rev. Joseph La Mar M. M. ⎬	*Shareholders of Conscience, dogged, prepared to be scorned*
Young men ⎫ Young women ⎬	*Ill-mannered protesters waving stolen document*
Mr. Chin (or Chan)	*Polite, well informed, grateful shareholder—mature*
Mrs. Pearls	*Park Ave (type)matron in Pappagallo flats and pearls*

Guards, Reporters, Board Members, Auditors, Vote-Talliers, and Senior Management in attendance upon Chairman Labrecque, plus an audience of Chase Staff and Chase Retirees.

In the background, the soothing voice of Chairman Labrecque summarizes last year's accomplishments and next year's strategies:

. . . rebuilt our core franchises . . . built distinctive market positions . . . upgrades from major rating agencies . . . prestigious customer franchise . . . acknowledged expertise in key world industries . . . global intermediation skills . . . relentless focus on building customer relationships . . . delivery capabilities . . . cross-border needs of wholesale clients . . . integrated delivery . . . team based culture . . . most of our businesses generating fifteen percent risk-adjusted returns on capital . . . head count reduction of approximately sixteen hundred . . . never finished improving productivity . . .

I hate to admit it, but some of this stuff was starting to make sense to me. Still, it might be better to translate. The chairman seemed to be saying that things were picking up because we have a plan. The plan was to go where the money is and do what we do well. Abroad, Chase was closing branches and offering its services directly to corporations, governments, and wealthy individuals. At home, the relationship principle would turn every customer, even the guy with a credit card he never used, into a source of many kinds of profits.

By applying these strategies:

The relationship bank is on the way to greatness in this marketplace . . . our vision, a vision shared by my thirty-five thousand Chase colleagues, has been to build strong, focused, wholesale and retail customer franchises with a balanced risk profile and an earning stream to significantly enhance shareholder value.

The plan, then, was to go on being a bank. We've made the changes that will make us more profitable—"non-performing assets have declined by eighty-four percent to less than one percent of total assets . . . dividends up fifty percent—now give us a chance," he implored, "to reap the rewards." But no one seemed to be listening.

Even before the chairman's opening statement, shareholder George Sitkah, a balding man with a high-pitched voice, had seized the floor to demand, "This fellow Mayor, this guy next to you [he was referring to the corporate secretary], when are you going to replace him and send him to Africa or the North Pole? Because he's so obnoxious it's pathetic."

That was the general level of shareholder participation. But at least shareholder Sitkah had acquiesced when asked to wait for the question period, adding only that "I want it noted in the record to send him to the North Pole!" ["Write me down an ass."]

It was harder to constrain shareholder Evelyn Davis, whose familiar accent was greeted with groans by regulars in the audience. The chairman, however, was exquisitely polite.

"Thank you, Mrs. Davis."

"Call me Evelyn . . . Tom."

Evelyn took off after that sorry example of affirmative action, the public-television woman on the Board of Directors. She was undeterred by the information that the woman director was retiring: "It's about time!" Meanwhile a group of young men and women at the back waved a stolen document which, to them, showed Chase instructing the hesitant President of Mexico to massacre poor Indians in Chiapas.

The stolen document turned out to be a routine memo to Mr. Delsman's loan committee containing background on Mexico—who's on our side (the PRI), who's running the country (the PRI), et cetera—plus analysis of the post-peso-crash situation.

The paragraph that caused the fuss was about the Zapatistas, a movement headed by the masked Subcomandante Marcos, that issued poetic communiqués—"Here we are, the forever dead, dying once again, but now in order to live."* The Zapatistas called for land reform, for basic services like roads, schools, and electricity in their area, for honest elections in Mexico, and for the preservation of cooperative, land-loving values planet-wide. Their program, their relative nonviolence, and their sophisticatedly neo-indigenous style made them popular in both the countryside and the capital.

That's my analysis, of course. The "stolen" memo described them neutrally but assumed that they were an embarrassment to be eliminated. Unfortunately, according to the Chase consultant, the economic constraints of the peso crisis made it impractical to pacify them with reforms. And so:

> While Chiapas, in our opinion, does not pose a fundamental threat to Mexican political stability, it is perceived to be so by many in the investment community. The government will need to eliminate the Zapatistas to demonstrate their effective control of the national territory and of security policy.

Two weeks later, Mexican President Zedillo sent in the army to burn houses, poison water and animals, and otherwise make the land of about 20,000 people uninhabitable. There were also some human fatalities.

---

*From Frank Barducke's translation of the communiqués of Subcomandante Marcos, available from the *Anderson Valley Advocate*, Boonville, CA 95415, $3.00. Published in an expanded version by Frank Barducke and John Ross, Monthly Review Press, New York, 1995.

I can see why this might shock people who are unused to the way banks propose and dispose. (The same memo discussed whether it would be better for the ruling party [our side] to win all the seats in the next election or let other parties win some.) But personally, I don't think one ambiguous memo means that Chase pressured the Mexican government into a military solution. (Of course I don't know how these things are normally decided.)

To me the "stolen" document seemed more relevant to the shareholder nun and priest who had submitted a formal resolution. Much of the Chase document described the wretched conditions in Mexico; "The fall in value of the peso severely undercuts the capacity of the average Mexican worker to purchase the bare necessities of life each day," the Chase consultant wrote. The religious duo asserted that structural adjustment economic policies forced on third-world countries by creditors, including Chase, entrenched the misery and in some cases actually made it more difficult to repay Chase loans. As shareholders (religious orders have to keep their money somewhere), they asked the bank to prepare a report giving its official position on the structural adjustment programs. Mr. Labrecque recommended a vote against.

I can tell you what the nun and priest were talking about because I asked them afterward for a copy of their resolution and I have since become sadly familiar with structural adjustment and its consequences, but at the time it was just another sideshow at an event without a main show.

After the protesters and somewhere between an Evelyn Davis resolution and more Sitkah invective, a man named Mr. Price got up and said that he held 11 million Chase shares (more than 5 percent), he had filed the required government documents, and he wanted more money. It was just about as direct as that.

I might not have noticed him among all the other shareholders demanding money except that Mr. Labrecque thanked him for his patience. With a jaundiced look around the room, Mr. Price called Mr. Labrecque's patience "remarkable."

"If you paid me what he's getting paid, I'd be patient, too," shareholder Sitkah interjected, underlining Price's implied critique of a chairman who gave the rowdies free rein.

In Mr. Price's brief statement he rejected Labrecque's business plan: "It is not sufficient to say you are going to run your business incrementally better." Selling the bank would be superior, he said, to the current management's strategy of running "a bank conglomerate dominated by global corporate banking that spends shareholder capital ineffectively." But there might be options even more lucrative than selling. "We [his mutual fund company] believe it is within management's power to create shareholder values that could exceed sale values."

He didn't claim to be "saving Chase" or "leading America toward global competitiveness," and he didn't care what "mission" or "vision" the directors adopted, as long as they unlocked lots of value and turned it over to shareholders. Price lifted his lance only in the penultimate sentence. "We challenge the company and the board to unlock the value, or let someone else do it for you."

When the challenger sat down (I hadn't caught his full name at that point), I rushed over, tapped him on the shoulder and asked if I could have his card.

"NO!" he answered.

At the same moment the men on either side of him [Guards? Aides? Vice presidents?] rose slightly from their seats and I fell backward. I wasn't menaced, just startled. Who says "NO!" when asked for his business card?

In stumbling back, I stepped directly onto a pair of Pappagallo flats (with bows)—"Oh, dear!" "So sorry!"—nearly knocking over a thin woman in her fifties wearing a blue dress and pearls.

"Is this what these meetings are usually like?" she asked when I said that I was writing a book.

I explained that Davis, Sitkah, Brown et al. make the rounds during annual meeting season. Some chairmen hold them more in check but they have a right to speak. Besides, some of their points aren't entirely absurd.

Mrs. Pearls had started out sympathetic to Chairman Labrecque, she told me, but it made him seem "ineffective," (I noticed she echoed Price's word) to let them get out of hand.

The rustics had the opposite effect on me. I'm not inherently sympathetic to multinational bank chairmen, but as Labrecque stood there, patient and sane before the onslaught, I felt, *Poor CEO, look what he endures for us.* Among protesters, shareholders, and now Price, thank goodness there was someone looking after *the bank.*

I assured Mrs. Pearls that nothing was supposed to get done at annual meetings. In a way Labrecque was using Evelyn Davis toward that goal. I started to explain the differences between the stolen-document protesters and the religious orders but I saw that Mrs. Pearls had her own concerns.

Her father had recently turned a portfolio over to her and her brother to administer as the future inheritance for her three and her brother's two children. It would be practice, her father said, for the money she and her brother would eventually inherit. "I wish he wouldn't talk that way."

Her brother, who the family assumed would make the decisions, thought the old man had been too sentimental in holding on to their poorly-performing Chase stock. It was up a little now and he intended to sell. But when the proxy material arrived she decided "to come and see."

From what she could tell, Chase was as "hopelessly old-world" as her brother feared. "That Mr. Labrecque is too gentlemanly. That Mrs. Davis!"

"Call me Evelyn," I joked.

So Mrs. Pearls was going to tell her brother that he was right: "Sell Chase."

That's when I told her to wait. "That man who wouldn't give me his card . . . "

"He seems to be a bit of a thug."

"Well, he owns over five percent of the shares."

Five percent didn't seem like much to her so I opened one of the proxy packets to the holdings of the board members and pointed out that the largest were in the tens or occasionally hundreds of thousands of shares. Not one of them had even a million.

"I wonder how many shares Mrs. Evelyn Davis owns?"

"Four hundred I think I read somewhere," I said. "How many do you own, by the way?"

"Well, I'm not in the chairman's category."

"But above Evelyn Davis?"

Mrs. Pearls would sooner tell me her sexual fantasies than her dollar number. Some people react that way because to them their dollar number is their true worth. But I came to feel, after getting to know her a little better, that Mrs. Pearls' reaction was primarily superstitious. She wasn't quite sure where the money came from or where it resided. To speak her number aloud might tempt a mischievous spirit to press some button and make it scoot around or vanish.

"I'd rather not say," she responded politely.

Later, when I asked her name, I got the same answer. "I'd rather not say." That's when I began to call her Mrs. Pearls in my notes.

"So you really think that man who pushed you could be important?" she asked as we parted.

"He didn't actually push me."

"Well, scared you."

"Yes, I said, "I think he could be important. I'd wait a little before I sold the stock." And I gave her my card.

Apparently Michael F. Price scared Chase even more than he scared me.

A while after the shareholders' meeting, Chase and Chemical banks merged. They would use the Chase name, but Chemical had essentially bought Chase. One day after the merger was announced, Michael Price's 11 million shares were worth 275 million dollars more—that's 70 percent more—than the price he'd acquired them for over the last five or six months. The 10,300 shares held by the religious orders that introduced the resolution against structural adjustment had also increased in value by 70 percent. So had an unknown number of shares controlled by Mrs. Pearls' family. Where had that "value" come from?

Two Can Live as Cheaply as One

Throughout the late 1990s, millions of Americans (not including me, as I mentioned) seemed to be growing richer as the value of the stocks in their mutual-fund portfolios increased by amounts like 15 to 30 percent per year— or more. (Maybe the really big returns were rare, but those were the ones you heard about.)

Some of the increased value came from dividends that companies gave to their shareholders when their ongoing business was unusually profitable. But a much greater part of the increase resulted from mergers, acquisitions, breakups, and so on. These financial reorganizations enriched shareholders either by distributing the one-time proceeds realized from selling off company assets or by simply making the stock *seem* more valuable to new buyers.

The most successful investors of the era were those who either anticipated or, like Michael Price, actively promoted such mergers. The odd thing about these well-publicized financial reorganizations is that the resulting new enterprises often yielded very modest new profits. Many of the mergers actually shrunk the volume of business at the company that was left after the transition. Yet these scaled-down companies were deemed to be worth amounts like 70 percent, in the Chase case, more than they were worth before.

Earlier in US history, acquisitions had been about growth, and mergers raised the specter of giant octopuses spreading their tentacles. But the Chase/Chem merger was definitely one of the modern, shrinking sort. As a relic of trust-busting days, however, a public hearing was required before the merger could be approved. But no one came to complain that the new entity, which would be the largest bank in the US (until the next spectacular merger), was going to gobble up their customers. Customers came, instead, to complain that they would be abandoned.

Representatives from community groups in poor parts of the Bronx and Brooklyn feared that their neighborhood branches would be closed and they would be left to the mercy of check-cashing operations. They reminded the regulators that before its merger with Manufacturers Hanover was approved, Chemical had said that it would close only 80 branches but wound up closing 177. Furthermore, fees on small accounts had been raised almost prohibitively after previous mergers. No one seemed to want their business.

The banks could only say that they would try to leave ATM's where they were safe.

I called Gardner Young from Chase to see how the merger would create new value at his Fed-funds desk. "Will there be bigger, more profitable deals you can make when you're trading for three hundred billion instead of a hundred and twenty?"

"Nah," he said, and explained that Chase had already extended the maximum reasonable credit lines to his Fed-fund customers. And most of them didn't use the money now, so . . . "

If there weren't going to be bigger or better deals, what was the advantage, I asked. "They can do it without the seven of us. . . . I run a reserve account for a bank; someone at Chemical runs a reserve account. Now they'll run one reserve account. It's like getting married and having a joint checking account. Only one person manages it even though it has bigger balances."

That same thinking had been systematically applied to departments throughout the two banks before the merger was announced. Indeed, the basis of the agreement was the calculation that 12,000 of the combined 75,000 employees could and would be fired. As to Gardner's personal future:

"I'm in the crosshairs. I'm a senior manager who makes a lot of money and there's someone at Chemical who does what I do. But I'm in a good position. I'm hearing that you get three weeks of salary for each year of service. And I've had twenty-three years of service, so that gives me a cushion to go out on."

But Chase is the relationship bank. Won't customers go elsewhere when longstanding relationships are ruptured? Yes. It's the common wisdom that banks lose customers after a merger.

In another era, a bank under shareholder pressure might have said "Our business is lending. We'll make more money for you by going out there and selling more loans." Or "We have a great team in the east, we'll merge with a bank that has a great team in the west. Then we'll be able to grow nationwide." But this was not a time of growth, at least not for banks. The Chase/Chem merger was about consolidation.

They answered Mr. Price's demand for money by saying "We'll do the same or a little less business, but with twelve thousand fewer employees, and we'll pass the savings directly along to you." Investors thought this plan made Chase a lot more valuable.

In an article subheaded "Nothing succeeds like unemployment, at least when it comes to stock prices," *New York Times* business columnist Floyd Norris wrote:

> The news of 16 percent fewer workers sent the value of the two bank stocks up 11 percent. Put these figures on a graph, draw a line, and the implication is obvious. Each canned worker increases the combined market value of the two banks shares by about $216,000. If the banks got rid of all their workers their share prices would go up another 53 percent.

That plan couldn't be carried out to its logical conclusion, Norris pointed out, first because "somebody has to be around to put cash in the ATMs" and second because "all those fired people are consumers and are probably going to buy less if their incomes vanish." But in the short run, the financial sector seems to grow, Norris noted, when the real sector is shrinking. "So for now, at least, there is no quicker way to get your stock price up than to announce plans to fire a lot of workers."

The Chase/Chem shrinking marriage was certainly popular with investors. "We love this merger," Michael Price told the *Wall Street Journal.* Mrs. Pearls loved it too—at least at first.

A couple of months after the meeting, Mrs. Pearls called to thank me. She'd followed my advice and held on to her Chase shares. It had been very exciting for a while to watch the share price shoot up. But now it had slowed down. She was wondering if there were any other meetings like that that I was going to.

I tried to explain that such things couldn't happen every day. Her gains were based on firing 12,000 people, but if every company on the stock exchange fired their employees there's be no one left to buy the things they made. Mrs. Pearls wasn't interested in generalizations. She just wanted to know about one or two more companies where such events were about to happen.

One good way to learn about dramatic stock movements in advance, I suggested, would be to follow Mr. Price around.

"But he wouldn't even give us his card," she quipped.

I explained that Price's company advises a group of mutual funds called the Mutual Series. If Mrs. Pearls became one of his investors ("But please, I'm not recommending any particular mutual funds."), Mr. Price would take her money with him when he went to meetings. It wouldn't be as exciting as picking stocks herself, but it would be a lot smarter than asking me for tips.

When I mentioned that mutual-fund advisors like Mr. Price charge investors about one percent for their advice, Mrs. Pearls seemed to think that was reasonable. As soon as I got off the phone I realized that I should have asked for a one-percent fee myself. Then I'd know how many Chase shares she had held on to at my advice.

Now, over a year later, while I was agonizing about my own first stock-market investment, Mrs. Pearls called to thank me again. She'd put a sizable part of her children's money into Michael Price's Mutual Series funds. One of them, Mutual Shares, had gone up 29 percent—but that was over the course of a year. It wasn't as exciting as watching her Chase shares shoot up. Besides, she now had the reputation in the family as quite a stock picker. So, more for the excitement than the cash this time, perhaps, Mrs. Pearls called to ask for another tip.

"Twenty-nine percent is enough," I said. "You mustn't be greedy."

The call may not have solved Mrs. Pearls' investment dilemma but it solved mine. As soon as she thanked me for my financial suggestion, I realized that I should take my own advice. By the next week I had $5,000 (the minimum investment) in Michael Price's Mutual Shares. I was too fearful to put the entire advance installment in the stock market. I also called friends to warn them that this might be the right time to get out of the market.

———

At the time that I invested, the Mutual Series had 12 billion dollars under management in a small "family" of funds. (It's up to 33 billion as I write.) Mutual Shares was the oldest of the funds and had about 200 securities in its portfolio.

As a Shares investor I had stock in 11 banks, about 30 health-care and insurance companies, some aerospace companies whose military contracts I had demonstrated against, and one company I was boycotting. I owned consumer companies whose products I recognized, like Dial (soap) and RJR Nabisco (cigarettes and cookies), and some with nondescript names like U.S. Industries. I had no idea at the time what they made. I was also invested in publishing, media, oil, US government securities, banks of course, and a potpourri of businesses in bankruptcy, liquidation, or reorganization.

Some stock pickers try to predict winners by studying a company's products, markets, and management; in other words, its prospects of making a profit from its productive activities. For that purpose, brokerage houses have extensive research departments staffed by analysts who specialize in the various industries.

Other stock pickers never look at the companies they're investing in. They look instead at their fellow investors. John Maynard Keynes, who handled the endowment of his old school quite successfully, claimed he made his picks purely by psyching out the other gamblers.

Michael Price is what's called a "value" investor. He knows something about a company's products and he certainly has an intuitive sense of investor psychology. But he and his team came into the office each day to search for the undervalued or "out of favor" companies whose total shares are selling for less money than the assets of those companies are intrinsically worth. Price buys those undervalued shares, then waits, or acts, to get the company to sell, merge, downsize, or in other ways "unlock" the value of those assets for shareholders.

Even more attractive than assets that can be sold off for cash is cash itself, that's already there, or cash flow that can be diverted directly to shareholders. In capitalist theory, the purpose of production is profit. The classic capitalist invests in setting up a facility, hiring workers, promoting, selling, and delivering his goods, and then he makes a profit. But there's many a slip betwixt that cup and lip. If a cash profit is the ultimate goal, why not go where the money already is and simply take it? Become the owner, then force your employee, the CEO, to sell off parts of the company or simply unlock the safe. If—and it's a big if—you paid less for the shares than the sales values of those assets, you're bound to come out ahead.

It may sound a little rough on the general economy to buy into underpriced companies and force them to sell off their parts and/or hand over the nest eggs they might use to modernize or expand. Won't that eventually cause the economy to stagnate or shrink? In free-market theory, no. In reality? It depends.

According to the theory, these undervalued companies probably weren't using their money or assets effectively. But the investors who take the money out of them will invest it in something else. Mrs. Davis, Mr. Sitkah, and Mr. Price, acting both for himself and for Mrs. Pearls, will take the 70-percent profit that they made from the Chase/Chem consolidation and invest it in some enterprise that will, again according to that theory, give other work to the 12,000 people fired from the two banks.

Okay, they may not create jobs in New York City and they may not relocate that admirable woman who struggled through night school to become a bank teller. Sometimes, unfortunately, there's just too much banking capacity (or too little banking business). But according to the basic tenets of laissez-faire capitalism, if we allow investors like Mr. Price to unlock some of the bank's *value* and move it, unhindered, to any country or industry where he thinks he can find the best returns, that will almost invariably produce the greatest real economic growth and usually (though this is not essential to the doctrine) the greatest good for the greatest number of humans.

That's the free-market premise, and I was about to examine it up close.

At the time that I became an investor, Chase and Chemical had already merged and Michael Price was getting publicity for another "unlocking." The Mutual Series funds owned over 20 percent of the shares in the Sunbeam Corporation. Investor Michael Steinhardt owned 22 percent. About ten years earlier, the two Michaels had bought out the creditors of a conglomerate that was in bankruptcy, in part, because of the debts it had incurred in buying Sunbeam. Along with a third investor who would actually manage the company, they initiated a restructuring in which 40 percent of the workers were fired. Then they brought the new Sunbeam Oster Company public and made a great profit. According to *Barron's Weekly*, the $125 million they paid for the bankrupt company turned into more than a billion. A couple of years later, the managing partner was ousted acrimoniously. Under the next CEO, Sunbeam's annual earnings hit 20 percent. But in the last 18 months earnings had dropped, and they were still falling.

I would have said, if anyone asked me, that a leveling-off was inevitable. There are so many companies all over the world making small appliances these days, and they sell for so little in megastores like Wal-Mart. A *Wall Street Journal* article pointed out that the price tag on a Sunbeam electric can-opener hadn't gone up since 1975. It was amazing, and should have been gratifying, that the restructured appliance company still made good products at a decent profit. But the two Michaels believed that there was more than a decent profit left in Sunbeam.

When Price confronted Chase, the business press called it David versus Goliath and awaited the result in suspense. But there was no doubt about the outcome when the two principal shareholders told the Sunbeam board that it was time, once more, to unlock shareholder value.

It's everyday business for mutual funds and other big investors to press a company for changes when earnings are down. It normally rates just a small story in the business section when a CEO is replaced under such circumstances. Sunbeam became a media event in part because of Price's slingshot victory over Chase, but mainly because the Sunbeam board brought in the renowned, self-promoting turnaround artist Chainsaw Al Dunlap.

Chainsaw Al had just written a book about his string of successful turnarounds called *Mean Business: How I Save Bad Companies and Make Good Companies Great.* During his first week at Sunbeam, Dunlap assembled the 60-person headquarters staff in a conference room, told them, according to the *New York Times,* that "surgery may be painful but it's better than death," and advised them all to buy his book.

I have to confess that I didn't buy Al's book. I phoned the publisher for a free review copy. So I feel honor-bound to at least describe it.

The core of *Mean Business* is the "Four Simple Rules" for "Dunlaping" a Corporation:

1. *Get the Right Management Team*

Al offers this help in selecting them

> Business is simple. It is not complicated. Like the football basics of blocking and tackling, there are a few simple things that you have to do. . . . What complicates business? For one thing, managers and employees do.

2. *Pinch Pennies*

Methods include outsourcing, renegotiating contracts with suppliers, eliminating all charitable contributions, cutting pay, and firing people. Lower-level Sunbeam employees may have been comforted by Dunlap's advice to:

... slice the real fat first; get rid of nonproductive senior executives and middle managers, headquarters, airplanes and so on. That sends a clear message that you are serious. Deal with the unions and workers last. They want the company to succeed as much and more than management does. In my experience they'll be more supportive of cutbacks if it means the general health of the company will be demonstrably improved.

3. Know What Business You're In—Lesson: Focus Like a Laser

Two questions you should always be asking yourself: What business are we in, anyhow? What business should we be in? When you have the answers, sell everything else and focus on the core business. . . . Try this process and you'll discover your company's "hidden" corporate bank, the money raised by selling non-core assets.

4. Get a Real Strategy—Lesson: Envision the Future and Plan a Route to It

That sounds like the most difficult task, but not if you remember that the basic goal is the same for all corporations.

If there was one overall theme that drove my vision for Scott as a consumer products company it was *creating shareholder value.* (Emphasis *his.*)

By following the four simple rules, Dunlap achieves results like these in his model turn-around:

The bottom line at Scott Paper Company: We cut back 70 percent of upper management and eliminated more than 11,200 total jobs, 35 percent of the Scott payroll. Another 6,000 jobs became somebody else's payroll responsibility as I sold off assets such as S. D. Warren (for $1.6 billion) and a Mobile, Alabama, cogeneration power plant (for $350 million). I sold the company's corporate headquarters for $39 million.

When December 31 came around I was true to my word. The bloodletting ended and 20,000 people had secure jobs once again.

From the start a few voices warned that the companies Al leaves behind aren't viable businesses. A union official compared Dunlap's reorganization at Scott Paper to slapping a coat of paint on a house before putting it up for sale. It's true that Dunlap's turnaround tenure usually ended when the "core" business was sold. And it's true that some purchasers complained afterward about surprises they'd found under the new paint.

But there'll always be customer complaints, and the union attitude was also predictable. The results of any restructuring are bound to be subject to interpretation. The question was, should I trust Al's?

Describing his success in reorganizing an Australian media company, Dunlap wrote, "The Australian press referred to me as 'Chainsaw' because of the way I cut through all the fat and left a great sculpture . . . "

It may be true that he left a well-defined business in Australia, and it may also be true that the nickname was coined by someone who meant to praise him for that. But I'm familiar enough with the way people use English (even in Australia) to judge that the media didn't go on calling him "Chainsaw" in appreciation of his craftsmanship. Had I been more familiar with the language of corporate structure, I might have been wary of some of Al's other self-evaluations.

But from an investor's point of view (and wasn't I a Sunbeam investor?) it shouldn't really matter whether Al Dunlap cut away fat to leave a beautiful sculpture, i.e., a focused, debt-free business, or merely cobbled something together that could stand up until sold. Shareholders would profit either way. So sure were these outcomes that the share price rose 59 percent *in one day* when Chainsaw Al's appointment was announced. And that, as he reminded audiences frequently, was a New York Stock Exchange record.

In bold type right under the chapter-heading "Whose Company Is It Anyhow?" Dunlap tells us that "THE PEOPLE WHO INVEST IN A COMPANY OWN IT— NOT THE EMPLOYEES, NOT THE SUPPLIERS, AND NOT THE COMMUNITY." Furthermore, "If a shareholder calls me and says, 'I want to talk to you,' I have an obligation to talk to him or her." So I wrote for an appointment.

In his first week on the job, Dunlap formed a central committee of himself, a couple of people from past restructurings, and one retained Sunbeam executive. Then, as in previous campaigns, he sent forth his faithful consultants, captained by Coopers & Lybrand partner Don Burnett, to survey all the Sunbeam factories, warehouses, and showrooms, then held a teleconference with hundreds of Wall Street analysts promising "a massive and swift restructuring." After the Burnett team returned from the field, he would announce what he'd keep, what he'd sell, and what percentage of both the keeper and nonkeeper labor forces could be fired. (For immediate profits it's just as important to streamline the divisions you're going to sell as the divisions you're going to keep.) Meanwhile he met with investment bankers, hired a new chief financial officer, reviewed products that were in the pipeline, convinced board members to take their stipends in stock instead of cash, added veterans from his past turnaround to the Sunbeam board, found new heads for marketing, manufacturing, R&D, and the household products group, hunted up foreign licensees, and hung pictures of predatory animals on his office walls.

While employees at some 50 Sunbeam facilities waited to hear whether they would be sold, downsized, or closed, I pursued my attempts to get an interview. Al's secretary, Sharon, aware of her new boss's emphasis on shareholders (she must have been at that pep talk where he told the staff to buy his book), had shown him my letter right away. Sharon was a pleasant woman and seemed to have good secretarial skills. The papers she needed were always at hand. But she may not have been right for Al. She didn't seem to know, for instance, how unimportant I was. We had had a few encouraging but inconclusive conversations.

Finally I tried to pin down a date by telling Sharon that I would be in the Fort Lauderdale area from September 27th through October 4th for my mother's birthday. She looked at Al's calendar and found that he'd be in Boston for two days that week as part of his book tour. She knew he'd be back by the 1st or 2nd because he had a bookstore signing scheduled for the 2nd in his home town of Boca Raton, Florida. Since I was going to be so near, he could probably squeeze me in.

But by the day I arrived she hadn't pinned him down yet, and a couple of days later Sharon was gone. The new secretary was also pleasant, but she knew exactly how unimportant I was. There was nothing I could do in Florida but visit my mother and see Al at the bookstore signing.

The Gleanings

Liberties Bookstore; chairs set out for an author's reading

I got there early and sat next to a man who happened to be doing a story on Al Dunlap for *People* magazine. "Is that him?" I asked when a tall man entered surrounded by friends. "You'll know when you hear him," the reporter answered without turning to look. I did.

"How ya doin' there! How are you?! Hi! How are ya! Hi, how are ya?" High, nasal, staccato, piercing. "How are ya! How ya doin'? Hi! How are ya! Hi! How are ya!"

"I've got two and three-quarters hours of it on tape," the reporter said when he saw me wince. It was the most piercing voice I'd ever heard.

As Dunlap made his way up to the speaker's table, he stopped for a confidential word with the reporter. "We made it onto the business best-sellers list. With your help we'll make it onto the national list." They began to make arrangements for a photo session. "I'll be in Orlando Friday. I'll be on the West Coast Monday." I didn't have to lean in to catch anything Al said. "Maybe Saturday morning at the house."

"Hi! How ya doin!" "How are sales going?" To the bookstore manager: "There's a fellow here from *People* magazine; they're gonna do a big story. *Fortune* is gonna do a big story. *Time* is gonna do a big story. "I was speaking to John—from Random House . . . " "Foreign countries, I heard, don't have tapes." Dunlap was proud of having made the cassette tape of *Mean Business* in his own voice.

I learned a lot, that evening, about selling books.

Al didn't give away much content in his talk. He'd start a story or mention a well-known financier, only to say "It's all in the book. It's quite humorous." "Written so that anyone can understand it . . . in a conversational tone." "It's a human-interest book. . . . As Ron Perelman said in one of the testimonies on the back, 'Love him or hate him, you can't ignore him.' Something like that."*

Dunlap isn't embarrassed to tell you how he's angled the book to sell it to you. "If you have your own business, if you have a job, want to know how to keep your job—there's something in it for everyone."

And why, indeed, should it be embarrassing to ask "Who is this product for; what features can I add to make more people buy it?" Al is right, you've got to *know what business you're in* and *get a strategy*. I'm in the book business. What kind of strategy is it to write a *business* book about Thai peasants?

---

*When Revlon Chairman Ron Perelman was introduced to author Susan Braudy, he said, "You write books? I don't read books."

After the talk I heard someone congratulate Al on the book. "Well, we intended for it to be a best-seller and now it is," he said. "So it's kind of a self-fulfilling prophecy."

I've been in the writing business all my adult life, and it never occurred to me to plan for a best-seller. I just vaguely hope that whatever interests me will interest others. Is it so far below me to "envision the future"—a best-seller—and "focus like a laser?" Al may sound arrogant. "Who's that new author back there?" he asked, pointing to another display. "Tom Clancy? He should be happy to have his book next to mine. If he comes in I'll autograph one for him." But my lack of a sales strategy may be just as arrogant as Dunlap's lack of a literary strategy. I resolved, that evening, to dump my self-protective indifference and do everything I could to make this book a best-seller. (But away from Al's bracing influence, I lacked the backbone, as you see, to edit out the Thai peasants.)

Al and I may have been thinking about book sales that evening, but some people were there to hear about Sunbeam. The first audience question came from a man who said he'd been reading about the two Michaels and how they expected to "cash out." I, too, had seen business-page stories speculating about Michael Price's "exit strategy." "Are you there," the questioner asked, "to make Sunbeam good or to get them out quickly?"

Al launched into a tangentially related story that he could tell on automatic pilot—I would see him do this often enough to recognize the pattern—while he decided whether to give a straight answer.

He complained that he'd saved 18,000 jobs at Scott (down from 20,000 in the book) and yet a TV piece concentrated on the people who were fired. "A woman whose husband had a stroke—somehow I'm responsible—says 'I wish Al Dunlap could come spend time with my husband.' But *she's* divorcing him." Another irony was the 52-year-old fired employee shown playing golf and complaining because he had to send his wife out to work. That was probably Al's genuine image of typical displaced workers.

Moving toward the point of the question, he explained that well before his, Al's, appointment, Michael Steinhardt had announced that he was liquidating all his American funds, so he sold stock to distribute money back to his individual investors. "But he kept his personal money in Sunbeam," and "Michael Price still has all of his holdings," Al said.

"Not to be arrogant, but on the naming of me CEO we had the biggest single run-up on the stock of a company, fifty-nine percent in one day, in the history of the New York Stock Exchange. We believe that by October 30th we will come out with a world-class restructuring plan and we believe we will announce it by November 15th and we don't think anyone will be disappointed with it."

The implicit response in this seeming nonresponse was a point that Dunlap made many times in his book: there can be no separation between building a good company and increasing shareholder value. But this didn't tell me how or when Mutual Shares would get out of Sunbeam, so I could either spend my profits or let Michael Price reinvest them.

In another form of stock boosting, Dunlap praised his winning team, including Rush Kersh and Don Burnett, and assured us that they would have the same success with Sunbeam as they'd had with Scott, Lilly Tulip, and other companies.

But another audience member suggested that the Scott turnaround happened when paper prices were going up, while Sunbeam faced stiff foreign competition at a time when appliance prices were stagnant.

Scott faced competition too, Al insisted. "With Sunbeam we have so many facilities. If we ever get down to the most efficient facilities we can be very successful." I couldn't help noticing that even though the fact-finding team was still in the field, Al already assumed that most new shareholder value would come from sales and consolidation, not from increased productivity and growth.

In what seemed like a lighter vein, to the audience if not to the questioner, a woman said "I have ten thousand dollars and I want to invest it in something. What would you recommend?"

"If it weren't for the fact that legally I couldn't tell you to invest in Sunbeam, that's probably what I would suggest. But I didn't say that."

As I write this sentence, Sunbeam stock is at $4.50. If the woman followed Al's nonadvice, her $10,000 is now worth around $2,000.

But that evening, Al was on a roll. Sunbeam would be his ninth successful turnaround, and his first book would make it onto the *New York Times* best-seller list. "I was born a poor inner-city kid." "I walked away from Scott with one hundred million dollars." "Hoboken to Palm Beach county. That's a long road." He told stories of his own early audacity and of employees who kept their jobs by showing Al Dunlap their can-do spirit. "The meek shall *not* inherit the earth and for sure they won't get the mineral rights."

If that's what he admired, I too would conquer by showing Al Dunlap my audacity and grit. When the line formed to get our books signed, I was determined to get that interview appointment nailed down. I don't remember exactly how I explained my project in the moments I stood before him with his book opened to the title page. Whatever I said, Dunlap just stared through me. When I paused for a response he asked who to make it out to. The autograph says "Barbara: I hope you enjoy the book! Best wishes, Al."

Mineral rights? I didn't even get the surface sharecropping rights. But if I'm not bold, I'm resourceful. I could certainly gather the gleanings. So I left my tape recorder on near the signing table and wandered back to talk to Al's entourage.

His wife, Judy, was explaining that people just didn't seem to realize how many jobs Al saves. A Boca Raton neighbor told me that Al and Judy were a very generous couple. The neighbor herself had made a lot of money on Sunbeam shares and was grateful to Al for that. Being a fellow shareholder should have given me a good opening to chitchat with her. But Al's way of staring through me had flattened my bubbles.

Two gawky guys in their thirties, one short, one tall, from MIS and HR systems, said they were confident that they could keep their jobs at Sunbeam by showing Mr. Dunlap that they were ready to make changes. "And showing up at your boss's public appearances," I thought ungenerously. I must have been smarting more than I realized.

I introduced myself to two men who seemed to be hiding among the book stacks. One turned out to be Dunlap regular Rush Kersh, now Sunbeam chief financial officer and one of the quadrumvirate running the business. The other, looking avuncular in suspenders, was Don Burnett! He had a couple of Coopers & Lybrand people with him, including the South African in charge of the whole Sunbeam team and a man who had been inspecting Sunbeam facilities in Mississippi.

"I—I—I guess you must feel bad having to close facilities in your own area," I suggested. I forget how I knew he'd worked in Mississippi. Some things there might close, he indicated, but others would stay open.

Pathetic! I thought as I walked away. *These people are going to decide how many thousands lose their jobs in Maine, Georgia, Tennessee, Texas, New York, Louisiana, et cetera, yet here they are, a claque, listening to their boss say things he's said a million times before.* "I may be some pathetic nut who thinks she's writing a book," I muttered. "But their boss Al Dunlap works for Michael Price. And Michael Price works for *me!*"

As you can see, I was in a very bad way that evening. The top men had probably been meeting all day and had simply taken a break for the book signing. Yet it still seems odd to me that all the heavies should have attended their boss's talk instead of turning to some other work or just relaxing. I had other occasions to see Kersh or Burnett with Al Dunlap, and they always seemed to be "in tow."

Eventually I might analyze the Sunbeam fiasco in terms of unrelenting investor pressure for high returns at a time of global overproduction (or underconsumption) of appliances. But looking back to that evening, I can see how Al's egotism or insecurity (whatever side of that coin you want to examine) also played a big part. Not to mention his preoccupation with book sales.

"What about the tape? You'll really enjoy it."

"Hi! How ya doin'?"

"It's my voice on the tape."

"Hi! How are ya!"

"They're great for your clients. They can listen driving around."

The people waiting for signatures had already bought the basic product, so Al was promoting the advanced model.

"I didn't do it with a professional reading," I heard him say on my tape. "I did it with my own voice, which I think makes a lot more sense."

"You're voice is very——." [I can't make out the book-buyer's adjective.]

"Very distinctive," Al agrees. "Very distinctive accent [formed] over seventeen states and three continents."

One of the signature-seekers suggested a unique promotional idea.

"Maybe if someone bought five or six Mixmasters—the Sunbeam ones—you could give them one of the tapes."

Quick as a flash Al goes him one better. "How's this. We won't let them buy the stock unless they buy the book. No book, no stock."

Someone else asked whether it was still a good idea to buy Sunbeam stock at $25 a share.

"I can't comment. *I* would. But I can't comment."

———

It had been a successful evening. As the crowd dwindled, the bookstore staff gathered round to take pictures. Al makes sure they get the book cover in the shot.

"Look this way and say best-seller—*National* best-seller," he corrects himself. Judging by the laugh, I'd say they got a lively photo.

As the evening winds down, Al introduces someone to "the owner of this fabulous establishment" and praises the bookstore as "a first-class operation."

"I've got a great team," the owner answers.

"Absolutely!" says Al. "It starts at the top. Top sets the direction. Then you put the team under it and that's how you win."

The Analysts' Teleconference

Sunbeam's restructuring plan was unveiled three days before the date that Al had predicted when he spoke at the bookstore. For all I know it was just about ready then. But it was announced to the public—that is to say, to the stock analysts at financial firms—by phone on November 12. I "attended" that telephone conference from my home phone. The opening monologue was, to use Al's phrase, "classic Dunlap."

"As you know, and as stated in my book—all us starving authors have to plug our books—I feel *business is simple*."

After explicating his four simple rules and listing Sunbeam's new dream team—"As you know, I eliminated seven of the top nine senior managers that were here when I arrived. Obviously the results weren't there; why should *they* be?"—Dunlap detailed the plan:

"We will divest all non-core product categories: furniture, time and temperature, Counsellor-Borg scales, decorative bedding, gas logs.

"We'll also sell our Biddeford factory, which makes blanket shells for our electric blankets. We'll keep the electric-blanket business but we'll outsource the shells, and hopefully from the people that buy Biddeford."

Sunbeam was the leading seller and only US manufacturer of electric blankets. It made the electrical innards in its own new factory in Mississippi. In

Mean Business Dunlap deplored the building of that facility by a previous management. He preferred to be in the more flexible position of outsourcing or ordering Sunbeam products from factories to which the company had no permanent tie. But given the investment in a plant that could not be used by anyone but a competitor, he decided to keep the Mississippi factory. He decided to sell the mill that wove the outer blanket to some purchaser who would then presumably supply Sunbeam—but hopefully not supply a competitor.

He summarized equally straightforward plans to slash the number of styles and models in the retained divisions, thereby decreasing the amount of working capital needed to make and distribute products by about $100,000,000. "We've just *given* ourselves one hundred million dollars."

"We attacked every aspect of the business with seventeen cross-functional teams. Seventeen cross-functional teams have been working for months. . . . And as a result of our studies we have identified two hundred and twenty-five million dollars in annualized savings. Yup, you got it right. Two hundred and twenty-five million in annualized savings which we expect to achieve through the following bold initiatives (and we expect the preponderance of this to be accomplished within the next year):

". . . We plan to consolidate fifty-three facilities to fourteen including reducing twenty-six factories to eight—four domestic and four international.

"We plan to reduce the number of warehouses we utilize from sixty-one to twenty-four.

"We expect to reduce head count by *fifty* percent [emphasis *his*], from twelve thousand to six thousand people.

"Once again, these items are expected to generate two hundred and twenty-five million dollars annualized savings, the preponderance of which is expected in this next year. The actions to be taken are happening *as we speak*."

I can confirm that. A while before the telephone conference, I'd phoned a Sunbeam decorative bedding showroom in New York City. The woman who answered said that she wasn't worried that the place might close; they did so much business out of that office and the bedding was so beautiful. When I called back after Dunlap's announcement, the number had been disconnected.

After a one-year *restructuring* program, Al launched into the three-year *growth* plan. (This is an important distinction for him. In his chapter "Real

Jobs, Real Cuts," Dunlap rails against the "addle-brained" fiction—"I hate fiction"—of three-year restructuring plans favored by executives who prolong the pain because they can't face the scrutiny. If a restructuring can't be done in under a year, he says, it can't be done. Growth is another matter.

At the beginning of Sunbeam's three-year growth plan, sales were expected to drop, due to the announced divestments, to one billion. But "by 1999 they will be, our goal is to be, at two billion in sales." International sales, Dunlap said, would account for almost half of that growth.

Sunbeam would "globalize . . . tripling international sales from $185 million to $600 million by 1997." We would create "counter seasonal" products, "sending grills to South America in the 3rd and 4th quarter, electric blankets to South American and the Asian Pacific in the 2nd and 3rd quarter." Al was already lining up 15 new distributors and/or licensees for countries including China, Thailand, Malaysia, Indonesia, the Philippines, Taiwan, Brazil, and Australia. (This was before the Asian crash, remember.)

Based on all that growth, Sunbeam would "achieve a 20-percent operating profit, up from 2¹⁄₂ percent . . . 20 percent vs. 2¹⁄₂ percent," he gloated; "achieve a 25-percent return on equity capital up from one percent achieved over the past twelve months—that's pretty pathetic; generate close to $600 million of free cash over the next three years."

Where is he getting these numbers? I wondered. Ah, well. It's easy to say with precision what you'll close and who you'll fire, but growth is necessarily speculative. Still, you've got to "envision the future and plan a route to it."

"Sunbeam's three-year mission—again the growth mission as opposed to the one-year restructuring—is to become the dominant and most profitable small-household-appliance and outdoor cooking company in North America with a leading share of Latin American and the Asian Pacific market."

Dunlap was very excited about new products, particularly a line of upscale outdoor grills and "The Blanket with a Brain—it measures your body temperature and adjusts the heat automatically to each part of the body." He even rolled out the new slogan for us: *Sunbeam: Now there's a bright idea.* I liked it. I got a little worried, though, when he announced that product-development time would be cut to six months. (Maybe I'm too sensitive about rushing the creative folks.) But the goal of 30 new products a year sounded reasonable. He concluded his formal presentation with a snappy aphorism.

"Cost-cutting gets you *in* the race. New products enable you to *win* the race."

Then the lines were thrown open for questions. The analysts showed no interest at all in the new products.

Andrew Shore of Paine Webber asked what percent of Sunbeam's goods would be outsourced after the restructuring. He seemed worried that the company was still overcommitted to fixed-manufacturing plants.

"We've gone from fifty-three facilities to fourteen," Al repeated defensively. "We've reduced from twenty-six factories to eight—four domestic, four international; we've reduced from sixty-one warehouses to twenty-four. We're in a unique position as opposed to other companies in this business. We'll have four facilities in the United States, three in Mexico, one in Venezuela, plus the ability to outsource...so we can make it in the US, make it in Mexico, and we can outsource it."

That wasn't good enough. The analysts wanted cash quickly. Will we see the cost savings (from selling divisions and firing people) "immediately?" "In this quarter?" "This year?" They questioned Al jealously about commitments to old factories or hidden plans to build new ones.

Over and over Al had to defend the remaining factories as "already built." "About the only capital requirements we have are for new tooling." "Our domestic facilities will compete with our Mexican facilities, which will compete with outsourcing." "This is a company that's going to throw off, we believe, a lot of cash flow without a requirement to build factories." But they kept after him. "About fifteen percent [only] of your sales are now outsourced. What do you think that *could* be?"

What do these guys want from poor Al?! He's getting rid of 50 percent of the employees. Sure, Chase fired 12,000, but that wasn't 50 percent; AT&T fired 40,000, but that wasn't 50 percent. Al Dunlap is cutting a record 50 *percent* of the labor force. Give the guy a break!

The analysts weren't braggadocios or excitable types like Al. They were difficult to quote because they spoke in abstract numerical terms. I take that back. Numbers, for instance numbers of grills or numbers of steam irons, are not abstract; they're concrete. The analysts spoke not in numbers but in *amounts*—"operating margins," "ROE [Return on Equity] targets," "growth margins," et cetera.

I had a dentist who used to say, "An empty mouth is a healthy mouth." He was kidding. But that seemed to be the analysts' philosophy. Factories and warehouses are so messy. Why couldn't it be a schematic company, money in/money out, without all that production stuff in between?

One analyst seemed to recognize that the cash flow they all wanted to capture came from the sale of concrete products that had to be made, sold, and shipped. She even seemed to know, though she didn't state it explicitly, that people were involved in making those products, people whose concentration might be disturbed in the course of such a rapid restructuring.

"On the consolidation of the facilities, Al," asked Lisa Fontenelli from Goldman Sachs, "coming into the sort of peak holiday season, are you folding them into each other to kind of mitigate any inability to meet demand around the Christmas holiday, or are they all coming out at once? Is there any concern there?"

"What's happening," Al reassured her, "as we speak, we have people at every single facility. This thing has been planned like the invasion at Normandy." (Did I forget to mention that Dunlap went to West Point?)

It may be that Ms. Fontenelli's subliminal image was not so much distressed employees as disjointed flow charts. But at least she knew that shipped goods were the source of future profits. The other analysts probably knew that, too, but they weren't thinking two quarters ahead. They were after that bird in the hand. They wanted to make sure that Al wouldn't fritter away the cash from cost savings and divestments on expensive hobbies like manufacturing appliances.

Andrew from Paine Webber dialed in again and tried to pin Al down about how much real money could be expected in cash profits.

Andrew: You never told us, of the two hundred and twenty-five million [cost savings] how much you will need to plow back into the company to grow. How much could we expect to see on the bottom line?

Al: Firstly the two-twenty-five million, I mean, that's real. That doesn't have to be plowed back into capital. . . . With the sale of assets, with the liquidation of inventory, with the new terms [stiffer credit terms for retailers), we put ourselves in a very advantageous position, plus this is not a capital-intensive business, plus we have the facilities, and most of the money which we'll spend—which will equal depreciation—goes into tooling and improvements in how we run our facilities.

Andrew: So it's fair to assume, then, that over the next two years, theoretically, the cost savings should be anywhere from like a dollar seventy to a dollar seventy-five per share?"

Al (coyly): We never comment on earnings, but you're a lot more clever than I am on that and I'm sure you'll come to whatever you deem is the proper number."

The $1.70 to $1.75 per share was left to float there before the analysts.

More important than the *amount* of earnings is what's *done* with the money, of course. It could, as Andrew Shore feared, be plowed back into the business. Al was reassuring on that point:

"Share repurchase is certainly one option. We're going to be a very cash-rich company. We could do lots of things. We could merge; we could acquire. I think my record speaks loudly that I'll be looking for what generates the next quantum leap in shareholder value—the people that actually own the company."

The owners' representatives were apparently satisfied. After the announcement, Sunbeam's share price continued to rise. By June the Sunbeam stock in my Mutual Shares portfolio was worth 165 percent more than when Al Dunlap came aboard.

What kind of calculation did investors make when they bid the stock price up that high? Could all of Al's cost savings, even if they were true, and all his future sales, even if they had materialized, make the Sunbeam company worth 165 percent more than before? Where exactly did the new shareholder value come from, and where did it go when it rushed out of the Sunbeam balloon as fast as it had been pumped in? Price and Dunlap would both have time soon enough to ask themselves those questions, but let's not get ahead of the story. Back then, there were properties to sell, costs to cut, workers to fire.

Anything that has a structure can be restructured, and it can be restructured in many different ways. But by the end of the 20th century, that broad word had been narrowed to apply to *corporate* restructuring of a fairly predictable form.

Starting in the early 1970's, many American and European companies noticed that their growth and profits had slowed down. There are many ways to increase profits, of course. But if other people in the world can make the same product, and if the total market doesn't seem to be expanding much, the most obvious option is to cut costs.

For a quarter of a century, American managers, under pressure from shareholders, had been presiding over cost-cutting reorganizations like the merger between Chase and Chemical. With a little prodding from my mutual-fund manager, Michael Price, those *restructured* banks were now prepared to do somewhat less business at significantly reduced costs and turn more profits over to me. Unfortunately, most of the reduced costs came from firing workers. In the Chase-Chem merger, 12,000 lost their jobs.

Ideally, Mr. Price would find some expanding industry in which to invest our Chase profits. In the meantime, the leaner bank would be better fit to compete for today's limited business and ready to expand when growth picked up again.

Every few months, government economists said that we had finally moved into the growth phase. But in the five years before I invested in Sunbeam, about 30 percent of all Americans who worked had lost a job due to restructuring.

That's why people who deplored the human distress from job loss often equated restructuring with the "downsizing" or "deindustrialization" of America. But those descriptions were slightly inaccurate or at least debatable, because American industrial output had not actually declined and most of the people who lost jobs found new ones.

But two-thirds of the new jobs were at lower pay. Even people who found jobs at the same or better pay brought a disquieting sense of impermanence to their new workplaces. People who kept their jobs at a restructured firm felt more transitory, too. And since restructuring hit workers of all ages, it was no longer statistically reasonable to count on steadily increasing wages throughout one's work life. In fact, it became statistically difficult to count on anything throughout one's work life except change.

So insecurity was the one undebatable result of restructuring. For some, that was its success.

Officially the US Federal Reserve Bank is charged with the double mandates of restraining inflation and promoting full employment. But like his predecessors, the Federal Reserve Board chairman at the time, Alan Greenspan, seemed to take only the former goal seriously. Indeed, he felt obliged to raise interest rates and thereby slow the economy whenever too many people had jobs. Anything significantly less than 5 percent official unemployment rate triggered fear that a tight labor market (i.e., a good job market) would lead to rising wages followed by price inflation. But one time when unemployment dipped, Chairman Greenspan did nothing to increase it. This is how he explained his inaction to congress:

> ... Despite the sharply lower unemployment rate and the demonstrably tighter labor market, the same survey [a survey of workers at large firms] found 46 percent fearful of a job layoff. ... as I see it, heightened job insecurity explains a significant part of the restraint on compensation and the consequent muted price inflation.

But fear alone wouldn't keep wages down indefinitely, or, as the chairman put it:

... suppressed wage cost growth as a consequence of job insecurity can be carried only so far.

Chairman Greenspan assured Congress and the world that he stood ready to curb wages by increasing unemployment at the first hint of inflation. But right then it wasn't necessary. America had come to have an affordable, competitive, suitably fearful labor force—at least for the time being.

I was soon to see the effects of job insecurity on "restructured" Sunbeam employees. Many felt depressed, frightened, and resourceless. But I never met a fired worker bitter or paranoid enough to believe that there was a federal agency dedicated to lowering his wages and/or increasing his fears.

———

Despite his pride in eliminating a full 50 percent of the employees, Al Dunlap's turnaround plan for Sunbeam sounded like a fairly standard restructuring. It was intended to produce immediate wage savings, fast cash for shareholders, and eventual regrowth. It if worked, the surviving "core" business would be more streamlined, more efficient, and more salable.

But Dunlap's CEOship was Sunbeam's third restructuring in the decade since my mutual fund had acquired its large stake in the company. Now, with appliance sales stagnant and no plan to automate production, we were looking for yet another big spurt of shareholder value. How many times can you squeeze the same lemon? That's one reason that I was dubious about the eventual regrowth. I had no doubt, however, about the insecurity.

Sunbeam had about 50 facilities that produced or warehoused electric blankets, clocks, can openers, blenders, hair clippers and a variety of other small appliances. At every one of those facilities, employees were waiting to hear whether their own workplace would be downsized, sold, or closed.

At the time, Sunbeam was America's leading producer of lawn furniture. Yet all three factories in the aluminum furniture division—Texas, Georgia, and Tennessee—were running well below capacity, sometimes producing less than half of what they were equipped to turn out if they had the orders. So it made sense to close at least one furniture factory and consolidate the work.

As it happened, a restructuring or downsizing of the furniture division had been in the works before Dunlap was hired. Jim Buckley, a decent, dogged, traditional-minded business representative of the United Steel

Workers of America, serviced the Sunbeam local in Portland, Tennessee. According to Buckley, a Mr. Dale Tabinowski from corporate human relations in Florida had contacted the in-plant bargaining committee asking them to voluntarily lower their wages if they wanted to keep their plant open.

"They average eight dollars and twenty-four cents an hour in Portland," Buckley told me, "but only six dollars and four cents in Georgia. The difference, they point out to us, is large. There are also benefits in Tennessee that amount to two dollars an hour more than in Georgia. Tabinowski asked them [the members of the bargaining committee] to make an offer."

"I was out of town," Buckley continued. "I didn't have a chance to confer with the committee. But my ladies [the committee was predominantly women] told them that they weren't going to start offering fifty cents, a dollar, okay, a dollar fifty. They said, 'you tell us what you want to keep it open.'"

"They pitched to me that the unemployment rate in Tennessee is only three and a half to four percent, but that part of Georgia offered them nineteen percent."

"Did they use the word 'offered'?" I asked. "Georgia *offers* us nineteen percent unemployment?"

"They definitely mentioned that nineteen-percent number. They also said they got breaks from the government of Georgia. They'd want the union to contact Tennessee officials for them if they stayed. I called someone in the state AFL-CIO and they were ready to put me on to the right people in the Economic Development Department of the state of Tennessee."

I was surprised at the human-relations man's bluntness. Of course I understood that the threat of unemployment gets people to accept lower pay. But I thought it operated as an invisible hand, not a fist in the face. Still, it sounded like the old Sunbeam management had given the Portland plant a serious chance to bid. That surprised me, since Portland was the only one of the three factories with a union, and getting rid of a union is usually regarded as one of the windfall benefits of restructuring. Perhaps the pre-Dunlap management believed that the Tennessee labor force had some skill or cohesion worth saving. They seemed to be trying to shape the ideal labor force—union workers with nonunion wages.

But once Dunlap announced that he would sell off the furniture division, it was obvious which plant would be closed.

I've never lived in a private house, so I don't know much about fixing one up for sale. But I do know that when a Manhattan landlord wants to get the most money for an apartment building, he tries first to get rid of tenants with long leases. A new owner doesn't want to buy obligations. And a factory with a union contract is like a building with rent-controlled tenants. They have too many contractual rights. It's worse than termites.

The Landing in Tennessee

In the course of the teleconference where he revealed his radical restructuring plan, Al Dunlap had assured the stock analysts that "this thing has been planned like the invasion of Normandy." By the day of that announcement— November 12—Dunlap had his own operatives in each Sunbeam facility.

At the Portland, Tennessee, furniture plant, the former Environmental and Safety person, Rosette Clarke, had been promoted, flown to Florida, and given a list of people to fire. On D-day she relieved the plant manager of his command, sent him and about 60 others of the 80-some supervisors, managers, and office staff home, and announced that the factory would be closed on January 12th.

"That gives the legal sixty days," Jim Buckley told me.

I asked the business rep if he'd like the tape of Dunlap's teleconference.

"No. I'm focusing my attention on what I need to do to prepare my members in terms of unemployment, any educational retraining they might be entitled to, and just making sure the company lives up to its closing responsibilities."

Like many US union reps in the age of restructuring, Jim Buckley had the plant closing drill down pat. So did the companies. "They're astute," he assured me, "they generally provide the notice."

But the legal requirement of 60 days' advance notice was more or less irrelevant in the Portland case. Most of the approximately 350 factory hands had been laid off since June. A summer layoff was normal. The workers were usually called back in September or October. "I didn't approve of the lengthy layoffs," the business rep confided, but "the ladies bought into it because they could be with their kids over the summer." This year's layoff had simply gone on. "So for everyone on layoff" Buckley explained, "it's just not calling them back."

It took a while for that to sink in. The people who made Sunbeam outdoor furniture collected unemployment insurance regularly for two or three months each year while the company did maintenance, retooled, and made samples of next year's models. The program that I thought of as emergency income maintenance for unemployed workers had become a standing subsidy that enabled the company to keep a trained workforce on retainer at reduced wages. To the employees, that was an acceptable summer vacation. But if they then became genuinely unemployed . . .

"Wait, does that mean people have used up their unemployment benefits?"

"Yes," Buckley answered. "The consequences of not working are much more severe."

There would be consequences for the rest of the community, too. The Portland countryside was dotted with more than 50 low, modern factories, including a couple of Japanese plants. So there were jobs to be found. But increasing the labor force by four hundred newly unemployed factory workers with no checks to tide them over meant that local employers wouldn't have to offer their own workers raises or benefits. They could just plug in the Sunbeam workers, preferably as temps.

The Committee

Lynda Caudill was one of the union "ladies" who had been approached by Mr. Tabinowski to "make an offer." She and others on the committee had begun polling the members on his invitation to bid against the Georgia plant. They found wide agreement that if they had to "go back to six dollars an hour" they'd rather do it at some other company. (Choice is the chief perk in an area of low unemployment.)

But once Dunlap landed, the question became moot. The only business left between the company and the union was the terms of separation. The union wanted severance pay even though there was nothing about it in their contract. The company wanted a signed waiver from every individual saying he or she relinquished any job claims against Sunbeam or whoever continued making the outdoor furniture.

Lynda Caudill had been negotiating the separation package on the day I first phoned her. "They're [Sunbeam] holding them [the negotiations] in this great big empty headquarters building in Nashville. They got it all locked up. We had to knock. They said they got to be careful."

She described the company bargaining team: "Dale Tabinowski—he comes in from Florida, Larry Dymowska, he's one of Chainsaw Baby's people [he had been promoted out of another Sunbeam plant to become part of Dunlap's plant-closing cadre], and Rosette Clarke—she's kind of running the plant now, the only one left in the office."

On the union's side of the table were Lynda Caudill, who was a welder; Cleta Ison, the local's secretary treasurer, whose job at Sunbeam was "cushions"; Business Rep Jim Buckley, and the local president, Wynn Caudill, who happened to be Lynda's husband.

At the time of these negotiations there were still 28 union members in the plant working to break down and prepare the furniture-making equipment for its move to Georgia and Texas. Wynn Caudill, a skilled tool-and-die maker, was one of the retained employees. It had to feel awful, I thought, to pack up pieces of a plant you'd worked at for years. But people must be desperate for a few extra weeks' pay, I mistakenly thought.

"They gave my husband a list of everyone's firing date," Lynda explained. "His is the thirty-first of January. But they intend to extend it."

"Oh, that's ... " ["good" I was about to say.]

"Wynn told 'em flatly, he don't want to work for them. Not him and nobody else. They wanted out."

"So why don't they just ... "

"If they quit they don't get no severance. And if they get fired they don't get no severance. They want to get on with their lives but they got to stay in and do the company's business. They can't quit."

I'd assumed it was a favor to be picked to stay on. But some of the people on the inside felt more like hostages, it seemed. Or rather, their severance pay was the hostage. The company naturally wanted the most skilled, capable people to help close up. These were the very people who were most anxious or least afraid to get out on the job market.

"Maybe I better not come till after the thirty-first I now suggested. I'd already mentioned to Lynda that I'd like to come to Tennessee and interview people. "If your husband's still working there, he may not want to ... "

"We don't mind. Wynn—usually when we're in negotiations he lets me do all the dirty work. This time, the first day in negotiations he just told them right good he don't want to work for them no more. That's the nicest way to put what he said. That was to Rosette Clarke. My eyes popped wide open when he said that to her. He told them off in the Miami *Herald*, too," she went on proudly. "That's right near where Dunlap's headquarters is. They can't fire him for that." Freedom of speech is an important union benefit.

Lynda Caudill encouraged me to come in time for the plant-closing meeting on January 12. Everyone would be there to hear about the settlement and sign their waivers. "Even the scabs'll be hanging around to find out what the union got for them."

Tennessee was a "right to work" state, which means that after a union is voted in, joining and paying dues are still voluntary. The union, on the other hand, was required to bargain for non-dues-paying employees without discrimination. That didn't mean, however, that nonmembers could attend union meetings. January 12, though it affected everyone, was a local membership meeting to ratify or reject the plant-closing agreement that Lynda Caudill and the others had negotiated. "I don't want to let them [the scabs] in, but Wynn says, 'Let them in, you may have to work with them somewhere else.'"

The day before the meeting Lynda Caudill was still arguing for scab exclusion. "'You call yourselves Christians?' I say to them. 'It's the same as stealing. Taking something you don't pay for, soaking up benefits for twenty years that ain't yours.'"

We were driving through open countryside on the way to the Sunbeam factory. Lynda, a generous, glamorous women with Nashville big hair, had a warm, open expression even when she remembered a whole family of scabs.

"The company fired the kid because he just don't make it to work. So Sue Adams, his mother, asks me, 'Can you help Darrell?' She is standing in the office with Rosette. So I'm doing it on my lunch while he is sitting out there drinking a Coke and eating a Moon Pie. Him sittin' and eatin' a Moon Pie and gettin' a union job!"

Yet on her next to last day as a union officer, Lynda was still working for the scabs on her own time. We were on our way to the plant to pick up copies of the settlement proposal that Rosette Clarke had run off for Lynda to proofread. Under the agreement, each production worker, union or nonunion, would get a cash settlement in exchange for abandoning any job rights un-der the union contract.

I waited in the parking lot while Lynda went in to pick up the documents. She seemed to be having a little trouble with the guard until a woman carry-ing a small dog in her arms intervened.

"New Security," Lynda said when she got back into the car. "Wouldn't let me in 'til he got ahold of Rosette first."

"That's Rosette Clarke? Running around with a little dog?"

"She's up here on a Saturday," Lynda springs to the defense. "It's her own time."

The new guard had warned Lynda that no one would be allowed in more than 15 minutes early the next day, but Rosette had instructed him to let the union officers in 30 minutes before the meeting. "The old man [the guard] asks me if I think there'll be any trouble tomorrow. I said, 'We got a good enough settlement. We're not gonna blow you up.' Rosette said to me, 'I am proud you all got what you got.'"

————

Rosette had been at Sunbeam for only two years when she was suddenly pro-moted by the Dunlap team to manage the plant through the shutdown.

"It got announced that I was the HR [Human Resources] specialist in a meeting that I didn't even know it was going to happen, in front of eighty people," she told me. "We [management and office staff] were sitting in the lunchroom getting the information that they're going to study about the clos-ing of either Portland or Waynesboro, Georgia, and 'if you have any ques-tions ask Rosette Clarke as she has just been named HR specialist.'"

"Who said that?"

"The vice president of Logistics, the one that said, 'I'll keep this one and this one and this one. . . .' The next thing I know I'm headed to Fort Lau-derdale, Florida, learning what the process is going to be. That was the eighth of October. Then on the twelfth day of November I interviewed fifty-seven or sixty-seven persons and gave them their terminations dates. . . . I even terminated the plant manager."

Rosette had helped to close two other plants that she'd worked in. "It's not unusual in this day and time," she assured me. I asked how this compared to the other closings she'd managed.

"Other places we left people in place to take care of all the functions. We didn't terminate everybody on the same day."

"You fired everyone, even down to the payroll clerk?"

"We kept the payroll clerk, but parts people, benefits clerks, timekeepers, people that just answer the telephone, clerks that did correspondence for us, engineering clerks, administrative assistants . . . "

"You don't have an administrative assistant?"

"No."

"But whose instructions was it to have so little management left?"

"That come from Coopers & Lybrand [the consulting firm whose team members I'd met with Dunlap at the book-signing; see page 199]. And when you terminate, uh, management-type people, it's hard to replace them with people with knowledge enough to go through the season. . . . When everyone was leaving they were taking the knowledge with them. There are processes I'm still not aware of."

Rosette insisted that she was simply handed the termination list and had no input to it, just as she had no advance knowledge that she was going to be made Human Resources Specialist.

"They didn't ask you first?"

"No. In fact there had been mention of it but it never had come about."

"So no one from Coopers & Lybrand formally interviewed you for the job?"

"Oh, absolutely not. It was by word of mouth because I had worked with the HR manager and he knew what I was capable of doing."

Rosette was working at least 12 hours a day, she told me, and was very shorthanded.

"When I go to bed it kind of rolls over in my head. You can't get the wheels to stop with all the stuff lying on your desk and you think about what you got to do in the morning, what you left, and the telephone calls you got to make.

"I heard there was a woman that collapsed in the bathroom today at Neosho, Missouri, and it was just from overwork and stress. They took her to the hospital and that's what it was."

The Neosho plant made Sunbeam's barbecue grills. Those grills turned out to be Al Dunlap's Waterloo, or at least the first *public* unraveling of his rough-and-ready restructuring. That's why I pass along an obviously hearsay story about pressure at a plant that was downsized and kept.

"In this particular downsizing (I'm not sure whether Rosette meant the restructuring of the furniture division or all of Sunbeam), it almost crippled the business. But I'm sure—hopefully—it'll come back and be better, strength-wise, than it was before. But anyway it continues to go on."

Her immediate task was to collect the waivers from all the factory workers after their January 12 union meeting.

The Union Meeting

The parking lot was filled early that Sunday. People got out of their cars to smoke and exchange a few words. The cafeteria (an area in the plant with benches and vending machines) was packed as the doors were opened.

"They're here," Lynda said to Wynn. "Dangle a scrap of meat and the scabs come out."

"First off, we're gonna ask nonunion members to step out of the room," Wynn announced. There was no movement. "We're not going to have a meeting 'til the nonunion members step outside." Maybe I'd just absorbed Lynda's prejudices, but it looked like the winos and the sad sacks shuffled out. Some scabs remained, as several members signaled to Wynn. But that was as far as he was going to go.

Brother Buckley began by thanking people for their unity: "I think we have an agreement, something to put some sun behind the gloom that's been in your life." Buckley seemed sensitive to a possible accusation that Portland wouldn't be the closing plant if it weren't the union plant. He described conditions in Waynesboro, Georgia, where, counting benefits, hourly labor costs came to 44 percent less.

"My beautiful new wife, Willie, asked me on the way up, 'What would you rather, to have been making eight twenty-eight for the last ten years or to be at six oh-four now but still have the job?'"

He recalled the offer to bid against the Georgia plant, and another rushed negotiation about moving the more expensive Samsonite outdoor furniture line from Florida into the Tennessee plant. That would have entailed giving up some of the members' seniority and accepting days of up to 12 hours, without overtime pay rates, to give the company flexibility. The deal had to be agreed upon immediately, according to the man who'd flown up from Florida. This was three days before Dunlap's appointment was announced.

"It seemed to me they didn't know what was going to happen anyway. They were just feeling us out to see what they could get from us and we weren't in a buying mood.... [Another possibility is that a group of company executives was hastily trying to put the furniture division together in an ideal form for buying it themselves. Insider purchases are not uncommon when companies restructure.] But then they put in Dunlap, and subsequent to that, all the talk about bringing the Samsonite people here was put off-limits." I don't think anybody cared about this history, but Buckley was troubled that he might have missed something that cost people their jobs.

"On November twelfth—the company didn't send us no warning note first—you got the sixty-day notices. You may be aware that this [the requirement for advance notice] is a piece of legislation signed by Clinton and vetoed by Bush. Immediately I wrote to the company and told them we want to start talking. And Cleta and her husband went down and loaded the food at Camp Justice [left over from a strike-support campaign] and we went and got a truckload of food and it's in Lynda-Sue Combs's beauty parlor—no, Cleta's house. [Cleta Ison, a middle-aged woman, had timidly corrected him.]

"We met with the company December ninth. I asked if we took a two-dollar cut would they sign something saying they would keep the plant here, and they said no, they wouldn't.... The reason the company gives settlements is so they can get rid of you, and they're willing to give a chunk of change to get you out of their hair. So we try to get as big a chunk of change as we can. It's normal. You gotta sign this paper getting rid of your seniority to get the settlement.

"The severance, it will be in a lump sum less withholding. Yes, Uncle Sam is going to get part. We weren't able to negotiate that out.

"In addition to this settlement you're entitled to any unemployment should you still have some coming. On Friday Cleta Ison filed for TAA. [Under the Trade Adjustment Assistance provisions of NAFTA, workers might be entitled to extended unemployment if they could prove that their specific jobs moved to Mexico as a result of the North American Free Trade Agreement.]

"I been negotiating for twenty years. Our standard request is one week's severance for each year's seniority and we ain't never got it except this time. So I'm pleased you ... "

One week's pay per year! The average seniority was eight years. Eight weeks of an $8.50-an-hour salary is not a golden parachute. I finally took a good look at the bargaining-unit list that had been handed out.

The most senior employee, there 33 years, would come away with $8,840 before taxes, while the largest severance, $10,036 dollars, went to a man who had 27 years of service but at a higher hourly wage. There was a knot of workers at 12 years with $4,080. The bottom 100 would collect around, or under $1,000. That included a large bulge of newcomers, a year or less on the job. Their "chunk of change" would be $502. It would have been less based on a week's salary for a year's work, but the union had insisted on the $502 minimum.

"It's a considerable amount of money," Buckley concluded, "everything being relative."

"You'll get it within ten days after you sign the release and give it to the company. We'll facilitate that by signing it here, witnessing it, and giving it to the company."

There were many questions after the formal presentation.

"How do you go about getting your pension from Sunbeam?"

"That gave me a lot of worry," Buckley answered. "I woke up thinking about it. Here comes old man Dunlap who has experience knocking out companies. He must have figured out that pensions cost a lot of money. Maybe he figured out a way around it. I called and I said, 'I know we already shook hands on it but *you* put something back on the table and now I'm worried about the pension.' I got a separate letter from them on it. Anyway the law should protect us and there's the Pension Benefit Guarantee Corporation."

A retiree said she'd called to change the beneficiary on her $4,000 life-insurance policy but they wouldn't take it from her. She didn't know who to call. Others, too, had trouble finding anyone at Sunbeam responsible for them.

"An important question. They used to do employee benefits in-house at Sunbeam. Now they have a company that does it outsourced, Hewett Associates. Unfortunately this causes delay. They have to come on-line and do new calculations. I asked Tabinowski how much time it will take. He said, 'I don't know.' I said, 'Well, I'll tell them to wait one month. After that I'll give them your home phone number.'"

Pensions and life insurance were future benefits. I'm not sure many fully believed in them. The most pressing questions were about medical insurance.

"COBRA," Buckley began a general explanation, "is another of the things the union has done for you that most of us don't understand." For readers outside the US or for future Americans for whom my generation's medical insecurity will hopefully be incomprehensible, I'll give some background.

There was neither a national health service nor universal medical insurance in the US in the 20th century. Individuals bought health-insurance policies to cover unusual medical expenses. It had become common for corporations, particularly those employing white-collar workers, to negotiate health insurance packages to cover all of their employees and to pay part of the premiums. Unions like the Steel Workers had won such insurance benefits for some blue-collar workers, but when people lost their jobs, whether they were blue- or white-collar, their insurance coverage was terminated. Insurance companies treated them as new individual applicants, and it was insurance-company policy to reject old and unhealthy applicants when possible and to exclude coverage of preexisting conditions. COBRA was a union-backed law that gave fired workers the right to continue to buy their previous health-insurance policies for a certain period, *at their own expense*. It doesn't sound like much of a benefit, but if you were already diagnosed with cancer, if your heart medicine cost hundreds of dollars a month, if your child needed ongoing physical therapy, if you were pregnant or simply middle-aged, COBRA could be a literal lifesaver.

Some of the healthier Sunbeam workers had gambled, letting their insurance lapse over the summer on the assumption that it would resume when they were called back. The union had arranged for such people to have the COBRA option anyway. One woman had never paid her part of the Sunbeam insurance premium because her husband had cheaper coverage. When he lost his job they elected to let his lapse and wait until she was called back to Sunbeam. Now they had seemingly lost both COBRA entitlements. Could they somehow be gotten back in? Another woman said she had tried to pay last week but the insurance company wouldn't let her. Still another knew she couldn't continue insurance payments and asked if she could get money back for prepaid weeks.

Buckley thought she could but advised people to take advantage of COBRA. "With the settlement, everybody will have the ability to pay these rates. Although this year is high," he acknowledged, looking at the family rate on a schedule that had been distributed, "four eighty-four." That was $484 a month.

The most common settlement was $502. Was Buckley advising people to continue their insurance month-by-month and hope that something (another union job?) would come along before the next payment was due? That's not what I think of as feeling insured.

There was no drama or ceremony around the vote on the plant-closing package. Somewhere along the way, Wynn ascertained that there were no objections. In a similarly anticlimactic way, the formal meeting broke up on its own as Buckley circulated to answer individual questions while members milled around union officers to get their waiver signatures witnessed.

Lynda Caudill wanted to introduce me to a friend and fellow welder, Mitzi Pitts. She spotted Mitzi's aunt, Mitzi's sister-in-law. "There must be a dozen of the Pittses working here." Giving up, she introduced me to another woman she thought I should interview. "She and me were also welders together."

"Uhm, have you found another job yet?" I asked lamely.

"Well, no. I'd like to find something with the pay I'm making now. It took me eleven years to get there. I don't want to go back to minimum wage."

Others had bitten the bullet. A well-groomed woman with short gray hair had registered at one of the temporary agencies in town and had worked for two weeks pulling orders at a distribution center. "Two weeks which we thought, me and this other girl, we thought we were doing very good. But they let us go. They were paying the agency nine dollars and paying us six or six-fifty."

Another woman tried to reassure her that this was no personal failure. "The temp places tell you like it's a tryout for a permanent job, but they want to move you around to keep making money for them."

"That's their way, alright," the well-groomed woman smiled painfully trying to take the bucking-up as it was meant. But alone with me, she was more inclined to go over what she might have done wrong. "They told us 'Don't rush, just don't make no errors.' But the temp people said, 'You didn't make production.' I didn't know we was on production! I went slow and careful like they said. But maybe I should have gone fast."

Sunbeam had been the woman's first employer. She'd left to raise children, then returned after her husband was killed in an industrial fire. Her severance, which was based only on the last ten-year stint, would be $3,400. Many women had a similarly broken work history.

Buckley, meanwhile, was handling exceptions.

"I was on administrative leave." "They wrote down my seniority wrong." "I was drafted in 'seventy-two." Army service was an exception to the rule that severance was based only on the last continuous work stint. Buckley was sure it could be cleared up.

"This beautiful lady on my left," Buckley stiffly charmed an elderly woman, "put her name on the list for retirement. Now they say she's not entitled to separation." His charm didn't always go over but his advice did. Buckley could tell most members what to do or who to see. "And if they don't help, you get back to me and brother Buckley will get in their ear."

"Excuse me," Buckley brought the group back to order. "Lynda Caudill's fixing to go to her new job. I'd like for us to give her a hand for all she's done for the union. [The applause was long and sincere.] And let us know when you get ready to organize there."

This would be Lynda's first day, or rather first evening, at The Gap warehouse. It could take years for former Sunbeam people to work their way up to day shifts at other companies. That might be hard on women with young children, but Wynn and Lynda's kids were grown up. The pay cut wasn't critical for them, either. The house was paid off, and they had one of the tightly rationed state tobacco-growing allotments. They'd made $18,000 this year on the crop, Lynda told me. And Lynda Caudill certainly wasn't worried about being new or going too slowly. An ordinary work shift should be relaxing, compared to the responsibilities I'd watched her handle. But Lynda had her own misgivings.

"It'll be so hard to work in a nonunion shop. I mean, I could be fired just for sticking up for somebody at The Gap."

Members began drifting away. I was staring into an enormous empty space with wooden pallets stacked up in the distance.

"What's it like in there now?" I asked Wynn.

"Like a graveyard. And we're digging the graves. We're in there making tool-and-die for them other plants."

Linda-Sue Combs's Beauty Parlor, Main Street—the next day

Waiver signing continued informally at Linda-Sue Combs's new beauty parlor. Linda-Sue was another of Buckley's committee "ladies." Her specialty was filing formal grievances for members. She'd shown me eight Avon boxes of union papers stored under her bed—"grievance first-stage, grievance second-stage." Her only serious failure was on restoring the Tampax machine to the strapping department bathroom. "Well, it's ninety percent women and you're there twelve hours a day." But the business rep had advised her that under the contract they didn't have to provide Tampax machines.

When Linda-Sue heard that the plant was closing, she'd registered for some brush-up cosmetology courses and rented this store. People had been calling Linda-Sue's new beauty parlor all morning with questions about their settlements. I'd stepped out to buy some cassette tapes and returned to find Linda-Sue deposing a woman of about 30 named Janie whose severance pay was being docked to cover the cost of a welding helmet that had disappeared from her locker.

Janie: I said, "Well, I didn't steal the hood." I said, "Why should I have to pay three hundred dollars for a hood that I don't even have?"

Husband: Then what she say *to* you? [Janie's husband had come along to back her up.]

Janie: She [Rosette Clarke] said, "Okay, you are *telling* me that you didn't take your hood." In other words she wanted me to say how can I prove to her that I didn't take it.

Linda-Sue: And you ain't been up there?

Janie: No, I haven't.

"Janie's not getting but seven hundred severance"—Linda-Sue stopped to fill me in—"and *she's* wanting to take two hundred and ninety-five out for the helmet that's in her locker. Here's how they do, they call you up there and escort you up to the locker like you're gonna steal something. And Janie sees her lock's gone, her helmet, and everything else, and she's not been there all summer and she's escorted. She comes back a squallin'. She says her helmet and lock and everything else is gone."

Janie: I never once since I been working there, I never brought my hood home, not once.

Janie's husband backed this up, but Linda-Sue ignored the routine denials and probed for solid information. Were there any witnesses who could confirm that the locker was left locked with the helmet inside?

Janie: Who's that short fat bald man with the glasses?

Linda-Sue's second line of defense was to establish that cutting the lock off wasn't standard procedure.

Janie: Well [X], he called and told them to cut his lock off because he had lost his key and they said, "No, we're not allowed to do that unless you're here."
Linda-Sue: They made a mistake. They shouldn't have opened the lock. You had a lock on it. Now that lock's been cut. Who's to say the hood ain't in Georgia?!
Janie: That's what I asked her.
Linda-Sue: They're moving copy machines and they're stealing copy machines. They blame it on everybody and they act like you're gonna steal something all the time up there. And they escort you back there. I mean if they escort you back there you say "I was escorted back there, how could I have got it?"

"You know," Linda-Sue said to me, "it's probably good that I got out of there. 'Cause if I was there and they kept *her* [Rosette Clarke] there, I'd get fired. I mean she ain't liked me since I asked her, 'What is your job, Health and Safety or checking under bathroom stalls?'"

Janie: And now she says she ain't sending me my severance pay. If they do they gonna take three hundred dollars out of it. And I ain't getting that much.

Linda-Sue: Anybody all summer could have cut that lock off and you're responsible for it.

Janie: They had the maintenance cut the locks, and . . .

Linda-Sue: And all them are scabs.

Linda-Sue witnessed Janie's signature and sent her up to the plant with the same advice she'd given others, "Don't go it alone. If there's any trouble say 'Can I call Wynn Caudill in here?'"

Frankly, I was a little worried about Linda-Sue's business. The shop was always busy but I hadn't seen one paying customer or heard her make one hair-cutting appointment. But she assured me that Thursday, Friday, and Saturday were the big days.

The self-effacing gray-haired woman who had picked up the union food donations was the secretary-treasurer, Cleta Ison. "Cleta with no GED," Buckley had told me, "keeps the books, files the W-2s, W-3s, the 941s, the 940s, everything for the Labor Management Disclosure Act, and she takes care of the membership money like it was her own."

I never heard Cleta speak about herself, but I learned from others that her husband had had a disabling heart attack so she was the primary support of the family. Before I left town, Cleta took me aside to ask: "If you hear anything about moving any of the aluminum furniture abroad, I would appreciate it if you would let me know. They didn't leave nobody in the union on this. It's just me and he." ("He" meant her husband, who did not work for Sunbeam.)

It was a practical question. If the next owner of the furniture division wound up moving Portland's part of the work to Mexico, the employees left behind might be entitled to additional weeks of unemployment benefits. But it was difficult to trace jobs unless the company cooperated and/or the local government assigned staff to prepare the application. What a responsibility for Cleta to carry away.

Wynn and Lynda Caudill, Linda-Sue Combs, Cleta Ison: not one member of the committee had even finished high school. But together they took on tasks that it made me nervous to think about. I guess it's true, as the song says, "The union makes us strong."

I asked Cleta if she thought the Sunbeam people would get together from time to time. "No. Everybody will be working different shifts. We'll be scattered." That's a cost of restructuring that's hard to measure.

Labor-Force Flexibility

It made sense for Dunlap to close the Portland factory. Labor-force flexibility is the great desideratum of modern employers.

In a competitive world where orders fluctuate, you want labor available as needed, with minimal commitment. Outsourcing, the system which allows you to use factories without owning them and workers without hiring them, puts a company at the high end of the flexibility scale. Slavery, which requires you to feed people full-time or lose your capital investment, is at the low or primitive end.

A company-owned factory with a union workforce definitely tilts a producer toward inflexibility. Commitments like severance pay or plant-closing notice, whether imposed by union contract or government regulation, make an investor think twice about buying a business. That's why Sunbeam would have an easier time selling the furniture division if it got rid of the union first.

Yet there must have been reasons why one large retail chain specified the Tennessee plant as the source for its goods, and why some insiders toyed with a consolidation plan that included the Tennessee facility. A cohesive workforce has real advantages. In Tenessee the union played a part in attracting skilled workers and keeping a nucleus together despite the seasonal layoffs.

Union uppitiness must have been a daily annoyance to some managers. Yet the union, as a second chain of command, also helped keep the plant running smoothly, just as it helped make the shutdown smoother.

At the closing meeting, someone asked if people inside could still file grievances against Sunbeam. Buckley answered that it was legally possible but "frankly, your severances will be held hostage." When it came time for the vote, he'd advised with regret that "from a practical point of view our options are limited." And above the noise, as the formal meeting dissolved, Wynn Caudill's last words as local president were, "Thank you for showing up. Sign this now in front of witnesses."

Because people trusted the union officers, the company would get a neat stack of waivers, delivered in a timely manner, absolving whoever ran the outdoor furniture division from unknown future obligations. That should raise the sale value.

———

After the plant-closing meeting, when almost everyone had left the lunchroom, Rosette Clarke came to check things out. Wynn thanked her for keeping the plant open for the union on a Sunday. The Florida headquarters was open, too, it seemed; Rosette had already phoned Tabianowski to let him know the results.

Dale Tabinowski was the pre-Dunlap human-relations man. It was he who had phoned from Florida trying to bargain the wages down. He was among the few executives retained after Dunlap took over.

"I don't know if that man's going to make it," Rosette said. "He hasn't had but two days off in six months. He went to his father's funeral. He just told Dunlap, 'I am going to my father's funeral.'"

When Wynn and I were well out of the building, Rosette called after us to double-check something. "Did y'all actually vote?"

"We held one," Wynn answered. "We said, 'Everybody in favor signify by saying "Aye," and everybody not in favor say "Nay,"' and we didn't have no nays."

"No nays? Okay, I just wondered. They wanted me to find out how many were for and against."

Those waivers were really important, it seemed.

There's another way unions help manufacturers, though it's hard for any single firm to appreciate the benefit. Unions help by making people less poor.

"The furniture on our patio and decks and our gas grills were all Sunbeam," Portland's mayor was quoted in the town paper as saying. "I'd say 95 percent of local people had their things." That may be an exaggeration, but if US wages hadn't been going down for 20 years, maybe Sunbeam's US sales wouldn't have leveled off. Then the three furniture plants wouldn't have had so much overcapacity. Perhaps then my mutual fund could have extracted value from steady profits on rising sales, instead of from these periodic restructurings.

There was a benefit from higher wages, or rather, a cost of lower wages, that might hit plants left in the Portland area more directly. After the plant-closing meeting, a woman stopped us in the parking lot.

"You Wynn Caudill? I didn't know y'all had a meeting," she apologized, "'til Edna come by and told me we had to sign some kind of papers." Edna had a telephone.

After witnessing her signature, Wynn asked the woman if she was working now.

"The temporary got me a job at Precision in second shift," she said. "But my son, him and Denise separated and he's living with me and they got him a job at Payton's. He's been out there six week now and he's on day shift and he ain't got a car so he's driving mine to work and I told them I'd have to have a day-shift job with but one car."

One car for two workers, and no telephone; this family had already slipped below the union income level, it seemed. Many companies had located in the Portland area counting on an educated, flexible, and *relatively* cheap work force. But if labor became so *absolutely* cheap that workers couldn't afford cars and telephones, what would happen to the flexibility? You can't tell someone "We want you tonight from seven to ten" if he doesn't have a car and a phone.

If everyone in the region goes from eight-dollar jobs to six-dollar jobs, I thought, *the companies will have to start supplying dormitories and transportation the way they do in Asia.* That was, of course, an exaggeration. There were lots of ways for American workers to make themselves cheaper, but still stay flexible enough to meet Sunbeam's needs. They just weren't pleasant.

OUTSOURCING

I never did interview Al Dunlap, but I attended a conference on Strategic Management where he was the luncheon speaker and I got to ask, from the audience, why Sunbeam was selling its blanket plant in Biddeford, Maine. (At the time, I was already in contact with people who were bidding to buy the plant.) Al's one-word answer—prefaced by many words urging his listeners to find out more by buying his book, on sale in the lobby—was "outsourcing."

There's nothing new about outsourcing. At the start of the industrial revolution, garment companies bought or "sourced" fabric from textile mills and "put it out" with workers who sewed at home, as independent contractors. But under the putting-out system it was hard to guarantee the quantity and quality that customers ordered, so the more successful businesses took to "insourcing."

As their industry took off, early garment manufacturers brought workers into factories, where they could be timed, supervised, and trained to use methods and machines that yielded predictable output. To make supplies reliable, some clothing manufacturers even ran their own textile mills. Later, for the same reason, some auto companies owned tire companies, and those tire subsidiaries owned their own rubber plantations.

This kind of "insourcing" helps a business deliver the goods on time. But when demand gets unpredictable, particularly in the downward direction, it becomes safer to outsource as much as possible. Let someone else maintain the fixed factories and payrolls.

Swings from outsourcing to insourcing are as perpetual as the business cycle itself. As I write, we seem to be at the height, or perhaps just over the peak, of an outsourcing wave. As Al Dunlap says in the book he recommends so highly, "You can outsource just about anything today." Of course, every enterprise requires a few key people to perform a few core functions. But who's "key" and what's "core"?

When he downsized Scott Paper, Dunlap got workers off the company's books by outsourcing such functions as payroll, truck scheduling, information systems, and human resources (personnel). When fired workers from Portland, Tennessee, called Sunbeam about their pensions, they found that "benefits" had been outsourced. Unfortunately, the new contractor didn't seem to have a phone number yet.

Urged on by the anorexic vision that you can never be too thin, today's streamlined companies may have their design, research, manufacturing, shipping, advertising, billing, paying, and collecting all done out-of-house. Perhaps the only "key" employees are a sales manager and a treasurer to perform the "core" functions of getting orders and rounding up the capital needed to commission outsiders to fill those orders.

The core corporate function, then, is financial control. But what happens when the contractors hired to handle production and distribution begin to accumulate capital of their own? How long can you keep control of control?

To answer these questions we have to think back to the decades in which this global era began. Starting in the late 1960's and early 1970's, when US and European profits were declining, many manufacturers tried to cut labor costs by producing in Asia. A decade later they would claim, and believe, that they sought cheap workers in order to compete with cheap imports. But in fact, US manufacturers created their current competitors when they outsourced in Asia.

Today's Asian businessmen served their apprenticeships in facilities set up by Western companies to produce for Western markets. When the subcontractors put together enough capital to go into business for themselves, they continued to produce for the export market with which they were now familiar. But displaced US and European workers couldn't buy all that could now be produced both at home and abroad, while Asian workers were paid too little, both by local and foreign employers, to pick up the slack. (That's one origin of today's manufacturing "overcapacity.")

Dunlap might be setting the same process in motion domestically, I speculated, if he outsourced to a mill that could become an independent competitor down the line. At the moment, Sunbeam was the only electric-blanket manufacturer in the US, and no electric blankets were imported, probably because they were too bulky (for their worth) to ship. So Sunbeam had 100 percent of the US electric-blanket market. Was Al Dunlap about to jeopardize our monopoly? (Remember I'm still a Sunbeam investor.) Was this one more indication that he wasn't concerned with our long-term profitability?

Of course, Biddeford didn't yet have the capacity to make an entire electric blanket. The Maine facility was a 150-year-old textile mill that Sunbeam had acquired during an "insourcing" phase, to assure its supply of blanket shells—the soft part.

Soon after Al announced his 50 percent downsizing, I phoned Mike Cavanaugh, a New England director of UNITE (the Union of Needletrades, Industrial Textile Employees) to hear how the Biddeford union local was coping with the planned sale of their plant. At the time, however, I had no intention of traveling to Maine, because the end of the story was bound to be the same as in Tennessee except that there'd be New England heating bills added to the worrisome health-insurance and car payments of the unemployed.

Whoever bought the business would continue to sell blanket shells to Sunbeam. But any new owner would, I assumed, take his equipment and his Sunbeam contract and move as far away from the union as he could get. Did I really need to tell that story twice?

People in Maine seemed to make the same assumption, though a few local officials expressed the hope that some new owner might find his way to keeping a part of the operation in Biddeford. Mike Cavanaugh described early meetings between union, state, and local officials.

"The mood was, whichever way it goes [move out entirely or keep some work in Biddeford] we got to get prepared to deal with a lot of unemployed people. In the meantime, what kind of package—tax breaks, wage cuts et cetera—can we put together to make ourselves the most attractive to a corporation? The philosophy was totally passive. If we sit in a corner, make our-selves as small as possible, breathe very little air, maybe someone wouldn't mind letting us live. I took the position that would be leading with our chins. We ought to inject ourselves as players."

Cavanaugh's idea was to put together a consortium of credible buyers that would include the union. "The union has no money but we have to make ourselves an element *somehow*, because no other buyer has a commitment to keeping three hundred and thirty-seven jobs."

The "somehow" that occasionally brings workers into a buyout is called an ESOP (Employees Stock Ownership Plan). Under an ESOP, both union and nonunion employees forgo some part of their salary and benefits, and usu-ally dip into their pension fund too, making that money available to the new company. In exchange they get shares proportional to their investment and, in the meantime, keep their jobs.

In some circles, ESOPs had the reputation of what the British used to call Lemon Socialism—that is, the practice of letting the public pay good money to buy what private companies want to get rid of. The hope of saving jobs had led both governments and unions into some economically dubious ventures. For that and many other reasons, an ESOP can be a hard sell.

"But you can't even make an approach to the owner," Cavanaugh ex-plained, "unless you can show a reasonable way to pay for what you're offer-ing to buy. We needed a business plan to present to Sunbeam's bank [which happened to be Chase]." So Cavanaugh brought in a firm that specialized in ESOP financing. "We did a feasibility study for which the city put up five thousand dollars, the state ten thousand, and the union twenty thousand."

By that point in my money travels, $35,000 seemed like an endearingly wee sum to bother mentioning. I thought about the years that Nigel Carlin spent scouting a refinery site for Caltex. The company spent five million dollars be-fore they decided to go ahead with the project. For a multinational oil company, that's a normal cost of doing business. But five, ten, and twenty thousand just to explore a possibility is money Mike Cavanaugh had to pitch for.

He also had to pitch the idea to potential partners like Maine investor Michael Liberty. "He's a local developer I used to battle with ten years ago when he wanted to put up co-ops on the waterfront. So Liberty and I were not particularly close. But he has some access to money and he has a working-class background, some feeling for working people so ... "

The pitch Cavanaugh seemed proudest of was the one the union made to the plant's manager, Rene Boisvert. Starting as a machine operator 45 years earlier, Rene had worked his way up at the mill and seen it through several restructuring crises. During a shutdown scare 25 years earlier, he'd made a convincing pitch to a major customer of the division that he by then ran, and the customer had bought the place. That's how it happened that for a quarter of a century, Rene managed the mill as Sunbeam's vice president of textiles. He'd quit soon after Dunlap's 50-percent announcement in order to do the same thing Michael Cavanaugh was doing—put together the financing to buy the mill and keep it in Biddeford. But apparently he hadn't thought of the union as a possible partner.

"He came in skeptical," Cavanaugh explained, "not because of his long relationship with the union but, he's seventy. Employee ownership sounded maybe a little new-age or something to him. But he said he'd be willing to talk to us and share what he knew."

Rene was apparently being wooed by other potential buyers, who included rival bedding companies and a not-quite-gelled group of Sunbeam corporate insiders, mostly from the southern plants. "But within two weeks," Cavanaugh told me proudly, "Rene made it known that he was willing to work with our team. Now we had it: the management and industrial know-how, the financial backing, and the union leadership, all put together. So Michael Liberty, Rene Boisvert and the union's local leadership—I was there with them—went to the plant like any other potential buyer to hear a presentation from Sunbeam and Chase about this factory they were selling.

"It was kind of comical," Cavanaugh remembers. "On one side of the table you had the man who established and ran the company for twenty-five years along with representatives of the [union] people who made it go every day. On the other side you had investment bankers who in two months had tried to get up to speed on the electric-blanket business, and sitting with them, Sunbeam management, all of who had worked for Rene till three weeks before. So when questions came up about the history, the markets, any question a buyer would need to know, they would all defer to Rene."

Sunbeam quickly accepted the ESOP bid. In his updated paperback, Dunlap describes it as a "win-win situation." "Everybody in Biddeford kept their job ... we continued a reliable high-quality supply source and unloaded an asset from our books. Don't be so sure I'm mellowing."

All things being equal (which of course they never are), a company in Sunbeam's position is better off, according to the common wisdom, selling to an ESOP than to a corporate buyer. That's because employees are far less likely to come up with the additional capital needed to turn their company from a supplier into a competitor.

"So it was up to the membership," Cavanaugh said. "It was their call." And he described what was, to him, the hardest pitch of all.

"On a Sunday in February we invited all the union members and their spouses, the nonmembers too—all the Biddeford employees and their spouses. We had three meetings, at nine, twelve, and three. Come to any or all if you want. Hundreds came. We had a slide presentation about ESOPs. People asked questions about ESOPs that failed. I could field those because I was involved with one they all knew about that failed [a New England suit manufacturer that closed three years after the employees bought it]. In that one everyone lost their jobs. In this case, I said, we have a viable business because Sunbeam has one hundred percent of the domestic electric-blanket market. [The suit company's major customer had gone bankrupt.] And here we have the top management with us. Having Rene Boisvert here—workers at the mill have a lot of respect for Rene—having Rene say 'I'm teaming up with the union on this because this is the best possibility for Biddeford,' that was it."

Actually that wasn't quite it yet. The local bargaining committee still had to negotiate a contract with the new company, and the membership had to accept it. "We'd played around with numbers—the results on cash flow of reducing labor costs ten percent, eleven percent—to see what we needed to make this viable to attract the loans we needed to buy the business and to run it. [They settled on $11^{1}/_{2}$ percent.] But exactly what sacrifices were we going to make to give the company the cash flow it needed? What would our new contract look like?"

That's when I became interested in visiting Biddeford. How do you bargain with a company that you own, I wondered? And where would the union stewards—now owners—stand in that ongoing tug-of-war in which workers perceive owners as demanding the exertion of every bit of mind and muscle, every moment, while to owners, the workers seem to want the eight-hour day with the seven-and-a-half-hour coffee break? A year after the plant-closing in Tennessee, the former Sunbeam workers in Maine still had their jobs. But did they still have a union?

The UNITE Office, Biddeford, Maine—weekday afternoon
"Michael likes to talk to the press," business rep George Csapo greeted me. "As far as I'm concerned they're just garbage-pickers."

George was the same vintage of bread-and-butter business rep as Jim Buckley in Tennessee. When I'd called Buckley, he'd automatically refused to let me come to the plant-closing meeting. It was the two Lyndas who said, "Oh, why not." In the course of strikes both men had probably wasted their good time on friendly-seeming reporters who called back to apologize that the union's side of the story had been cut at the last minute. For reasons both sociological and individual, neither of these men found it easy to chitchat with someone like me. Besides, they'd come of age at a time when a union didn't need favorable press or gimmicks like ESOPs. "In 1955 we had ten thousand dues-paying members in Biddeford!" George told me. [In those days, the union made you strong.]

"If the garbage-pickers call I just say 'We've already said what we have to say.'" And George turned to the work on his desk. Still, he tolerated me hanging around the headquarters, and even gave me a good summary of the ESOP's contract terms.

Union members accepted 5- to 6-percent wage cuts along with benefit cuts that brought the company's compensation bill down by 11½ percent. The cuts averaged about $2.01 per hour, per union employee. "Total cost, about seventeen thousand dollars per person, over five years," George calculated.

"Yeah, we're locked in for five years," said local union President Phil Bourassa. "But they will get a twenty-five-cent raise in April—twenty-five cents a year for the next five years. They didn't even want to give us that. But I said, 'I will never be able to sell it to the people.' I says, 'If I bring this to three hundred people, I'll never get out alive.'"

While George, as business rep, was a full-time union employee, Phil was a full-time production worker who drove a taxi after his shift, three nights a week. Like many of the mill's employees, including Rene Boisvert, Phil's ancestors were French Canadians who'd been brought to work in New England mill towns in the 19th century. The memory of company stores, company houses, and 14-hour days was living history in Phil's family. So were the union's battles against them.

"From when I was a little rugrat, when people visited, the women would go into the kitchen, the men would have coffee in the living room and talk the union, the union, the union. That's why I didn't get involved on the Board. [The union has two representatives on the Board of Directors of the new company.] It's not my job to understand management's problems that well."

The union activists Phil introduced me to, including men who had negotiated the new contract, were divided about the ESOP. But the conflicting assessments—"We were had," and "We saved the day,"—weren't hurled between factions. Each person was divided within himself.

The same seemed true of people who were less involved with the negotiations. I talked with two friends who were having coffee together. The first woman criticized the ESOP. "We opened up the pension funds. Now they have the use of our money for fifty years." "Yes," the second defended, "but at least we have our jobs."

They sighed, sat for a moment, and somewhere in the silence, exchanged positions. "Anyone else who bought it would have moved it," the erstwhile critic said. "We don't know that," the defender now attacked. "We're the only place in the country that makes the shells. They needed us."

The seesaw continued to move on its own. When the first woman remembered the pay cut, the second remembered that she could still take the kids to the doctor with the "ten-dollar card." When the second remembered the lost vacation days, the first said, "Yes, but otherwise we'd be on permanent vacation." After several more ups and downs they hit upon a balancing formula.

"It was all unknown and we made it the known." "Yes," the second agreed, "we made the unknown the known."

Eventually I would visit Sunbeam towns, without unions, where workers had drifted helplessly on a sea of rumors. Long after the restructuring was completed, they knew only that the layoff had been extra-long that year or that the place just never reopened. In Biddeford, the union provided information and options that gave people the sense of shaping a known future. Even in Tennessee where the known—a shutdown—was unpleasant, it helped a little that the union had given the threat a name and date, not to mention a little cash to tide people over.

I asked Phil what the atmosphere had been like at the mill when everything about the restructuring was still unknown. No one from Sunbeam headquarters ever contacted the union, he told me. But Rene had informed them about Dunlap's teleconference with the stock analysts. Phil and George had listened in just as I had, and heard exactly when I did that their plant was up for sale.

"Those were hard days for Rene," Phil said, "because he had to check in every day with Dunlap's people."

"Were they in the plant?" I asked.

"No, they weren't in the plant. He'd call down to Florida. But they kept a tight handle on everything. And they'd pop in. There was a big blond guy, when Rene said he would quit, they said, 'You're out already!'"

"Don Foley [director of manufacturing, who became interim plant manager] told me that's a normal precaution. They're afraid of sabotage so they put you out." Phil shook his head. "I've been in this plant twenty-four years. It's always been Rene. Rene started it. All I know is Rene. And they put Rene out because they're afraid he'll sabotage?"

I asked Phil if rumors went flying around the plant after Dunlap's announcement. Biddeford had weathered several changes of ownership, he reminded me. "So people got accustomed to being bought and sold. The big scare came for us in December when Rene resigned. Then it was like Good Friday: you work, you don't talk. Rene resigned. What's going to happen next?"

"This is a five-year deal we're locked into," Phil summarized his position on the ESOP. "Just because we're part-owner doesn't mean nothing.... We needed Rene and Rene needed the union to pull it off. But now we got this contract, we're locked into it for five years and what I say is 'let Rene be Rene and let the union be the union.'" And he turned to hear from a shop steward about a grievance.

Rene Boisvert

Biddeford Textiles had two facilities in town. Rene Boisvert's office was in the original, long, 1850's brick mill building. A new sign near the old time clocks said OWNERS ONLY BEYOND THIS POINT. It seemed ironic that the only reference I'd heard to the workers as owners came at the time clock where they still had to punch in. But Biddeford employees hadn't invested in the ESOP to change their class status. Like Rene, they just wanted to keep the place open.

"My great-grandfather, my grandfather, my father, and I all worked at Sanford [a nearby town]. My grandfather, my father, and I, plus brothers, sisters, aunts, uncles, you name it, were all there when the mill shut down. Five thousand lost their jobs. A town of eighteen thousand with five thousand working there. That experience [50 years earlier] has guided my career."

I told Rene what happened when my husband lost his job at the newspaper where he'd worked for 25 years. In that restructuring, the new owner not only fired everyone, he also appropriated their pensions through a technicality. "But we weren't going to go hungry, we weren't going lose our apartment. Yet we wound up at the hospital emergency room twice in those first few weeks. He thought he was having a heart attack."

"My father died about six months later," Rene said.

"But I'm a writer, he's a photographer. We both knew all about downsizing and plant-closings. And he could find another job. He did, at much more pay. And yet . . ."

"Five thousand in a town of eighteen thousand," Rene said. "It's never the same."

"Every decision I've made in my career has been guided by Sanford. Everything I do is about keeping this damn place open."

With that sentence, Rene confessed to violating the most basic tenet of laissez-faire capitalism. He was trying to channel capital to achieve a social end. When Michael Price "unlocked" Sunbeam, it was to make the highest possible returns for his shareholders. No one could sue him when the entire restructuring later collapsed. His motives were proper. He merely made a mistake. But if the new Biddeford Textiles had been a publicly owned company and a director suggested that he was willing to make less than the maximum profit in order to help the current work force, it would be the same as admitting that he was stealing company money to give to his friends.

Keeping the mill open in Biddeford is not a legitimate use of investors' money, nor is making good blankets. But these were Rene's passions. To achieve his two illegitimate ends, he'd kept the mill profitable over the years, not by looking for cheaper labor, but by constantly modernizing.

"The talents of the people, the work ethics of the people are so important, but what keeps them on their job is modernization. The company must continue spending money on new equipment, new procedures, and development of new processes. We have the largest installation in the US of Dref machines," he suddenly said, and looked around for someplace to draw something.

The diagram Rene sketched in my notebook showed how the Dref spinning machines he'd bought in Austria combine three different fibers into a single thread. The precise placement made it possible to keep the artificial fiber on the inside. Until then I'd snobbishly rejected blends because I don't like the feel of polyester. But according to Rene's diagram, I could have the strength of an artificial fiber while nothing touched me but pure cotton or wool. I didn't quite believe it.

The spry but slightly bent seventy-one-year-old jumped up to get a couple of blankets to make his point. And indeed, the Biddeford cotton blend that I've been using ever since, is durable, washable, and feels dreamy.

From spinning, Rene shifted with equal enthusiasm to dyeing and carding. The innovations he described were all designed to increase the sales of conventional blankets. He said nothing, whatsoever, about competing with Sunbeam in the electric-blanket business. But I knew it was on a lot of minds.

Shortly before the restructuring, Rene had convinced Sunbeam to move one wiring line to Biddeford. It was an experiment to see if they could avoid shipping bulky blanket shells down to Mississippi by doing more of the assembling at the mill. When Dunlap took over, the wiring line was quickly moved out. Several people who had no way of knowing assured me that Rene had hush-hush plans to produce an entire electric blanket in Biddeford. But with Dunlap still riding high, I wasn't going to ask any questions whose response could sound treasonous.

I did, however, express my general concern about the ultimate weakness of companies that outsourced themselves down to nothing but financial spinal cords.

"The producers aren't going to stand still," Rene said. "We'll learn how to sell things ourselves. We'll learn how to borrow money ourselves. The financial group may think they can outsource and run it, but we, in manufacturing, are taking notes. We'll have to become financial people. We'll have to do it all ourselves. We'll do it and at lower cost too . . . But I don't like to talk about those things."

And he took me into the laboratory to meet a chemist experimenting with dyes. According to Rene, the company's new computer-programmed dyeing machines not only doubled productivity, they halved energy use, cut chemical use by 75 percent and cut water use by 80 percent. They also improved the local environment by reducing dyeing effluent by well over half.

The mostly silent chemist turned out to be Rene's son. The grandmotherly secretary who'd come in with a tea tray was, I later learned, Rene's wife. Since Rene's return, the plant had been running six days a week. A mechanic told me that he sometimes saw Rene up there at 6:30 A.M. on a Sunday, too. Perhaps his wife and son decided they'd have to work there themselves, if they hoped to see much of the old man.

Many Sunbeam and ex-Sunbeam people loved swapping Dunlap horror stories, but I knew I wouldn't hear any from Rene Boisvert. It wasn't in the company interest to say anything about their largest customer. Besides, Rene was not only too disciplined to vent his feelings, he was also too farsighted, after 45 years at the mill, to waste them on a passing CEO.

For 150 years, as he reminded a local reporter, the Biddeford workers had been "at the mercy of out-of-town corporate boards." In a speech to the local Rotary Club, Rene described the advantages of being independent at last.

"The topic for today's meeting" he began, "covers my most favorite subject—that of manufacturing blankets in the city of Biddeford, Maine." After listing the partners in the new corporation, he said: "This forms a rather unique group of owners who, for the moment, do not have to report to large corporate conglomerates whose operational procedures are based mainly on downsizing, plant-closings, mergers and acquisitions. Large companies who are strictly Wall Street–driven and who place the price of their company stock above all else."

So the problem wasn't anomalous CEOs like Al Dunlap, but typical investors like me.

In contrast to Wall Street-driven companies, "We . . . plan to remain market-driven," Rene explained to the Rotarians. "Our desire is to operate our business for the long term. Securing our jobs and our futures here in Maine requires us to quickly respond to global competition with innovation in the key areas of product development, product cost, and product quality."

Rene Boisvert was interested in making blankets in Biddeford. Shareholders like Price, demanding 20 percent returns NOW, could keep him from making the real investments necessary to keep the company competitive. But if Price was the problem, hadn't he also been the cure, in this case? After all, Michael Price forced Sunbeam into the restructuring that leaves Rene free today to make long-term investment decisions. There's only one hitch. Buying that freedom had cost ten million dollars.

I asked Rene how the workers had financed their part of the purchase and what sort of interest payments the new company now had to make.

"They sort of bought it as you do a house or a car," he explained. "They bought it with a down payment. The down payment came from their pension. That's the hard cash. The remaining money is borrowed from local banks. The cost of the interest is somewhere between eight and nine hundred thousand dollars a year."

Let me try to put that figure into perspective. In the balance of his talk to the Rotary Club, Rene described, in loving detail, how he'd invested $10,843,005 in modern equipment. That investment increased the output of blanket shells per employee, per year, from 5,000 to 15,000, yielding a payback of over $9,000,000 a year, which meant that the money was recouped in only 1.2 years.

That kind of modernization would produce roughly the same level of debt that the purchase from Sunbeam produced. But the acquisition loan didn't buy equipment or operating capital, so it can't be paid off quickly out of increased productivity. That's why workers were absorbing the costs for at least five years.

Rene may now be free from the obligation to unlock cash for Michael Price every time my mutual fund needs a shot in the arm. But the sale that gave Mutual Series a nice jolt of cash created a nonproductive debt that will limit Rene's ability to borrow for real investment. Interest of $800,000 to $900,000 a year is not an unusual or crippling burden for a company the size of Biddeford Textiles, but it's quite a handicap when it comes off the top like protection money. In the 1970's, a wave of leveraged buyouts created debts that doomed many otherwise viable US businesses.

Under Rene's management, Biddeford Textiles will survive, I predict, and may even be able to pay back the employees' pension money someday. But after most ESOP buyouts, workers continue taking lower salaries for a long time in order to pay off the acquisition debt. The same is usually true, by the way, for a buyout that doesn't involve employee ownership. Restructuring almost always means firing people and cutting wages because, regardless of who buys an existing company, the workers are usually elected to pay the debt. The kind of restructuring that my fund managers forced on Sunbeam is an economically nonproductive transfer of ownership that succeeds (when it does) because workers pay the financing costs.

That said, I believe the ESOP was the best option for the people of Biddeford. But why should it matter to anyone else? As long as Sunbeam continues to sell electric blankets, it's going to require mill workers to make the shells. If the blanket division had been moved, the work would still generate jobs and income somewhere. It's noble of Rene Boisvert to try to hold together a group that so many people described as "like my family." But since the work still has to be done, another family, it might be argued, would be formed, perhaps in Mississippi, or Mexico. Why should I prefer one family to another?

One reason, I suppose, is because I now know the Biddeford people. Another is that there may not be any recognizable new family formed at the new location. Outsourcing is designed to let companies like Sunbeam travel light. The advantage of limiting commitments isn't going to be lost on Sunbeam subcontractors who must themselves operate with short-term contracts in a rapidly changing world.

Sunbeam was only one of the many downsizing/outsourcing sweeps my fund had promoted since I became an investor. After the Chase restructuring, I ran into a data-entry clerk who was transferred from the bank's payroll to that of a contractor who now supplied her services to Chase. She worked at the same location and at first her hours were the same. Her greatest loss seemed to be the security of benefits. But eventually, as hours grew more "flexible" and people began to feel their tangential relationship not only to

Chase but also to their new employer, being outsourced seemed to distance her from people she'd worked next to for years.

Data entry is an isolating job to begin with. Clerks stare into a screen and pass work along, not to each other, but to the center. Still, there are lunch hours and coffee breaks. But somehow, after the restructuring, birthday cards and mutual favors at lunchtime started to disappear. Like many workers I met in Asia, these outsourced employees were making the reasonable, self-protective adjustments to a world in which so many employees are disposable temps.

On the positive side, temps aren't as likely to suffer heart palpitations or die when their employer shuts down. If there's no work family to begin with, there's no traumatic family breakup. Of course the same might be said about real families—the less the attachment, the less the separation. But some of us are old-fashioned enough to think that both kinds of families, in their deepest forms, are worth preserving anyway.

Portland, Tennessee

Six months after the Portland plant closed, I phoned some of the people I'd met there to see how they were getting along.

Cleta Ison was at church but I spoke to her husband. As a matter of fact, I couldn't help speaking to her husband. He told me, without my asking, that he had had a heart attack. "I'm one of those, they brought me back from the dead." He needed 16 different medicines, he said, including a very expensive blood thinner. "I'm out of it right now. Four of my medicines need to be re-filled and I can't afford it."

"Maybe your doctor could get you samples or something," I suggested. "Does he know you can't fill his prescriptions?"

Mr. Ison had worked most of his life as a tree-trimmer for a firm that sub-contracted to the telephone company. He liked it much better than factory work, but "No insurance, no retirement, all you had when you left was your last check. We relied on Cleta's insurance from Sunbeam."

"What does your doctor say?" I asked.

"He says I need my medicine. But needing is different than getting."

He tried to explain to me about the insurance that stopped after three months and the TennCare (state Medicaid) he'd been turned down from three times. The forms, the eligibility, the empty medicine bottles must have been running through his mind terrifyingly, for he couldn't stop talking about them. But I couldn't follow the details.

"A doctor wouldn't write prescriptions he knows can't be filled," I kept saying foolishly. "There must be some . . . I'll call back when Cleta's home."

Cleta explained their situation. She had been working at a local factory for five months through a temp agency. She had stuck with it, believing they would make her permanent at six months. But instead, they'd reduced her to four and now three days a week. So tomorrow she was going to apply at the factory where her daughter's mother-in-law worked. They were definitely taking on permanent people. She would have gone there earlier except that she'd already invested the time "working toward the insurance" at the first place. But if she got the job tomorrow, it would be only a few months before she'd be eligible for their health insurance.

Cleta was not a person to talk about her troubles, but when I dug a little, the medical situation sounded as frightening as her husband had suggested. They had at first bought the COBRA insurance, but when they could no longer afford over $400 a month, they switched to a plan that turned out not to cover drugs beyond $500 a year. "That's not the way they explained it to me at the meeting I went to."

Cleta, remember, was the woman who had handled the union's books so diligently even without a GED. Was she at a loss now because of a misleading sales pitch or because there simply were no good options? I had several for-profit health-care companies in my Mutual Shares portfolio. I hoped Cleta wasn't dealing with one of them.

Though her husband's doctor visits were paid for on the new plan, he'd used up the drug coverage in three months. But they had been turned down for state Medicaid because Cleta's salary, at $6.50 an hour, was too high. "They count it as forty hours, two hundred and sixty dollars a week, even if you don't get forty hours."

Apparently they did have prescriptions that they couldn't fill. "He's supposed to take his blood thinner twice a day," Cleta said.

When I asked what she was going to do, Cleta began talking about trees. They sometimes sold wood from the trees around their place. Unfortunately there were none at the right stage then. But she was reasonably confident about the job she'd apply for tomorrow. "My twenty years at Sunbeam should prove I can do something." If it didn't come through? "We have to take it day-by-day."

———

I spoke to one of Lynda Caudill's fellow welders. Mitzi was that single mother who'd found a new job even before the Sunbeam plant closed. But the health insurance hadn't kicked in yet when, in the same week, one child came down with strep throat and the other got a piece of hot lead through his eyelid in shop class.

"It went right through into his eyeball. I was out three, four hundred dollars," she told me. "I just had to borrow from Peter to pay Paul. I wouldn't have made it if some friends hadn't helped out with food."

Four hundred dollars sounded low, I said, for the eye and the strep throat.

"This may sound mean of me," Mitzi faltered, not sure whether to go on, "but I could only take them one time. They were supposed to go back for another visit but I just couldn't and they was getting better so . . ." I think she wanted absolution. It's the kind of decision a mother freezes remembering, even if she got away with it safely that time.

But there was one positive change in Mitzi's life. Her mother, a diabetic, who'd also worked at Sunbeam, had given up looking for a new job and moved in. Mitzi still didn't like having to be away in the evenings, but at least there was someone home with the children. Anyway, she hadn't lost the house (a new double-wide trailer), and she would become a permanent employee on the tenth, so "Things are getting themselves together."

It was a relief to talk to the Caudills. "I ache all over," Lynda said cheerfully. On her job at The Gap warehouse she lifted 30- to 70-pound boxes and swung them eight high onto a pallet. "You have to pass a hard written test to get on there, then the jobs are mostly no-brainers."

On the other hand, she'd never worked for any company that treated their people so well. If they needed an order quickly and the team managed to get it done, the supervisor might buy pizza for everyone and give them 20 minutes extra to eat it. One time when her group of newcomers broke the record by stacking 13,000 boxes in an eight-hour shift, the big bosses themselves cooked steaks for them on the outdoor grills. But the most important way that the company showed they valued their employees was by eschewing temps and giving medical insurance "from day one!"

Lynda was still on the lookout for a welding job. But she wasn't going to give up that health insurance until she or Wynn had another job that covered the whole family. Meanwhile, "Wynn is busy using the unemployment out. First time in his life he ever drew it." It felt good to talk to people who weren't desperate.

Though the union local was dissolved, the Caudills were still taking calls from former members. They sometimes woke Lynda up in the morning. "Been up worrying all night they sound like, waited 'til eight to call. But I get home from work at two now."

Many of Lynda's callers wanted to draw their retirement money in a lump sum. I had tried phoning the Sunbeam benefits office myself, and gotten a succinct no-longer-in-service message, so I knew why some of Lynda's morning callers would be panicky.

"Sometimes I can do something for them," she said, "sometimes I give 'em Buckley's number."

Two decades of restructuring had systematically reduced union membership to less than ten percent of the private labor force. As I recontacted people I'd met at the plant-closing meeting, I heard a couple of complaints that Jim Buckley never calls back now. But how can the thinly spread US union reps service their millions of ex-members?

―――――

Linda-Sue's beauty parlor wasn't doing well. "There's eight others in town now," she told me. As a last resort she'd taken to subletting a couple of chairs to would-be competitors just out of beauty school.

She had also leased her house and was living with her sister. In my callbacks I encountered a whole family—mother, two daughters, one brother, and one sister-in-law—who had all worked at Sunbeam. "So we couldn't borrow from each other. Too many eggs in one basket." As house and car payments came due and went unmet, some had moved in with others. Maybe the extended family is ultimately a better living arrangement. But people who had to move in with their relatives for financial reasons felt like failures at the time.

Linda-Sue's stay with her sister was definitely temporary, however. Her husband was almost finished fixing up an old house for them. It's a funny thing, but union activists are often the best workers. And people like Linda-Sue, with the energy to act for the group, are often the most personally resourceful, too. If Linda-Sue can't make a go of the beauty parlor, she'll find something else, I feel certain. She and her husband and child will land on their feet and in their own house. But that doesn't mean without a loss.

In the course of our conversation I mentioned that I'd called the number I'd been given for the Sunbeam benefits office and gotten that no-longer-in-service message.

"I know! I know!" she said with annoyance that covered guilt. "But I can't be making long-distance calls for everybody."

Linda-Sue was stretched too thin now to do for others. The Sunbeam shutdown means that for a while, at least, all her managing will be strictly for one small family. That's a big loss, I think.

—————

The shutdown had its success stories, too. When the plant-closing meeting broke up, a group that gathered around the guard shack talked about registering for the free high school diploma classes at the library. A number actually did enroll, and a few had already gotten their high school equivalency degrees.

When these people had started working, no one needed a diploma to get a factory job. Their new degrees would allow them to leave applications at some of the better factories, where they'd probably do the same sort of work they'd done at Sunbeam. So maybe that wasn't real advancement. But a couple of people I spoke to were genuinely enjoying the course. "I got married at sixteen," a woman told me "because I'd have to take algebra the next year. Now I discover I like math." That strikes me as progress.

Rosette Clarke liked to talk about the successes. She knew of a supervisor of 32 years who hadn't had a high school degree but was now taking college courses. A couple of women were taking computer courses and might soon be working in an office. "Not that there's anything wrong with a factory. You have to have people that work in a factory. But they're going to upgrade their skills and they're going to work in an office, which I think is great."

By then, Rosette seemed to feel that she'd done a favor to most of the people she'd fired. But not everyone was capable of seizing the opportunity.

"I know these people. I terminated them all. I guarantee you that if it re-opens, and manufacturing of some kind comes in here, there'll be a lot of folks that have gone to work elsewhere that will be tempted to put an appli-cation there just because of the feeling that it had of being where I've always been—home."

Rosette may be right. Whether such attachment was admirable or pa-thetic, there were a lot of ex-Sunbeam people still drawn out of their way to drive past the plant.

"You can go by and see some activity," a man said hopefully. "See some cars outside. Always a bunch of them in that office."

"Cars up there galore," said another. "They're not telling anybody any-thing."

A few still maintained that the plant-closing had simply been a trick. "I be-lieve all that was just to get rid of the union," one man declared. "They'll open with another name." That suspicion was fostered when the name on the closed plant was changed from Sunbeam to SunLite. But most of the fired workers understood that the plant had been sold.

"I seen Rosette Clarke outside weeding with a weed eater," one woman re-ported gleefully. "She told me, 'I put in for human resources once and didn't get it because I didn't have a college degree. But look at me now. I'm doing everything, plant manager and all.' I said, 'But Rosette, there ain't nobody there for you to manage.' There she is a weedin' in high heels to suck up to the new owners. I laughed all the way home."

Apparently the weeding worked. The new owners kept Rosette Clarke on while they completed their own consolidation. The plant-closing had not been a trick. The division sold for somewhere between 120 million dollars (according to a confusing Al Dunlap statement), and 84.5 million (according to the buyers). In either case, Sunbeam was out of the outdoor furniture business. The name-change from Sunbeam to SunLite may have sounded suspicious, but the actual owner, I learned from Rosette was now U.S. Industries.

That rang a bell. I checked my Mutual Shares annual report. U.S. Indus-tries was a holding in my portfolio. In fact, it was listed directly under Sunbeam in the Consumer Products section. That made the sale sound sus-piciously coincidental to me, too, for a moment. But they were, after all, two companies in the same line of business. Perhaps Michael Price facilitated the arrangement by mentioning one to the other. Why shouldn't he?

Once the Sunbeam furniture division had been downsized, Sunbeam could make money selling it, and U.S. Industries could make money running it.

"Although this division has not done well recently," the president of U.S. Industries said in a press release, "a restructuring begun last year will be completed at our direction in the initial year of ownership. We believe that our acquisition goal of a return on capital of 20 percent will be achieved within three years."

If so, the sale would be a good deal for both companies, creating double shareholder value for me. As long as everyone was working honestly to increase the shareholder's bottom line, there was nothing shady about it.

———

My callbacks to people in Portland were hardly systematic. Still, what I heard made statistical sense. Temporary or contingent jobs had been on the increase in the US for several decades. They'd gradually come to outnumber what I was used to thinking of as "regular" jobs. But US employment, overall, was going up. So it was predictable that the fired Sunbeam employees in Tennessee would find new jobs quickly, but as temporary workers with minimal benefits and security.

Since workers, including older employees, were frequently starting over, and entering salaries were low, people could no longer expect to move slowly up the income ladder in the course of their working lives. To keep their standards of living constant, or more simply, to hold on to the house and car, workers had to have other sources of income to tide them over. But 80 percent of Americans had less than a month's salary in the bank. So the desperation I encountered among fired Sunbeam workers was also statistically predictable.

Finally, as the secretary of labor, Robert Reich, had told the bankers at the Waldorf, US real wages had been going down for 20 years. Actually, they had started back up since I heard him speak. The turnaround was widely noted. The Federal Reserve Bank was poised to go into action against inflation if wages kept rising. But the much-publicized wage hike meant only that real wages had finally reached the level they'd been at in 1954. And Portland, Tennessee, brought the average down. So the fired Sunbeam workers were apt to be poor.

I used to think it was hypocritical, or at least inconsistent, when champions of traditional family values opposed unions and minimum-wage increases. After all, you can't maintain the traditional nuclear family—father out working; mother at home with the children—if one income won't feed and shelter that family. But when people get poor enough, the inconsistency disappears, for then they rediscover the extended family. That's even more traditional.

In Thailand and Malaysia I interviewed people who'd left traditional homes to work in the city or on one of my refinery construction projects. Often they were sent by their extended family to bring back cash for the communal establishment.

But Alfalfa and his wife lived apart from his parents. So did the young woman who worked, off and on, in Penang electronics plants so that her father could remain a traditional fisherman. Squirrel was originally sent to the city by and for her family, but she now had a life, if not a home, of her own.

When wages are high enough for long enough, people come to think of themselves in terms of their paid occupations: as a welder, for instance, or a Sunbeam employee. But in Portland, Tennessee, many were falling back onto (or crawling back into, as some felt) their extended families. When employment affiliations are insecure, the larger group can patch together a stable living from a variety of income sources. It's the poor man's way of diversifying his portfolio.

I distrust analogies and I try to stop myself from generalizing, especially when the patterns look too neat. Tennessee workers and Thai peasants weren't going up and down on opposite ends of the same seesaw, or exchanging places in a choreographed do-si-do. But as my bank pumped money into Thailand and my mutual fund extracted shareholder value out of Tennessee, one economy expanded and the other contracted. They hadn't yet leveled out into something that you could call a global village. You can't get green papaya salad in Portland. But as their economies converged from different directions, some things in Thailand and Tennessee started to feel similar—at least at that time.

Financial Follow-up

Waynesboro, Georgia, was the workforce that had underbid the Portland, Tennessee, work force by $2.20 an hour. Actually, the Georgia workforce, which consisted largely of former sharecroppers, hadn't actively bid. They'd simply stood by during an unexplained long layoff ready to come back at the same low wages whenever the plant reopened. But the state of Georgia and the county had bid for the furniture factory in the form of tax breaks. The county had also done $250,000 worth of earthmoving for a recently built Sunbeam warehouse. That was real money for a poor county in a region with 19 percent unemployment, but it was worth it to keep 575 jobs. Or at least it had seemed worth it to local officials while the plant was still operating.

But within a year, U.S. Industries moved what was left of the Sunbeam furniture division from Waynesboro, Georgia, to Paragold, Arkansas. Since there was no union, there was no need to bargain about severance pay. They simply shut down. U.S. Industries had already sold a small North Carolina resin outdoor furniture plant they'd acquired as part of the Sunbeam deal to U.S. Leisure, a subsidiary of a foreign-owned plastics company. Soon after the Paragold move, they sold the entire SunLite Casual Furniture line to the SunLite Acquisition Corporation, which they described as "a New York investment group."

I'm not sure exactly what that last restructuring was about, but I guess it was good business, because a while later, U.S. Industries' Board of Directors approved a $100 million share buyback. [For discussions of buybacks, see pages 88 and 277.] That meant that they were passing one hundred million dollars along to shareholders. How much of that windfall came from all the buying and selling of the former Sunbeam outdoor-furniture division would be hard to say.

But between the hundred million from U.S. Industries, the increased value of the Sunbeam shares since we'd installed Al Dunlap as CEO, and similar profitable deals, the $5,000 I'd invested in Mutual Shares had by then grown to more than $7,500.

FELLOW SHAREHOLDERS

Mutual-fund companies aren't required to hold annual shareholders' meetings, and generally they don't. But Michael Price had arranged to sell his Mutual Series manager's contract to a larger fund-managing company, Franklin Templeton, for 550 million dollars in cash plus contingent payments that could net him a couple of hundred million more down the line. Price was already listed among the 400 richest people in America, but even for him, half a billion of personal profit was a coup. The sale, however, required shareholder approval.

We, the Mutual Series shareholders who could make it on a weekday morning to Short Hills, New Jersey, were hardly the big investors with the crucial votes. But we weren't completely irrelevant either. Franklin wasn't buying anything from us; we didn't stand to make money from the sale. Nor were they buying any stock or even purchasing Price's services as a stock picker. He might or he might not stay on. What they were buying was his contract as our advisor. Under the contract, the advisor gets a percentage of each dollar he manages. But those fees could quickly evaporate if the people who left this meeting began phoning their friends to say, "Things are going to change. I think it's time to diversify."

Meeting Room, Business Hotel, Short Hills, New Jersey—9:00 A.M.
At the Chase annual meeting, most of the "shareholders" I'd tried to interview turned out to be employees, retirees, or protesters. But the Mutual

Series meeting was attended by bona fide investors, most elderly or middle-aged, who had enjoyed impressive returns through good stock market years and bad, and counted on Michael Price to see them comfortably through life.

"Did you select these funds yourself?" I asked a woman from Queens who'd been on trains since 7:00 A.M. to get there.

"I was just lucky," she answered. "I've been with Michael a long time." Like most of the other people in the room, she was there to pick up any clues about the funds' future. She was concerned that with the sale, Michael would abandon her.

In response to that anxiety, Price assured us that his own stock-picking team would remain in New Jersey following the value investment philosophy they'd learned from him. Only our financial statements would come out of Franklin's headquarters and Franklin would probably handle that more efficiently. Furthermore, we, the original Mutual Series investors, would enjoy, in perpetuity, the privilege of putting money into the funds or moving money between funds without paying the up-front fees that the Franklin newcomers would have to pay. But most important, he, Michael Price, was required by the terms of the sale to keep his own money in the funds. That, he assured us, was the ultimate guarantee that he would keep an eye on our money.

From the Franklin press release that I read later, it seemed to me that Michael was required to keep only one hundred million of his five hundred and fifty million in the funds, and that for only five years. But even if it were all his money, should that be enough incentive for a man to spend the rest of his life minding it?

If I asked you to invest in the production of a play that I wrote, you would be unwise to assume that our interests coincide simply because I, too, would be paid out of the net profits. My pleasure as a playwright comes in the actual writing, and my sense of power comes from seeing the audience laugh at just the moment I planned. So I might press the producer to hire more expensive actors or pay for longer rehearsals, regardless of the bottom line. And once the production was running, I'd probably let others handle the touring company, the foreign rights, et cetera, and move on to a new project.

Was it unreasonable to assume that having nurtured a small, quirky mutual fund into impressive adulthood, Michael Price was ready to take up a new challenge or simply enjoy leisure?

Worse than his abandoning us for other interests, what if Michael was selling the Mutual Series in obedience to the inflexible rule he'd always followed on our behalf—"buy cheap, sell dear"? When Price put his collection of ancient coins up for auction, a newspaper article wondered who would buy whatever Michael Price was selling, or sell whatever Michael Price was buying. If Price was selling mutual funds, perhaps we should assume that the market had peaked and get out with him.

But the Mutual Series investors, at least those at the meeting, seemed satisfied by his assurances that he and his money would remain involved. Besides:

"You're entitled to sell," one gentleman said. "If I had the chance, I would, too."

"Thank you," Michael answered. Long applause expressed the sentiment of the group. How different *this* Michael Price seemed from the thug who nearly knocked me over at the Chase meeting and later told a *Wall Street Journal* reporter that he sits up close at football games because he likes to hear bones crack. But of course, his job as our fund manager is to talk tough in public. Here, Michael was among appreciative friends.

At one point, a white-haired man came slowly to the front of the room.

"Michael has done well for the family," he quavered. "Since I got to be over eighty, I started to shake a bit so bear with me. To show our appreciation to Mike for the effort he's put forth on our behalf, something we have around the family." He offered up a Tiffany riding club trophy. It was dated 1903 and had belonged to Diamond Jim Brady. "I don't know how it got in the family," the old man said. "But Michael is interested in polo ponies . . . "

The only even slightly challenging query came from a shareholder who held up his copy of Al Dunlap's *Mean Business* and asked Michael if he'd seen it.

Michael answered that he had. "Al sent us the copies—autographed."

The shareholder said that he and his brother had almost all the family's assets in the Mutual Series. He wanted to know whether we were considering adopting Al's precept of paying our board entirely in shares and options, thus aligning their interests more closely with ours. The man was particularly disturbed to notice that two of the new board members owned no shares at all.

Michael assured him that they would become investors, probably in one of our new funds. (We were starting a European fund.)

Whatever criticism of Al Dunlap Michael Price had implied in the head-tilt and eye-roll he made when he referred to Al's autographed gifts, Michael assured us that Sunbeam's new management was going to "sell assets, close plants, and pull production together." Our millions of Sunbeam shares were already up to 24, "and we think it should be at the midthirties to upper-thirties."

People would like to have gone on listening to Michael, but he was anxious to introduce the young men who would soon be taking over the day-to-day stock picking. It was important that shareholders have confidence in them.

Before Michael could turn over the microphone, an investor near me reminded him that he usually gave them an idea or two at these meetings. Michael Price never uttered a sentence without giving me an idea or two. But "idea" had a special meaning in this context. Michael put the man off, promising us all an idea later. Meanwhile:

"I would like you guys to hear from these guys. Maybe *they'll* give us some ideas. These guys work hard," he assured us. "It's difficult to realize that underneath are people actually creating the value."

I'd been thinking the same thing. It was difficult to realize, at a meeting like this, that underneath are people actually creating the barbecue grills, electric blankets, and ground-to-air missiles whose sales allowed many in that room to live without working. Michael was not, however, about to introduce the engineers, foremen, and welders who make our companies' products. To him, value, meaning shareholder value, was created by the team of young men that came up with what I was learning to call "ideas."

"The group we've put together has the ability to put a lot of money to use," Price said proudly.

One of the idea men whom he introduced was our railroad expert David Winters.

"He's cute," said a woman behind me. "Adorable," her neighbor agreed, and so did I.

David, a curly-haired kid with cherubic cheeks and a wide, almost goofy smile, told us about the British railroads he'd recently bought for us. When he'd heard that they were being privatized, he'd rushed over to London to examine the offering and had made a successful bid. Then he opened the package and discovered treasures that the British government had no idea were in there. "There's all kind of hidden stuff there," David enthused, "and they were basically giving it away."

On another occasion, I got a chance to ask David exactly what treasure he'd found in our British Railroads surprise package. It was land!

"Lots of land along the railroad lines, undeveloped but valuable, in almost every town in England." It wasn't, of course, as extensive as the land grants that the US government had given to the old-time robber barons, but it was enough, according to David, to make the British Railroads the largest real-estate interest in the United Kingdom: "Prime commercial land downtown and the stations themselves."

The sale of the railroads had been organized and rushed through by the British Conservative Party as it was leaving office. There was so much protest that the Labour Party had threatened to renationalize the railroads when they came in. That, to David's great glee, drove the price down. But we got to keep the railroads we bought, along with all the extra goodies in the box. A deal is a deal. Furthermore, you only had to put up half the money, David told me. "So the British Government essentially lent us the other half at no interest for a year."

I asked David how he became involved in all this.

He'd always been a railroad buff, he told me. As a kid he heard that Max Jacobs, then in the firm, had shares in a bankrupt historic railroad. David phoned to ask if he could buy some shares.

"Max said, 'Sure, how many do you want?' I asked could I buy five. 'Sure.' Gradually I became a customer."

Max continued to encourage little David over the years. Eventually (time passes) someone in the office needed an assistant and Max suggested that he hire David. That's how it all began.

———

Another team member with ideas was Rob Friedman. Rob had moved to London on our behalf three of four months earlier and was excited about getting in on the ground floor of European restructuring. Europe was an entire continent of 350 million people, he reminded us, and restructuring was just beginning!

The place where he was spending a surprising amount of time, he told us, was Sweden. We (the Mutual Series Funds) had taken a substantial position in a Swedish holding company that owned 40 percent, by value, of the shares on the Swedish stock market. That gave us interests in many of the electronics and manufacturing companies that exported, worldwide, from this nation of less than nine million.

After the meeting, Rob Friedman and I chatted about our mutual love of Stockholm. "Sweden is the most advanced country in Europe," he told me (Is he a secret Socialist? I wondered), "and they really speak our language."

"They certainly do speak beautiful English," I answered.

"I mean," he said "they speak the language of business." And he reeled off some of the tax advantages investors enjoy in Sweden. I think he was prepared for me to be surprised. After all, in the 1950's, Americans were frequently reminded about the "90-percent taxes" in socialist Sweden.

I wasn't surprised, however, because I knew a bit about 20th-century Swedish history.

A few years after the Russian revolution, the Social Democratic party came to dominate the government in that miserably poor, cold country. With the frightening example of Bolshevik Russia next door, Sweden's near-feudal privileged classes accepted the Socialist electoral victories peacefully. Once elected, the Social Democrats fostered the growth of Sweden's private industrial corporations, including many of the giants that my mutual fund was now invested in. It was largely through the wealth of these private companies, distributed as wages and generous benefits, that Swedes raised their living standards.

In other words, Swedish socialism is capitalism in a country where powerful unions and an accountable government oversee the transfer of wealth, not as welfare for the poor and unemployed, but through full employment at good wages and through public services available to all.

As part of that strategy, Swedish firms had high wage and benefit costs but low taxes on profits. The goal was to have them reinvest. The infamous

90-percent taxes were on money that left company treasuries in forms like high salaries, bonuses, or as large dispersements to individual shareholders.

The hundred million that Al Dunlap got for the Scott paper company turnaround would have been prohibitively taxed in Sweden. But as long as money was kept in the business, and salary ranges stayed narrow—executives getting no more than, say, five or six times the pay of an average worker—Swedish taxes were not confiscatory.

The system was sustained by an egalitarian ethic and the uniquely Swedish virtue called *lagom*, which translates roughly as "moderation" or "only what you need." As a matter of lagom, Sweden's well-organized unions (they currently represent 90 percent of workers, including white-collar workers) bargained nationwide, by industrial sector, for what they called the solidarity wage. To keep their firms internationally competitive, workers in particularly profitable companies didn't ask for higher wages, but the weak or inefficient firms in an industry were not allowed union dispensations to lower wages, which is to say, workers were not permitted to subsidize their own employers. If a company couldn't afford its industry's solidarity wage, the Socialists let them go out of business.

Swedish capitalists, meantime, seemed content to follow these rules. They could run their companies, but not raid them.

This understanding began to break down in the 1970's when economic growth slowed in all the Western countries. At that point, Swedish management was not above (or below) using the Euromoney pioneered by Walter Wriston, et al. [see page 28] to transfer jobs and corporate capital abroad.

Today the Swedish government is under pressure from people like the bankers we met at the Waldorf to "liberalize," or be more flexible about how capital can be moved. That, after all, is the direction that the countries of the new European Economic Community were moving in together. Despite the pressures, Swedish workers still manage to keep a bigger share than American workers.

Now Rob Friedman and Michael Price were working on ways to channel some of the capital in Swedish companies over to me. But I've met quite a few Swedish workers who consider it *national* capital, that is, *their* capital in some way. After all, they voluntarily left it in the big firms by refraining from taking more than the "solidarity wage" in good years. Even if I don't agree that it belongs to them, how can I explain that it now belongs to me, and that Rob Friedman means to extract it?

I didn't say all this to Rob at the time. I believe what I said was more like "Oh, really. Well, I just love Sweden." And I recommended an expensive Stockholm restaurant that serves traditional Swedish food. To be honest, I'd only dined at the restaurant's "bak fikan" (back pocket), a less expensive annex down the block. But I didn't mention that, and I certainly wasn't going to tell Rob that at lunchtime the annex served simple meals that employees could buy with the meal coupons that many employers issued as a benefit.

Personally, I'd prefer coupons to a subsidized company cafeteria because I'd get to choose where I ate. Competition improves quality, right? Now that I think of it, subsidized choice is the democratic socialist counterpart of the expense-account lunch. I know there's no such thing as a free lunch, but there can be a *shared* lunch. And in Sweden, where almost everyone worked, employee benefits were a favored way of sharing.

But what will become of the socialist lunch if Rob and Michael decide, on my behalf, that Sweden's excess corporate capital should be converted from meal coupons to shareholder value? Is it possible that European restructuring could eventually reduce Scandinavians to the insecurity of workers in Georgia and Tennessee?

––––––

After the investors' meeting broke up, I spent some time talking to a trim man with pure (prematurely?) white hair. His wife and his father-in-law were math professors. One child in his wife's family, her brother, had been brain-damaged at birth. The white-haired man was there on behalf of the whole family, but he was particularly concerned about his brother-in-law's IRA.

"The family invested heavily in his education," he told me with admiration. As a result, the brain-damaged man was able to work and put money into a retirement account.

"He worked sorting and delivering the mail for twenty years at Hoffmann-La Roche [a drug company]. When they had a promotion available for someone to deliver to the different plants by car, he worked determinedly with special help to get a driver's license. Then, in 1985, Hoffmann-La Roche had a restructuring—a bloodbath."

"But isn't that what Michael and that man in London who's buying us Swedish companies are talking about?" I objected.

"Oh, we don't . . . "

"You think there are any retarded mail sorters left at Chase?" I demanded. "Or there'll be any in Sweden when we get finished?"

"I like to think we take over things in worse condition," he answered. "When they're already not functioning. I don't think it's about firing people."

"What about Sunbeam?" I probably snarled it with an implied "Oh, yeah?" But the truth is that I admired this man's family and the care they'd taken to make a disabled child independent. There were surely many admirable people at the meeting. Mutual-fund investors aren't predators.

I calmed down, and the man told me about his brother-in-law's present job. "He cares for animals now. They even give him the key to lock up."

Aside from being decent, the white-haired man wasn't necessarily wrong about our investments. A restructuring doesn't have to be about firing people and pocketing their salaries. It could be about making a nonfunctioning company work. After all, Price originally bought Sunbeam shares as part of a bankruptcy. And the subtitle of Al Dunlap's book is "How I Save Bad Companies and Make Good Companies Great."

In the right circumstances, financial restructuring may promote growth. Mergers can help a company acquire new facilities and personnel quickly: the spinoff of one division can provide cash for the rapid expansion of another division: even a pure downsizing, in some economic climates, puts money into the hands of investors who use it to finance growth in other enterprises.

But none of those benefits seemed to be coming out of the Sunbeam or Chase restructurings. Our paper profits from those deals were high, but the clamor for our Chase and Sunbeam shares seemed to be based solely on the fact that those companies had fired a lot of people. And it was difficult for Michael and his young men to find other undervalued American companies in which to invest the returns if we sold the shares.

Ideas, I realized—places to invest—were scarce and precious. That's why Citibank and Chase fought for the right to send dollars into Asia, free of capital controls. At both banks, the people who gathered money were far less prestigious than the people who found uses for it. And at this meeting, Michael Price praised his team for their "ability to put a lot of money to use."

From the day I entered the Chase trading room and returned home on the subway, I'd been moving rapidly back and forth from a financial world where there's plenty of money but not enough to do with it, to the real world where that relationship is almost always reversed. No wonder I've been feeling so disoriented.

—*Wall Street Journal*, October 20, 1998

Suddenly Al Dunlap was fired and Peter Langerman, Michael Price's protégé at my mutual fund, replaced Dunlap as temporary Sunbeam CEO. Sunbeam's share price, which had hit 53 at the height of the Dunlap era, dropped precipitously in the days preceding his ouster, and finally stabilized after his departure at around 5. As I write, Dunlap is suing for 5.5 million dollars of severance money that the new Sunbeam board of directors refuses to pay. Meanwhile, shareholder groups have initiated their own suits on various grounds.

A few headlines may suggest how the story unfolded:

"Sunbeam Acquires Three Publicly Traded Consumer Products Companies: Coleman [stoves], Signature Brands [Mr. Coffee], and First Alert [smoke detectors]" (Sunbeam press release, March 2); "Ace Hardware Announces They Will Not Order Any More Sunbeam Grills Because of Defects" (CBS Radio, March 22); "A Big Sales Gain for Sunbeam Proves Costly to Investors" (the *New York Times*, May 7); "Did 'Chainsaw Al' Dunlap Manufacture Sunbeam's Earnings Last Year?" (*Barron's*, June 8); "Sunbeam Corporation Denies False Accusations in *Barron's* Article" (Sunbeam press release, June 8); "Sunbeam's Board in Revolt Ousts Job-Cutting Chairman" (the *New York Times*, June 16); "Sunbeam's Accounting Is Investigated by SEC" (the *Wall Street Journal*, June 22); "...And Take the Chainsaw with You!" (*Barron's*, June 22).

A lot of information is unavailable because of pending lawsuits, but I piece the story together this way. Al Dunlap tried to sell Sunbeam—the core company, all that hadn't already been sold off—just as he'd sold other turned-around companies, but there were no takers.

The company that was left after Dunlap's restructuring couldn't bring in the returns he'd promised, so he tried to delay the reckoning by buying businesses that would either yield profits and/or permit another round of spectacular downsizing. But it takes money to make money. In order to get the mergers and acquisition loans needed to buy other companies, Dunlap had to show his banks that Sunbeam would have cash coming in to pay them back.

So the company announced what it called its "early buy" program. Retailers who usually order barbecue grills in the spring were encouraged by unusual credit terms to order $50 million worth of grills in December. They didn't have to pay for the grills until June, they didn't have to take delivery until they needed them, and they could return whatever wasn't sold.

With those December orders on the books, Dunlap could show Sunbeam's banks remarkable sales growth in the last quarter of the year—the very quarter in which he'd implemented the restructuring. The generous sales terms were surprising, especially from a cost-cutter who had promised to rationalize Sunbeam's credit policies. Still, the scheme was legitimate up to that point.

In addition to offering good terms, Sunbeam also offered to pay storage fees to some of the retailers for holding the "early buy" grills. That may be legitimate, too. But some customers were apparently paid for storing grills that never left Sunbeam warehouses. Maybe that was due to errors because of the big staff cuts at Sunbeam, but it looked like retailers were being paid simply to place orders—orders they could later rescind. If that wasn't deceptive, it was certainly desperate.

As it turned out, Sunbeam reaped neither a jump in sales nor even the normal sales, because many of the barbecue grills turned out to be defective.

The first time I heard officially about defective grills was when Ace Hardware, a buyer's cooperative for local hardware stores, refused to order any more. But I'd already picked up gossip.

The Neosho, Missouri, plant, which in previous years sent out about 250 million dollars' worth of outdoor cooking products, had had its D-day landing like the one in Portland, Tennessee. But since this plant wasn't being sold, workers were surprised that the managers who were summarily fired included the kind of seven-day-a-week Stakhanovites that Dunlap presumably wanted to keep at Sunbeam. The executive in charge of shipping was one of those hard workers so dismissed.

With the plant so shorthanded, there were complaints about pressures and errors. Neosho is the factory where, according to Rosette Clarke, a woman collapsed in the bathroom from overwork and stress.

Of course, after any shakeup, some workers will say that the best people were fired, the quality will suffer, and their department will never recover. However, in the Sunbeam case we can surmise, not only from the complaints but from the outcome, that the restructuring plan gave almost as little consideration to running these factories in the future as it gave to minimizing pain for the employees who ran them in the past. As far as I can tell, Dunlap did worse than just slap on a hasty coat of paint to cover flaws. He also used his chainsaw to add new structural damage. Then, when he couldn't sell the company, he couldn't run it.

———

I phoned Andrew Shore of Paine Webber, one of the stock analysts who'd questioned Al Dunlap during his restructuring teleconference. [See pages 204–206.] I wanted to know what Andrew thought happened at Sunbeam. I began by suggesting timidly that the turnaround had been perhaps "too facile, I mean . . . "

"It was a joke! That's all," he cut me off. "It was a joke."

I mentioned that I'd followed events at a couple of Sunbeam plants. "They were actually turning out barbecue grills in the grill plant but . . . "

"Well, they produced enough grills for every man, child, baby and animal on this planet. That's the problem, not that they weren't producing grills. They just had no clue."

"As to whether they could sell them?" I asked.

"They didn't care about selling them. They just cared about shoving them all out to the retailers, making their numbers look good, and getting the highest price selling this company and moving on. But they couldn't find a buyer and everything they did came back and haunted them."

That was more or less my own conclusion. What I wanted to know from an analyst who'd followed previous turnarounds was why Dunlap's formula hadn't worked this time. "Was it because his reputation was bad from previous sales," I suggested, "or because his reputation was so good that it drove the stock up too high? Or maybe ... "

"It was both."

Actually, I was most interested in my third alternative, that Sunbeam had already been downsized and restructured beyond any further squeezing. "Even if Dunlap had been perfectly honest," I suggested, "maybe his *Mean Business* rules wouldn't have worked this time because there wasn't a big headquarters to sell, there wasn't a lot of excess staff. With his other turnarounds ... "

"They were *all* a joke," Shore dismissed my gropings in that direction.

So I congratulated him on getting his company out of Sunbeam before the shares tumbled, and asked how he'd known.

"'Cause any man that goes to an analysts' presentation and wears sunglasses is a man who's afraid to have us look in his eyes."

I'd read that after one of those analysts' presentations Dunlap had screamed abusively at Andrew Shore, who had been asking the same sort of questions he'd asked at the teleconference. I asked Andrew what Al had actually said. "It's not the kind of story I'm writing, but ... "

"He said, 'You son of a bitch, if you want to come after me I'll come after you twice as hard.'"

"And other people heard that?"

"Yup."

I wondered out loud why anyone had ever believed in Al Dunlap, and why my own mutual fund held on to their shares.

"Because he's a very persuasive speaker."

"Really? I guess I heard him saying too many different things to different audiences."

"Anyway, when the final book is written, we'll find out how bad he was."

"When will the suits ... ?"

"I don't know. I have no idea when the lawsuits will be settled. I don't even follow Sunbeam anymore," Shore said. I let a busy man get off the phone.

There's more than one way to restructure a company. In a sweet, idiosyncratic business memoir called *On a Roll,* Howard Jonas narrates the ups and downs of IDT, the internet and discount telecommunications firm he founded. During one of the downs, which he responsibly attributes to his own unwise ideas for expansion, Jonas oversaw large-scale firings and reorganization.

Though entire products and their divisions were eliminated, he tried not to lay off whole departments.

> The fact that one person might be in a profitable telecom division while another was in a money-losing group was only because, on the basis of their particular talents and our particular needs, we, the management, assigned them to one group or the other. For us to penalize the workers for trusting our decision making and doing their best job wherever they were assigned, would have been both foolish and wrong.

So rather than letting everyone in a dead division go, he kept and fired individually throughout the company, letting the remaining staff know that they were the chosen.

Jonas's goal was to keep the business, and as much as possible of its precious workforce, intact, independent, and ready to regrow. Unlike Al Dunlap, he'd built the company and intended to continue running it. So of course he wanted to leave a functioning enterprise. He also had personal and religious beliefs—Jonas is an orthodox Jew—which influenced his sense of responsibility to his staff. In writing about his own downsizing decisions, Jonas digresses to describe another type of downsizer:

> Recently, in America, a new kind of financial hero has been getting some good press: the turnaround artist. The hired gun goes into an older, faltering company and just starts firing. The marketing and advertising department, bang. Corporate jets and country clubs, bang, bang, bang. Middle management, bang. Senior management, bang.
>
> By the time he's finished nobody but a few Joes on the assembly line, wearing earplugs to block out the shooting, are left standing. The company is profitable. (Of course it probably has no long-range viability other than to be merged

into a real organization, but that's another story.) The stock price soars and the hero is interviewed for the cover of *Business Week*.

"Well," he says, "it was a hard job letting all those people go. Really hard, but someone had to do it. Someone had to save the jobs for everyone else. It was rough. It was horrible. I'm so emotionally drained I need to take off six months (and write a book about it) before my next turnaround."

Despite Al Dunlap's one-hundred-million-dollar package at Scott Paper, he remains, to use Howard Jonas's phrase, a hired gun. At Sunbeam he was hired by my mutual fund to do the second kind of turnaround. It was a job he'd done often enough before that he could practically write the final report in advance.

As a matter of fact, sometime between the publication of his book in hardcover (slightly before he took the Sunbeam job) and its appearance in paperback (after the restructuring was implemented but before he was fired), Dunlap wrote a new chapter on his latest success.

"Sunbeam was a fun turnaround," he wrote, "because every place you looked there was something to do." Here's the full description of his success with barbecue grills:

"We sent our own version of SWAT teams from our South Florida headquarters into each of our major facilities to ensure that customer orders were processed and shipped on time and that manufacturing schedules assured production of the right inventories. Our logistics director, Bill Bloomfield, did a wonderful job of lining up trucks so that the order commitments were met. Rich Goudis led the team that went into Neosho, the small Missouri town where we manufacture our grills. It was the middle of the grill season for manufacturers, so we knew it was the one business we could certainly drive. Retailers were stocking up. It was important that their stores and warehouses were full.

Neosho is a small town and Goudis even arranged to have the local police force guide our trucks through town because there were so many of them. This went on for more than a week, captivating the entire community. It worked. Sales and logistics not only met the goals they were committed to, but exceeded them. It was a tremendous team building effort."

Dunlap's epic continues from victory to victory until:

Now you know how we turned Sunbeam around. What were the results?

A company that had fallen short of its financial forecasts for eighteen straight months finally exceeded its forecast in our first quarter at the helm, after we completed the restructuring. . . . [This was the quarter that included the December early-buy orders.]

And from the final page of the Sunbeam chapter:

Naturally these improvements did not occur in a vacuum. We were subjected to the same choir of criticism, the same incoherent and wrongheaded analysis by certain segments of the business press, politicians, academicians, consultants and a new flock of ex-employees who said our plans wouldn't work—then took posthumous credit when they did.

. . . During the same period in which we fixed Sunbeam, several other high-profile companies couldn't repair a leak in the board-room ceiling. . . .

We took a company that was an absolute basket case and restructured it in seven months. Maybe someone should buy copies of this book for all the CEOs and boards of directors out there with three-year restructuring plans. *Mean Business* is still the cheapest, most effective, time-tested method there is.

The semifictional Sunbeam restructuring that Dunlap described in his new chapter is the one my mutual fund hired him to do. "In fact," he writes in *Mean Business*, "Michael Price can be credited with convincing me to take the top job at Sunbeam. He is, today, one of the most influential people on Wall Street. He singlehandedly forced the merger of Chase Manhattan and Chemical Bank . . . and created $500 million worth of value for the investors in his funds."

Had he succeeded, Dunlap would merely have dismantled Sunbeam, leaving behind fewer jobs, greater insecurity, less manufacturing capacity, reduced output, and more money for me and other Mutual Series investors. That would have been painful to the people I met in Tennessee and to many in places I didn't visit. But if Sunbeam profits had been declining because the firm was run inefficiently, and/or because the world had more small-appliance manufacturing capacity than it needed, then a successful Dunlaping might be considered, if not constructive, at least in obedience to the laws of the market.

But Dunlap failed, and while floundering to make things look okay, he bought three smaller companies (Coleman, First Alert, and the maker of Mr. Coffee) and began restructuring them. The result was more job loss, more insecurity, and contraction at firms that had no serious problem, at the time, selling their output. He also moved some manufacturing to Mexico, but the operation was so hastily put together that it was moved back. That surely meant additional disruption and insecurity, this time in two countries.

But Dunlap wasn't fired for what he did to people or production; he was fired because he didn't do his job for me. For a time Sunbeam stock soared, but in the end my mutual fund lost so much on Sunbeam that our total return was less than half a percent during a bull market. Not that I'm complaining. A year later we were far ahead again. But during the year of the Sunbeam fiasco, I would have been better off keeping that money in the Bank of Millbrook.

Quite a few other people we met would also have been better off if money that Michael Price invested sat quietly, instead, in the bank. But money, as we've seen, can't just sit. And if the Bank of Millbrook couldn't find local loans for its depositors' millions, what could it possibly find to do with the billions in Price's mutual funds? The Whalens would have to have passed a lot more on to Chase as Federal funds, or perhaps become another Chase themselves. But someone would have to have found a profitmaking use for the money.

I should have been used to large numbers by then. Still, it startled me to remember that Michael Price and his tiny team in New Jersey had more money to invest than many banks did. And there were private investment funds, hedge funds like those run by George Soros (whom I would soon run into), that required minimum investments of $250,000 to ten million dollars. Some funds manage more money than the treasuries of many nations, more than the gross domestic products of quite a few.

All that money was a constant pressure on Price and other fund managers. I mentioned before that there were more than 7,000 mutual funds in the US. That means there were more funds investing than there were companies on the New York Stock Exchange to invest in. The cash in those funds bid up share prices until market capitalization, the number of shares times the price per share, of US corporations was far beyond the underlying value of the companies' assets.

Price's value approach kept him away from the most inflated shares. That presumably meant that if the ballooning stock market deflated, his holdings would go down less. That's one reason that so many investors left some of their money in the Mutual Series even in its occasional bad years. But it was getting as hard for Price to find good stock buys in the US as it was for the Bank of Millbrook to find safe loans on "Main Street."

Maybe that's why Price tried to squeeze Sunbeam a third time. Maybe that's why he was willing to go with a CEO as extreme as Al Dunlap. And, as I still suspect, maybe that's why the *Mean Business* formula didn't work, at least not so automatically that Al Dunlap could restructure Sunbeam between stops on his book tour.

At that point in US financial history, there were few established firms left that hadn't already fired people, cut back production, lowered wages, sold assets, merged, or in other ways downsized. Perhaps the botched Sunbeam restructuring represented the end of a trend. But it was far from the end for my mutual fund. We may have been running out of easy domestic targets, but there was still one wealthy, yet-to-be-tapped continent, where many employees were well paid and reasonably secure, and where company managers sat on cushions of assets that had been piled up over generations.

When Chase couldn't find good commercial loans to make in the US, it expanded into Latin America and Asia. When Price couldn't find enough value to unlock at home, he expanded into Europe. The last Mutual Series event I attended was a press conference and luncheon to introduce the new Mutual European Fund.

By the self-imposed rules of my money odyssey, I had to follow the trail wherever it led. Yet I wanted to illustrate the typical effects of a mutual-fund investment. Could I really do that starting with the atypically aggressive Michael Price?

All stock pickers try to buy cheap and sell dear. They could do so, at the time, by capturing the windfalls from US restructuring—*if* they picked right. But only a few attempted to eliminate the "if" by buying as little as five per-cent of the shares in a company like Chase Manhattan, then publicly challenging the management to restructure. That's why Price was known as the David who took on Goliaths.

But Michael Price couldn't have made money for his investors if the shares of the companies he forced to restructure hadn't quickly gone up. That meant that other, less aggressive investors agreed that downsizing was the surest way to profits for those firms, and rushed in to buy those shares.

Price's periodic challenges may have gotten publicity, but ongoing pressure for downsizing was exerted by ordinary investors whenever they sold the stocks of companies netting a steady profit from their ongoing business to buy the stocks of companies that fired people. Furthermore, many fund managers, including those representing union pension plans, privately made the same kind of downsizing demands on corporate boards and CEOs that Price made publicly.

After his success with Chase, Michael Price told a *Wall Street Journal* reporter that he sits up close at football games because he likes to hear bones crack. I choose to believe that most investors don't enjoy hearing bones crack. But if the companies they're invested in can't seem to increase profits by doing more business, then lowering wages and firing people is the next obvious plan. That is, of course, a self-limiting strategy for any economy. Eventually there would be no one left to fire and no one left to buy. But some time before the field is completely grazed down, some of the herd will start a move to other pastures.

A while after the Sunbeam fiasco, Mutual Series called a press conference to introduce its new European fund. I hadn't expected such a turnout for the launching of one more mutual fund. But in a way, this press conference, without Michael Price, would introduce the team that had taken over the day-to-day management of the whole Mutual Series. I suppose the financial press wanted to see whether the young Turks would prove as aggressive as their mentor.

The reporters would also be looking for the next trend. Starting from practically nothing five years earlier, Mutual Series now had almost ten billion of its 33 billion dollars invested in Europe. Now it had created an *all*-European fund. It's true that there were laws and unions in Europe that made downsizing costly. Still, if that's the way Michael Price was going, Europe could be the next America.

If the failed downsizing at Sunbeam and the launch of the European Fund signaled that the restructuring trend was petering out in the US, then perhaps American workers could feel more secure. But for me personally, as I learned from one of the speakers, Price's move to Europe brought restructuring closer to home.

Manhattan hotel meeting room: muted conversation of reporters and hosts mingling before a press conference
"Oh, you're from 'XYZ.' " The woman at the door checked her list and identified my corporate affiliation. I hadn't exactly lied my way into the press conference, but I used my husband's fax address at work to get the information and I didn't correct the assumption that I worked for his firm, a trade-magazine publisher.

"They just went public," one of the young Mutual managers said, hearing the company's name. (They know my husband's company?) "Didn't the stock go down to thirteen?" Yikes, these guys keep their eyes on everything.

"They make a lot of profit," a second manager said, "plow it back."

"But the stock's still ninety-percent family controlled," the first manager explained the barrier to buying a stake in the enticing little company with spare cash. "And the public shares are nonvoting."

"How are they doing?" They both turned to me, hungrily.

"Well, the founders' son took over and . . . " What should I tell them? That he brought in his old school friends to play Rupert Murdoch? I don't want to talk the stock down. They just gave us 100 shares. But if I say "Doing great, selling ads hand over fist," one of these guys might get an "idea."

". . . the company still has a day-care center," I finally answered. And I began babbling about the adorable toddlers that run around the office. That turned them off.

"My name is Peter Langerman. We've invited you all so we can tell you basically what we're doing in Europe."

Langerman is the Mutual man that took over at Sunbeam when we fired Al Dunlap. He announced that we would hear from Rob Friedman (the man who liked Stockholm), David Marcus, and David Winters (the railroad enthusiast), all of whom were now spending almost half their time in Europe. Then there would be time to talk to them over lunch.

All three stock pickers explained, using different examples, how Mutual Series had in the past unlocked the shareholder value in US companies. "Our bread and butter has been breakup value," as Rob Friedman put it. Friedman cited Sears Roebuck. (None of the three chose Sunbeam as an example.)

Now "it's going to happen even more aggressively in Europe," Rob assured us. And Mutual Series had gotten there early.

David Marcus emphasized that Europe was "a fresh market, a new market." That's why we were able to spot values that local investors couldn't see, like the Swedish holding company, Investor, AB. A holding company is an entity whose entire business is holding shares in other companies. Investor, with its large stakes in Ericsson, Saab, Scania, SAS, et cetera, controlled 40 percent of the Swedish stock market. Yet its own stock, when David Marcus discovered it, was selling at 30 to 40 percent below what the team had calculated as the value of those underlying companies. That was because European investors hadn't, at that point, grasped the changed environment that would permit the extraction of more shareholder value from Swedish industry. "Today it's up a hundred and twenty-five percent."

Marcus also talked about our successes with a couple of French water companies that were restructuring. But he warned that you had to be careful in that bureaucratic and union-ridden country. "In France people have learned what the Americans want to hear, the buzzwords: shareholder value, buybacks. They know all the secret words that get people excited."

That's why Marcus and the other members of the Mutual Series team had to "get over there and actually hear them say it and look them in the eye and see if we believe. . . . Because too many companies just say it, they don't do it. We want to buy the companies that are cheap, that say it and do it." ("Do it to whom?" I wrote grammatically in my notebook.)

———

"I'm a big railroad investor," said David Winters, and he described past successes. "In the US there's been a whole series of deregulations and consolidations . . . and railroads have been a fabulous place to make money. . . . And then it happened in Canada. When they privatized Canadian National Railroads we bought a big stake and that worked out." Finally he talked about the privatization of British railroads.

"I went over there before the prospectus came out and the Labour Party, which was the party out of power, basically said, 'We're gonna renationalize this and we're gonna kill anybody, basically, who buys this stock.' . . . So all the local investors were scared about this stock. When the prospectus came out, buried on page 250 was a little note in the smallest lettering possible that said that they had transferred all the real estate to the company for zero. And the company is basically the largest real-estate owner in the UK. . . . So you had, basically, the largest real-estate company and new management which was going to come and do good things. And you had a stock price that was— basically you had a government that was a forced seller—and a stock price that was depressed by basically spooked local investors.

"And we came in and we bought the largest stake in the company and the thing that was really neat about it too, they did it in such a way where . . . for a year they essentially loaned us the money for free.

"So our average cost of the stock is probably about four pounds and it trades over ten pounds today. It's clearly not as good of a discount [now] as it was [when we bought it], but there's still a lot more to go."

―――――

I'd learned a bit more about the British privatization since I first heard David describe his coup at the Mutual shareholders' meeting. [See page 257.] The privatization that occurred hastily at the end of the Conservative Party's term in office had been sufficiently controversial that Labour Prime Minister Tony Blair, halted further sales of the British Railroads on the day he took office. But the gesture was primarily symbolic. The railroads had already been sold in some hundred jumbled lots separating contiguous lines, awarding tracks and rolling stock to different bidders, etc.

David may have snagged the largest piece of a lot that included the valuable land along the rail tracks, but local investors had not been entirely scared off. Scandal after scandal erupted over windfalls reaped by well-placed British "investors" who acquired their bit of the railroad for almost nothing down and held it only long enough to turn the ownership over at huge profits.

Popular resentment was also directed at some of the companies that actually undertook to run their newly acquired trains. The railroads continued to receive government subsidies (these were written into the sales contracts), yet fares and profits went up while breakdowns and delays increased. Apparently neither the old public subsidies nor much new private money was going into maintenance. Public hilarity reached a crescendo when key figures in the Labour Party arrived at their national convention hours late because they'd traveled together on privatized British Railroads. The laughter soured after a disastrous train crash.

Though David liked to describe how he beat out British investors, the story of British Railroads reminded me that European restructuring was not a matter of Americans, *in general*, imposing their economic rules on Europeans, *in general*. Some Britishers benefited from rail privatization, and others lost. British investors pushed for privatization on their own behalf and got their own politicians to act for them. One significant difference between Europe and the US, however, was that in most European countries, workers, the likely losers, were organized well enough that a major political party had to take a stand against the new economic rules—at least officially. But David assured me at lunch that regardless of its threats, the British Labour Party hadn't actually impeded any of our acquisitions in their country.

From trains, David moved on to candy and soda. The shares of the British company Cadbury Schweppes had been so undervalued in Britain, he told us, that "you were almost getting the US soft-drink industry for free." That included 7-Up and Dr Pepper (which was, as David reminded the assembled financial press, "a great drink").

"We bought our stake at about five pounds . . . today it trades closer to nine pounds. Again the discount is not as huge as it was. And at that type of situation, you—we—start exiting."

Finally David told us about a Dutch acquisition.

"One that is still really cheap, that we own eleven percent of, is actually a newspaper company called *The Telegraph*, in the Netherlands, which trades for between half and a third of what comparable US companies trade for. . . . This is a company that hasn't been very shareholder-conscious, but it's beginning to change.

"In the Netherlands at some point," David predicted, "they're going to allow stock buybacks. And when that happens a company that's overcapitalized and generates lots of cash, like *The Telegraph*, hopefully will buy back their stock."

"Buyback," as David Marcus noted above, is one of the buzzwords that gets investors excited. When a company buys back its shares, it pays cash from the company treasury to buy shares from investors at current prices. Then it generally retires or destroys those shares. As a result there are fewer shares, hence fewer claims on the company's future profits. Since each of the remaining shares is worth more of the company, share price inevitably goes up after a buyback.

I hadn't realized until David mentioned it that stock buybacks were illegal in some European countries. In the US, corporations were buying back their own shares at a rate of about two percent per year.

At first, those buybacks occurred primarily at companies with big profits whose managers couldn't figure out how to reinvest that money profitably enough in their own line of business. In such cases the management was essentially turning the cash over to the shareholders, while shrinking or freezing the size of the enterprise.

But increasingly, US companies that didn't have unused capital were also buying back their own shares—but with the company's cash flow. Then they would borrow the money that they needed to run the business.

Borrowing money and issuing shares are the two basic ways of raising corporate capital. They both have their uses. But borrowing to buy back shares is simply increasing stock prices short-term, by imposing long-term debt on a company, without using the borrowed money to create a means to pay that debt back. In other words, it's looting from within. If it became a common practice, it could hollow out a nation's corporations, dispersing wealth and destroying productive capacity that had accumulated over generations. I could see why cautious capitalist countries like the Netherlands might make buybacks illegal.

At the time, Sweden also restricted stock buybacks. But I just read that they're thinking of easing the law. I also read that the Danish tax code had been amended so that, as in the US, stock options aren't taxed until they're exercised. This isn't the kind of news that makes headlines. But both of these small, dry-sounding shifts were reported with approval in the US financial press.

Easier buybacks and stock options, less protection for fired workers, and a host of similar rule changes would make the European game more like the American game. Europe had centuries of wealth accumulated in her mature companies, and her own investors were just as anxious as American investors for the chance to unlock it.

But there was still that organized opposition. In comparing restructuring prospects in Europe with the US, one of the Mutual managers said:

"The good news is there's a lot more fat to cut out. The bad news is there's not the political will to let it happen and it's very expensive to downsize in Europe.... There's cash sucked out of your business at a multiple of what it would cost you in this country to do the same."

My first response was "Good for them." Good for the French and Swedish unions that make it costly to downsize. Why should their discarded workers be left like the people in Portland, Tennessee? And good for the cautious Dutch burghers who slow down the process of shifting capital out of their nation's established business. Why should European lives become more insecure so that I can get 29 percent returns on my money?

Swept along on this egalitarian wave, my back stiffened when Peter

Langerman fielded a question about how a flood of American investors coming in behind Mutual Series changed the rules of the game in Europe.

"... Americans have led the charge and the locals are following," Langerman said. "The blueprint of what's happened here [in the US] seems to be happening even faster in Europe because they already have the game plan."

So having already restructured the US—as a game—they can now do it more efficiently in Europe. The barbarians pillage one continent, leave rubble, and sweep through the next even faster. That was my emotional reaction. At the same time, I'd listened to so much investor talk, by then, that on some shallow, logical level it was starting to make sense.

Sure, these protégés are callow. They're playing a game for points and percentages. The pain they've caused at Sunbeam will never mean anything to them. Nevertheless, America is not rubble. Maybe we went too far at Sunbeam, but how else can you tell that a business trend is over except by going that step too far? (Turn the rubber band until it snaps, then go one less.)

Sunbeam notwithstanding, when old US companies like AT&T were broken apart, innovators sprang up. Yes, half a million people lost jobs and basic home phone service became more expensive. But look at all the new telecommunications companies providing cheap long-distance and Internet business services. After two decades of lowering real wages, US manufacturers were competitive and a high percentage of our people had jobs. Cowboy capitalism may be a rough ride, but it certainly is dynamic.

Besides, the Mutual managers didn't claim to be social benefactors. That's the thing I like about them, just as I liked Michael Price when I heard him at the Chase shareholders' meeting. Price didn't talk about stimulating the economy or saving the bank. He just said, "Give me more money."

The young men conducting this meeting may not be particularly warm or subtle human beings. But doesn't that illustrate the essential tenet of capitalism: that the worst people acting from their worst motives will somehow bring about good?

Even though I'd seen the pain in America up close, I was open to the notion that these young men might nevertheless implement a rational redistribution of capital on another continent. "Some of these European companies undoubtedly need a good restructuring," I said to myself. Then Rob Friedman gave the example that gave me such a turn.

"Another situation, my personal favorite of the last two years," Rob said, "is a UK company called Pearson, which owns a competitor of yours known as the *Financial Times*. [He was addressing the *Wall Street Journal* reporters.] It also owns fifty percent of the *Economist*. . . . [Wow. The *Economist* is so well written. I hope we don't change it.] It owns one of the most underutilized brands in the world, Madame Tussaud's [the famous wax works?]. . . . It owns the largest US textbook publisher; it owns Penguin Books; and is now the largest publisher of English books in the world. Now this company . . . "

Penguin Books?!

". . . has not made sense in years."

That's my publisher!

From England, Rob moved on to the Continent. ". . . situations we're working on in Sweden and also in France, a number of holding companies that were trading in huge discounts to their breakup values . . . " And on to Finland . . . "Recently we were involved in a Finnish insurance company known as . . . its interest is that there's a part of the world that hasn't restructured yet."

But I was still back in Britain with Penguin. What if Rob Friedman or Peter Langerman found out that I'd been holding on to a Penguin book advance for four years?

Rob was describing a particularly profitable Finnish investment: ". . . thirteen divisions; stripped it down to three. . . . We bought that stock back in '94 . . . trebled the price . . . "

I had $48,000 of Penguin money. Think what Rob could have turned that into, by now, on the Finnish stock market.

"These easy ones for the short term are gone," Rob concluded regretfully, "but still we're finding good breakups. . . . Finland is restructuring. We're there early."

———

Funny how different things look from close up. Finland, Sweden, France, and the British railroads may have needed restructuring. Even Sunbeam may be better off in the long, long run. But Penguin! Those orange spines mean *classic*. Besides, I'm writing a book about a predatory mutual fund, and the vandals now own my publisher.

It's not that I was afraid of censorship. Rob wasn't going to drop in at the

Penguin office to leaf through next year's manuscripts. But if you were interested in Pearson's profit, which would you suggest they get rid of, the *Financial Times,* or a division that advances money to people who produce products that are almost always commercial duds, except for the unpredictable few books that "take off"?

Literary publishing is a ridiculous business. People go into it because they like books. They're successful if they sell enough of them to pay expenses, pay their own salaries, pay interest on borrowed money, and have enough left over to publish more books. Publishing doesn't "treble" anyone's capital.

Come to think of it, very few businesses do. A successful business may make an 8-, 10-, or perhaps 12-percent return on investor's capital; 15 or 20 percent is remarkable. Very few honest enterprises can keep that up. Yet these twerps, having destroyed two-thirds of the share value of Sunbeam, expect *us* (I've had books in print with Penguin since 1977) to pull coins out of the air so that they can deliver 29 percent returns despite their Sunbeam loses! Whippersnappers who know no more about publishing than they know about barbecue grills are going to tell *us* how to squeeze money out of a company into which *they*—I suddenly realized—*had never put a penny.*

Why have I been calling them investors? When I sent my $5,000 check to Mutual Shares I assumed in some fuzzy way that my money would be going to the companies in the fund's portfolio. But, under the clarifying influence of self-interest, I realized that the entire premise was wrong. Stock-market investors don't give their money to the companies they're "invested" in. Except on the rare occasion when Michael Price gets us in on an offering of new securities, he doesn't give my money to a company like Pearson, to run Penguin. Nor does he give it to anyone who's responsible for making the British trains run on time. He gives it to individuals and institutions that currently own Pearson stock or railroad stock. Unless, by chance, those former shareholders splurge their capital gains on books, Penguin won't see a penny of that money.

Of course, someone, way back must have bought shares directly from the company. That original investor provided capital to the business. And he assumed he could sell his shares when he wanted to. He also hoped for a profit, I imagine. But a resale market was a sine qua non. Faith in a smoothly functioning market with future buyers certainly helped Western companies raise new capital when they needed it. In that sense, Mr. Price's willingness to buy shares today played a constructive role, retroactively, in the companies he owns.

But the real investment was so long ago. Does the freedom to buy, sell, and profit have to be so absolute that Mutual Series can fire directors and close down divisions just because it holds the pieces of paper that someone purchased thousands of transactions ago? Can these nouveau shareholders decide that a bank should become a brokerage, or that Penguin should sell its backlist of titles and go into the greeting-card business, or better still, give the money directly to shareholders?

At the time of the Chase merger I wondered exactly how Michael Price conducts himself when he presents alternatives to the CEO of a company in which he holds a stake. Fund manager Harry Keefe (of Keefe Partners L.P. Fund) told a reporter about a meeting he had with a bank CEO who said that the bank's return would probably be 9 percent that year, 10 percent the next, and "maybe" 15 percent a few years after.

"I told him that's not satisfactory.... That's yesterday's game.... If three or four years from now you're not at 18 percent, you'll be gone and I'll be there to make sure."

At least that's how Keefe told it to *US Banker*. Since Michael Price often carries a bigger stick, he may be more courteous.

At lunch I asked David Winters about the tone of the meeting between Price and Chase Chairman Labrecque. David hadn't been in on that one, but he told me about a Canadian lumber firm whose management "was not used to having to answer to shareholders. So Mutual had to apply pressure." This was a situation that David handled personally. I asked what those meetings had been like. "I can't see you pounding the table and yelling at Canadians." (Despite his exploits in Britain and the Netherlands, David was still that curly-headed kid with the goofy smile.)

"I didn't yell at *them*," he answered. "*They* were yelling at *me*. I was calmly saying 'I have the votes.' Of course you have to know the local laws. We hired local council. The management pulled—did—various things and eventually were thrown out."

So David Winters and Harry Keefe used the same argument. I have the votes (the shares). I can stop your salary checks.

"The key thing is," David concluded, *"the value has to be there.* It doesn't do you any good to beat your chest unless the value is there. You have to be right on the facts, and Michael is right."

I imagine Michael Price is right about Pearson too. The value is there. Some of it derives from a backlist of books (including mine) that Penguin has published over generations. But books aren't that different from barbecue grills. It would only take a few months (a few weeks a la Dunlap) to dismantle that list.

Even if Penguin-style publishing is profitable at the 10- or 12-percent level, shareholders have a right to demand the maximum possible return right now. And they don't need Michael Price to organize that demand. All stock pickers, whether they represent the one percent of Americans who own 95 percent of the shares, or they represent the rest of us, exert that pressure. And they exert it on almost every business whose shares are publicly traded.

My husband's company was an exception for a while. The founders frustrated the Mutual Series managers by holding on to 90 percent of the shares and selling the other 10 percent without voting rights. They did that because they wanted to keep the firm (and its employees, we liked to think) in the trade-magazine business. New investors would have to wrest control from the family before they could fully extract the value that had accumulated in the company and use it for something else.

As it happened, the benevolent founders soon sold their shares to another publishing company and my husband's magazine became part of a larger corporation. The founders used the cash to expand their charitable foundation. The business they left behind is now experiencing normal layoffs, spin-offs, et cetera. It still has that day-care center, however.

So the exception that frustrated my fund managers was only temporary. As a rule, investors can buy into almost any big business and immediately exercise the prerogatives of owners. In a sense, all the companies with widely dispersed voting shares, on all the stock markets of the world, are financially one business, whose owners are constantly shifting its assets into whatever they guess will bring the highest returns.

But what if I want to go on writing books? What if the Penguin employees want to go on publishing books? What if the world, I mean the non-shareholding majority, wants to keep Penguin-type publishing around even if it only makes 5 or 6 percent? Who does that hurt?

It would be a pretty static society, I suppose, if all businesses stayed as they were because their suppliers (that's what authors are), their employees, and their present customers liked it that way. On the other hand, it's a harrowing world where jobs and businesses disappear because Michael Price thinks he can make more money restructuring them.

In some European countries there was still a political climate that slightly slowed down capital extraction. My mutual fund was betting my money that that climate was going to change. I don't think I want them to win.

Après Moi

One morning, thousands of currency traders went to their computers to sell baht. Some had a vague feeling that the Thai economy was rickety. A few may have had specific knowledge that there was a building glut in Bangkok, which meant that there would be bad loans on the books of many banks.

But for the astute currency traders, the sell signals had to do with currency more than anything in Thailand's real economy. For the benefit of foreign investors, Thailand had undertaken to keep its currency linked, within a narrow range, to the dollar. But when the financial officials of the rich countries agreed to let the dollar rise rapidly in order to head off financial problems in Japan, the dollar-linked baht seemed to be getting overvalued. That made it the perfect target for what's called a currency attack.

Big foreign-exchange traders, like those at the Soros hedge funds, committed themselves to future currency trades whereby they stood to gain fortunes if they could drive the price of baht down by selling them and getting others to sell. A former British finance minister compared foreign-exchange traders to wild dogs. "They hunt in packs; they seek out wounded currencies; they savage their prey."

From the end of World War II until 1973, currencies traded at set rates—so many baht to the dollar—as a result of an international conference held at Bretton Woods, New Hampshire, in 1944. The post–Bretton Woods free market in currencies is characterized by normal fluctuations, orchestrated attacks, and spontaneous panics. The three merge. Fluctuations tend to be wider, pack attacks easier, and panics more likely if the victim is genuinely weak.

But most of the foreign-exchange traders knew no more about the Thai economy when they sold their baht then when they bought them. They were selling because everyone else was selling, which is not an invalid reason if your job is to preserve your own or your client's capital.

The Thai government struggled briefly to keep the baht at around 24 to the dollar, the rate they had set as their goal, but they had limited means to do that. Pressed by Western governments and by banks and investors like those we heard at the Waldorf baying for (okay, calling for) the free flow of capital, Thailand, like Mexico, had made its currency freely convertible. It had also abandoned once-standard regulations (capital controls) on the amount of currency people could quickly send in or take out of the country. The baht could be traded as a Eurocurrency anywhere in the world and was worth whatever people would pay for it that day.

In an attempt to maintain the price of their currency relative to the dollar, the Thai treasury used its store of foreign currencies to buy the baht that the attackers were selling. It must be frustrating to hurl money hand over fist at people who are trying to run you to the ground. Your victory means they will simply walk away with most of the money in your treasury. It's also usually futile. Sweden is the only country I'd seen outrun a full-scale currency attack.

Certainly Thailand's resources were no match for the huge hedge funds and others (including its own citizens) who were dumping baht. Once the Thai treasury ran out of money it had to stop buying, and then the price of the baht fell nearly 50 percent. Soon after, the stock market declined steeply as investors rushed to get out of anything Thai. Eventually, in fact quickly, the currency attack and capital flight spread up and down the Southeast Asian Peninsula.

After the crash, most Western pundits declared that the Asian Tiger economies had been corrupt and structurally unsound all along. Of course, some Southeast Asian sore losers blamed the crash entirely on currency traders. But as in most contests, it's difficult (and perhaps meaningless) to judge whether the losers were defeated by their own weakness or by their opponents' strength.

I'd gone to Thailand following Chase loans to two American companies that did business in Asia, but my bank deposit also supported Chase loans to Thai companies. I didn't encounter these loans back when I was asking individual businessmen, "Do you have a loan from Chase?" because most of them went indirectly, through Thai banks and finance companies. Because there were no capital controls, these Thai financial institutions had been free to borrow any amount of dollars that Chase would lend them.

Now Thai companies had vast short-term debts denominated in dollars, pounds, deutsche marks, yen, et cetera, to pay back with baht that were worth half as much as before. Chase and other US banks turned out to have over fifty billion dollars of loans in jeopardy.

As the baht crisis spread, pundits debated whether it was another containable implosion, like Mexico's peso crisis, or part of a global meltdown. While they speculated about what it meant down the line for Western investors, I decided to find out what it already meant to some of the people I'd met in my travels. [Here's where you may want to look back at my last days in Bangkok, pages 91–99.]

Squirrel and the Vendor

I wrote to Squirrel at her dormitory asking how she and her friend the vendor were making out. I enclosed a self-addressed envelope and a $20 bill, saying it was for stamps. The money was a mistake but I got a reply in my envelope.

Dear Mrs. Barbara Garson,
I do not know where Squirrel is. I will tell you to where I know.

Her factory closed. Other girls stayed outside it to try to get their money but Squirrel in two days went to sell food in front of another factory. She sold the new papaya salad you like but hot like Thais like. The factory women have not so much money now but her selling went OK. Squirrel is smart and works very hard. Also I introduce her to people at the market so she has best food to sell.

After one week some people came back and said it was their place. They sold in front of a building but when they stopped building it they wanted Squirrel's place which was their place used to be. Squirrel fought them and went back next day. She did not tell me this. I would say not to go back maybe. I do not know what happened. Squirrel came back and took her clothing.

I learned this from the lady who rented her room. That lady brought me your letter. She did not go home. Her father came to Bangkok to look for her.

The lady who brought me your letter said maybe she does not come back because she owes money for her room. But now everyone owes money. My business is still OK but some of the companies inside the building closed so I sell not so much. But worse for me is missing Squirrel.

I will holding the money for her you sent to her because the man who writes this letter for me said that is best thing to do. I will write if I know where Squirrel is.

Sincerely

Squirrel's Friend

P.S. I work in the building where Kuhn P— sells food in front. She brought your letter to me and I translate her answer since I have study English in Singapore. I have take it upon myself to advise Kuhn P— that you would like more to hear from her than to receive money back. I have tell her that this money is small amount in America especially now that baht is so low. Kuhn P— is an honest person who I see run to return small change to people. If you write back she would be most happy if you tell her it is true that she was right to hold the $20. It very much upsets her mind that you will think she is not honest. I have told her that you know she is good person. But if you tell her that is better. The problem is it is not good to put dollars in the mail or you will not get this letter maybe.

There was no return address. I wrote back to the vendor at Squirrel's dormitory hoping that someone would again deliver my letter. I also sent a copy care of "the landlady." No answer to either. I thought I remembered the name of a supermarket in the building near the vendor's stand. I lined up a translator to help me call. It was unlikely that whoever answered would happen to know a man in one of the upstairs offices who studied English in Singapore, but someone could at least tell me the names of the companies in the building. Someone in the supermarket, if it was the right one, might even run out and get the vendor for me. But the supermarket's phone had been disconnected. "Probably out of business," the operator told my translator.

In the course of one answered letter and one incomplete phone call I'd heard about a factory that closed owing wages, a factory still running where women were earning less than before, building construction that was halted, two street vendors fighting over a corner, a medium-sized office building out of which some tenants had moved, and a possibly shut-down supermarket. The newspapers weren't exaggerating.

Based on no more than you know, I suspect that the vendor had given Squirrel some money to start her street cart. Squirrel might have been ashamed to see her friend if she'd lost any of the savings for their market restaurant. But where did she go?

Shortly after the crash, Dr. Angkarb Korsieporn, a researcher intending to study rural people in Pichit province, noticed that "To my surprise I was talking to field laborers that had been recently laid off from construction jobs in Bangkok. They were dispirited and they were hungry."

There are few reliable postcrash statistics, but based on similar anecdotes it appears that millions of Thais were returning to the paddy farms which up until then they'd helped to support with their remittances. But the two Chase loans I followed, one to import shrimp and the other to build an oil refinery, had both had the effect of decreasing the amount of farmable and fishable land. So had many other development projects. This meant that there were fewer and poorer paddy farms to go back to. Still, the government promoted the hope (calling it a policy) that the Thai farmer would find a way to sustain the country back to prosperity. Who knows, perhaps he will. Besides, where do you go in troubled times if not home? A popular postcrash interview genre featured former city people saying that they'd forgotten how much they missed village life.

But Squirrel had declared herself a nonpeasant with such youthful conviction that she may have felt she'd burned her bridges. Does she know that her father came to Bangkok to look for her? Where is she and how is she living?

The Burmese Pipefitter

In response to unemployment, the Thai government announced a deadline for foreign workers to leave the country. After that, all illegals would be rounded up. CNN televised a forced march in which the Thai military conducted about a hundred Burmese men, women, and children on the three-hour trek from the town of Karnchanaburi to the Burmese border.

But things the Thai government announces don't always happen. There were anywhere from a quarter of a million to several million illegal Burmese in Thailand, so it's possible that the pipefitter whom I interviewed at the Burger King is still in Bangkok. Burma's military government was so oppressive and pervasive that an illegal existence in post-crash Thailand might seem preferable to going home. He's not likely to be doing construction work, though. His position had been precarious before, but now almost all building has been halted. Everyone who's visited post-crash Bangkok mentions the petrified cranes that stick out above the tall buildings like fossilized dinosaurs. He can hardly go back to repairing cars. With 100,000 vehicles repossessed in the first six months after the crash, that's a shrinking trade, too.

Because he was illegal, I had no address for him. In fact, I deliberately didn't know his real name. I wrote to the Burmese human-rights activist who translated for us, thinking that he might have gotten a dispensation to stay. So far no answer.

Alfalfa

Last, I wrote to the sweet young man from northeastern Thailand who worked on my Singapore refinery—the one that I met with his friends at the Golden Mile mall. It took a while to get my letter to Alfalfa translated because the Thai students I knew in New York were by then working full time. With the baht worth little more than half as many dollars as before, their savings got used up quickly and middle-class parents, who may have prospered during the boom, now couldn't send enough. The problem must have been widespread, because the US Immigration Department gave Thais on student visas a dispensation to drop out of school and work full time.

But eventually my letter went out in beautiful Thai script, and I assured Alfalfa that there were lots of Thais in New York who could translate for me. But his answer, too, came in English.

> To Barbara
>
> I'm very surprised about a letter from America that my mother brought me, but when I saw your name I'm very glad, because I'm still remember you.
>
> I came back to Thailand on February 5, 1995 not so long after I meet you at Golden Mile Complex in Singapore, very lucky I came on time my son was born. My son was born on February 6 1996 only one day after I came back.

Thank you for you anxious about my health, since my asthma its only a little not big matter for me.

A big problem for me is a job, because I'm unemployed now. Someday I have a little job it's can make money 100–200 baht but only one or two days a week. Only my wife has daily work. She work for government employee, she get 4,700 baht/month.

Since Thailand has to face for economic problem every where in Thailand also same. It's a big problem for my family, because we have so many expenses but only little bit income. We must be careful to spend we are money every baht.

Every Saturday & Sunday I must go to study at Rajabhat Institute Sakhon-nakhon, I study in English major. This year is second year. I must study about four years for get academic degree.

For this letter if you see about wrong spelling or wrong grammar, let me your suggestion please and next your letter, please writing in English language. I Want to learn English from your letter.

[...]

I wishes for success in your book as you want. And let you well know all the world.

> With warmest regards & Sincerely,
> "New Student of English"
> N—N—

So I hadn't needed the translation. But I was right to put stamps on the return envelope. If Alfalfa now works for 100 baht a day, the stamps on a letter to American cost over a quarter of a day's wage. At the baht/dollar exchange rate of this writing, his wife, a schoolteacher, earns a little under 30 dollars a week, and his Singapore savings are so devalued that it's as if 11 months of the two years he spent living in that metal container away from his family to work on my refinery had been unpaid.

But such baht/dollar translations can be misleading. Neither purchasing power nor the comfort of daily life are uniformly affected by changes in foreign-exchange rates. Though a Sunbeam small appliance may have become unaffordable, neither Alfalfa's school tuition nor rent in a provincial city had doubled.

But there were few businesses that didn't have supplies to buy or debts to pay in dollars. That's why even enterprises that hadn't overbuilt were failing.

And unfortunately, despite Thai hotel ads offering royal feasts at a third of the old prices, basic food costs hadn't gone down. In the year after the collapse, the price of rice nearly doubled. That's partly because the world crop happened to be poor. But it's also because rice can be sold abroad, and every private and government mechanism was now geared to garnering foreign currency to pay debts. To hasten that process, the IMF (International Monetary Fund) attached conditions to their emergency loans that prohibited the Thai government from subsidizing food prices. Thais who had to pay for their rice in devalued baht must bid directly against people who could pay in dollars.

In Bangkok, the price of cooked food from vendors was held in check, however, by the many newly unemployed people selling on the streets. So while government rice subsidies were prohibited, street sellers subsidized meals for the urban poor by taking less for their labor. Vendors had been the heroines of the boom; they were also the heroines of the bust.

But Alfalfa may yet be a hero of the recovery. As I write, the Thai economy is still in recession, but many of the businesses built during the boom will eventually get going again. When they do, quite a few will have new foreign owners, many of whom speak English. [See pages 312–314 to understand the mechanism.] That should make Alfalfa a desirable employee. (I hope he's learning to speak English as well as write it.) In the meantime, at least he's with his family. Happily for Alfalfa, unhappily for Squirrel, family support is the best predictor, everywhere, of how individuals will make it through a crisis.

The formulaic newspaper story after a standard third-world currency crisis (and they do seem to be becoming standard) features plucky former investment bankers peddling their designer clothing on the street or turning their BMWs into taxis. It's easy to understand why imported luxuries are unaffordable after devaluation, but necessities that were available before the crash also become scarce and unaffordable. Indeed, for poor people, a superficial currency crisis may mean going hungry and staying hungry long after the crash stops making headlines.

———

I hadn't understood that at the beginning of this odyssey, when I dismissed the peso crises as a fluke that I was lucky to have avoided. But having followed my money full-circle in and out of Southeast Asia, I can now see the repeating pattern. It was too late to backtrack and trail my bank deposit into Mexico, where it had gone briefly at the end of the previous emerging-market cycle. But fortunately I'd already interviewed a man who had not only survived several cycles, but was credited with pioneering many of the financial mechanisms that facilitated the era's unregulated capital flows. To me, Walter Wriston, Citibank CEO emeritus, is Mr. Global.

—*Walter Wriston—maybe*

By a coincidence, the publisher of Millbrook's weekly town newspaper, the *Round Table,* happened to be a retired international banker. "Citibank's man in Riyadh," Hamilton Meserve called himself in a column about his former boss. "Walter Wriston, Chairman of Citibank from 1967–84," the column began, "is the 20th century Moses of American banks ..."

In this affectionate essay, publisher Meserve tells us that Wriston developed and/or put into play some of the brilliant devices, like floating interest rates, money market checking, bank holding companies, and of course Eurodollars [see page 29], that liberated banks from the chains of government regulation. Most of the chains, as he explains, were put on after the crash of 1929.

Wriston's workarounds were developed starting in the 1970's, as the "Golden Age" of economic growth that followed World War II subsided and Western investors went "global" to chase diminishing profits. The innovations that facilitated this move so weakened government regulation and strengthened the financial sector that nowadays, as Wriston loves to remind us, it's *capital* that disciplines *governments.*

Here are some typical Wriston quotes on the new relationship:

The President of the United States goes out in the Rose Garden and says something dumb. The trading lights of the world light up, and it's all over. In France

Mitterrand announced all those ridiculous moves, and they lost a third of their foreign exchange in a week.

... There are 60,000-odd terminals out there in the trading rooms of the world and those guys are about as sentimental as a block of ice. If they're going to sell, that's it. This is new in the history of the world and I don't think it can be structured or contained ... there's no place to hide.

... The gold standard, replaced by the gold exchange standard, which was replaced by the Bretton Woods agreements, has now been replaced by the information standard. Unlike the other standards it is in place, operating, will never go away and has substantially changed the world. What it means, very simply, is that bad money and fiscal policies anywhere in the world are reflected within minutes on the Reuters screens in the trading rooms of the world. . . . You cannot renounce the information standard and it is exerting discipline on the countries of the world, which they all hate. For the first time in history, the politicians can't stop it. It is beyond the political control of the world, and that's good news ... *

The "bad money and fiscal policies" that Wriston refers to include food subsidies in poor countries and the assorted employment, health, and retirement protections once common in rich countries. It also includes any form of capital control or tax that governments might use to restrain the movement of money in or out of countries.

The specific "ridiculous moves" in France were a package of economic reforms aimed at unemployment. The capital flight instantly triggered at "60,000-odd terminals" by "those guys" who are "about as sentimental as a block of ice" forced the French prime minister to rescind his reforms before they were tried. Since they constituted the platform he campaigned on, you might say that Wriston's global voters overrode the French electorate. These same Wriston voters used my money to implement the currency trades and capital flight that triggered first the Mexican and then the Asian crashes.

Fifteen years earlier in the global era, before international banks had perfected mechanisms to have governments absorb 100 percent of their loan

*Those quotes come from Jeffrey Frieden's *Banking on the World,* Harper & Row, New York, 1987.

losses, an earlier Mexican crash forced Citibank to write off some of Wriston's third-world loans. The US government policed third-world repayment and absorbed much of the loss through a mechanism called Brady bonds, but not 100 percent. When third-world losses were followed by heavy losses in a domestic real estate boom and bust, Citibank was technically bankrupt and Wriston was retired.

But he wasn't ousted in disgrace like Al Dunlap. Whatever he cost taxpayers, Walter Wriston was straight with shareholders. A society of construction engineers awards their highest honor in the name of the man who designed the Tacoma Narrows bridge, even though it crashed with traffic on it. It was their way of saying that they honor the grandeur of his vision. It's also a way of saying, "This could happen to any of us."

———

"I'll be going from *Who's Who* to 'Who's that?'" Walter Wriston predicted at his retirement party. But he still had a spacious suite of offices at Citibank headquarters. There, tall and unbowed, he obliged me by repeating some of his global plebiscite lines.

"Through the global marketplace there's a lot of people out there, thousands of them. They look at the policies of the United States, of the UK, or Germany, or Japan, and they decide whether they think the dollar, yen or deutsche mark is going to go up or down.... When a politician says something dumb, traders on 60,000 screens all over the world can vote yes or no that instant. That's information democracy."

"Do I get a vote?" I asked.

"No," he answered. (You have to like the guy.)

"I mean, proportional to my deposit." I brought my thumb and forefinger together and shrunk down. But he took no pity.

"You gave your money to a fiduciary and his contract is to give it back to you any time you want. That is your only participation. If you want to have a vote you'll have to take more risk."

"But I need the money to finish my book."

He shrugged a "that's life" shrug and repeated, with no palliation, that I neither got, nor deserved, a vote. He's right. I entrusted the Whalens at the Bank of Millbrook to find interest-paying uses for my money. They in turn trusted Chase. I can't expect either bank to let *me* choose their borrowers and still guarantee my money back in full whenever I want it.

Since US corporations seemed to have all the money they could use, my fiduciary agents decided to lend some of mine in Asia and Latin America and to gamble with it at their foreign-exchange desks. Those uses may be riskier than blue-chip loans, but they have bigger payoffs. Especially if someone else will absorb the losses after the crash.

In the final years of Walter Wriston's swashbuckling CEOship, when Citibank was lending money holus-bolus in the countries then known as Less Developed and now called Emerging, Wriston reminded the Nervous Nellies that most of his Less Developed Country loans had been made to governments, and countries don't go broke.

"You know that famous thing you said? I'm not sure I have it right because it's quoted so many different ways but . . ."

"You mean, 'Countries don't go broke'?" Wriston answered.

"Right! I've seen it as 'Sovereign entities don't go bankrupt,' 'Nations don't default.' [He nodded in weary recognition of the many variants.] Well, did anyone ever apologize for making fun of that?"

"You won't live that long!"

"Because however you put it, it turned out to be true."

"I may not have said it at all," he shrugged.

"Well, you got the last laugh anyway."

———

Wriston got the last laugh because no matter how ill-advised their loans, countries rarely disappear. When a private company goes bankrupt there may be no one left to collect from. But a country's assets are still there.

"The assets of a country," Wriston explained to me, "are their people, their skills, their natural resources, their . . ."

He painted such a stirring picture of a nation's riches and a people's deep well of strength and resourcefulness that I didn't think, at the time, to ask him exactly which Mexicans paid back his LDC loans and what it entailed for them. But now, having recontacted some of the people I met in Thailand, I understand more viscerally that life after capital flight can be painful, particularly for people who didn't do the borrowing.

Through Chase, my book-advance money had gone into Mexico at the tail end of their last boom. People there were feeling the effects of its sudden withdrawal and still paying, at the same time, on some of Wriston's loans from the boom before. But since I never physically followed my money to Mexico the way I did to Thailand, I had no one to check back with. It happened, however, that my friend Anne Lewis was doing the research for *Morristown,* a documentary on relationships between Appalachians and Mexican migrants in Tennessee.*

One of the Mexicans Anne interviewed was a young man who came to the US illegally after the peso was devalued. Before that, he and his father had traveled around the state of Guerrero repairing machines used to make "something like popsicles—I don't know the exact name in English—a frozen dessert that's sold from carts."

The dessert-making machines were wooden, but the cost of the small metal pieces to repair them had gone up after devaluation, as had everything with any imported component. Salaries, meanwhile, had gone down and people couldn't afford treats, so vendors stopped repairing their machines. At that point, the father and son crossed illegally into the US. There must have been many Mexicans doing the same thing, because migrant remittances became the second-largest component of the national income after oil.

The young man's first job in the US was working in the fields. "Something he'd never done in his life," Anne told me. "He's a city kid."

He must have been a very bright kid too, because he passed US college entrance exams even though he'd only gone as far as middle school in Mexico. A Catholic priest who befriended him and a Tennessee farmer who agreed to hire him part-time arranged for him to go home and come back on a legal student visa. (Maybe something wonderful like that has happened to Squirrel. She's bright, too, and Bangkok, like Dickensian London, is cruel but full of hidden corners for coincidences and happy endings.) But of course the father couldn't stay on as an illegal.

So the young man, alone in Tennessee, now puts himself through school and helps support a family back in post-crash Mexico. He reminds himself that when he gets his engineering degree he'll be able to take care of them

*For information on Morristown contact Anne Lewis annelewi@airmail.net

well. In the meantime, though, his father is 70, his mother is ill, his sister has a crippling spinal problem, and he's working several part-time jobs while going to college full-time in a foreign language. Those aren't the things he complains about, though.

"It's been a long time living by myself," he said to Anne's camera. "Keeping my thoughts to myself.... When I'm with my family I can spend the whole day talking about anything. And I sure like to talk."

There were so many echoes of my Asian migrants in the interview that Anne recorded that I might have gone off in a dozen directions making comparisons. But the thing that caught my attention was the frozen dessert. "He must mean snow-cones," I said, thinking of the shaved-ice doused with colored syrup that children buy in New York's Hispanic neighborhoods. But snow-cones are only sugar and water!

I understand that the Mexican government made loans denominated in dollars; I understand that they have to pay back in dollars; I understand that Mexicans who never signed for those loans have to work hard and cut their consumption in order to export more of the country's mangoes, cotton, oil, et cetera, to earn dollars to pay Chase back. But we're talking about sugar and water. How did it happen that when the beneficent flow of capital receded, it left Mexican children so much poorer that now they can't buy snow-cones made out of Mexican sugar and Mexican water?

Actually, they weren't snow-cones. Anne and I both know how easy it is to extrapolate inaccurately, so she checked it out for me. They were *glaciellas*— small popsicles made of water, sugar, and usually some fruit. They were popular with both adults and children. "It's hot down there," the young man explained. "Everyone bought the popsicles but now no one can afford them."

———

Comparing postcrash newspaper stories from Thailand and Mexico, it sounded as though the Mexicans were worse off.

> One out of every five workers loses job. (It was one out of seven in Thailand.)
> Tortillas up 50 percent. (In Thailand rice was up *almost* 50 percent.)
> Calls on suicide hot line go from three hundred a month to three thousand.

Consumption of grain, meat, and milk down 30, 60, and 40 percent respectively.

Rural people decide to feed their children instead of their draft animals so hungry beasts come to town to forage in garbage pails.

A report produced by Banamex, a leading Mexican bank, said that half the people in Mexico were eating less than 1,300 calories a day. The solid, thoughtful, stolen Chase memo that protesters waved at the annual meeting [see page 180] painted an equally grim picture. Taking the two bank reports together it sounded as though Mexicans were worse off after the capital flow receded than before the wave came in. Based on what they did with the money, that unfortunately makes sense.

In Mexico, 80 percent of the money lent by foreign banks was borrowed by the government. Very little, as we saw, reached the company *presidentes* whom I met at the Waldorf. In the period during which the billions were flowing in, somewhere around half of the amount flowed back out to become deposits in US, Swiss, or other foreign banks. There it could be used to write checks for imported cars, Miami condominiums, or humbler imported goods.

In other words, some Mexicans borrowed money to go on foreign shopping sprees. But the entire nation, not just the shoppers, must now pay these loans back with interest. Since so little productive investing was done with the money, Mexicans working with the same old tools and equipment they used before now had to produce for themselves while setting aside extra for interest payments to Chase, Millbrook, and me. That's why many are poorer than before.

In Thailand, by contrast, over 80 percent of the foreign loan money reached private businessmen. It may have gone only to those who knew the right people and/or paid for the introductions, but once they got the money, most Thais used it to build. The unfinished condos, abandoned shrimp farms, and ghost malls they created are still there. So are hundreds of thousands of sewing machines; metal presses; canning, dehydrating and freezing plants; et cetera.

Much of this production capacity was created with Japanese capital in the first half of Thailand's dazzling decade. In the second half, profits from such businesses were often siphoned off into quick-return investments like real estate and auto finance instead of being retained in the original businesses to upgrade machinery and train workers.

My book-advance money came into Thailand in the second half of the decade, and most of it went through Thai finance companies into go-go ventures like Bangkok office buildings.

A bust is the predictable end of any boom; in fact, it's the hindsight definition: if it busted, it was a boom. The Mexican bust seems inevitable with hindsight since it was based on government loans and portfolio investments, neither of which produced anything with which to pay the loans back.

The Bangkok real-estate boom was more like the US mall-building boom of the early 1990's which culminated in the crash of so many savings-and-loan banks. Both were exacerbated by "crony capitalism," and each was "solved" by bailouts that the nation is still paying for.

But in Thailand, like the US, something concrete—all too concrete in many cases—was done with the money. Five-year-old factories and half-finished buildings are assets that should make a country richer than if nothing at all had been built.

Because the Mexican and Thai loans had been used so differently, and because their underlying economies were so different, the bankers who want their money back must devise different repayment plans, it would seem.

In Mexico, Chase and the other banks demanded the same sovereign—that is, government—debt remedy after this crisis that they had demanded in the earlier Mexican crisis that Walter Wriston presided over. The Mexican government must spend less, tax more, and use the surplus for debt repayment.*

In the meantime, the International Monetary Fund [IMF] would lend Mexico an emergency 40 billion dollars, 17 billion of which came directly

---

*That's why the stolen Chase Emerging Markets memo assumed that President Zedillo couldn't afford to pacify Chiapas with economic reforms. The Zapatistas were asking for roads, schools, hospitals, and electricity at just the time that foreign banks demanded government cut spending and amass more dollars. That meant delivering fewer services while pressuring people to use less and export more—primarily by working for lower wages.

from the US treasury. That way Mexico needn't miss a single payment to Chase, Citi, and the other banks.

In return for that favor, the IMF would have the right to look at the books and make sure that the Mexican government was complying with the strict fiscal austerity required to pay back all the old loans and this new one too.

Further, the Mexican central bank was required to increase short-term interest rates to the point that international investors would think it worthwhile to risk getting back into pesos. The IMF seemed to be aiming for interest rates of about 60 percent in Mexico, but at some points it went as high as 100 percent. Such interest rates cripple local businesses. They also make consumer prices go up just when people are losing their jobs. But banks don't care about local businesses that fill local needs, because that commerce is done in the local currency. The banks are concerned that the debtor earn the foreign currencies with which to pay them back. So local business must be sacrificed. Posting up high interest rates may tempt the flown flight capital to realight.

It works on the same principle as the cargo cult magic on Pacific islands. During World War II the American military established temporary air bases on many formerly isolated islands. After the war, islanders who had enjoyed the chocolate bars and Spam that GI cargo planes had brought tried to lure them back by building runways and full-scale model planes that could be seen from above. In the same way, high interest rates posted in very large letters are supposed to lure the capital that's winging around the world looking for a place to alight.

So austerity and high interest rates are the traditional regimen for poor, sovereign debtors. There are nations in Africa that spend 75 percent of their revenue for debt service under IMF structural-adjustment programs without any hope of getting out of debt and resuming growth. That's why the nun and priest at the Chase annual meeting had begged their fellow shareholders to reconsider their insistence on structural-adjustment programs. Now that I've seen their effects in Asia, I understand the religious duo's dogged persistence at a meeting where no one was listening.

If the only possible debt repayment plan for Mexico was to squeeze the last pesos from peasants, then taking away their popsicles was an appropriate element. But what should the banks have required in Thailand? A lot of the debt there was owed by businessmen who still had factories that could produce goods to sell abroad. The problem was to get them running again. A temporary debt moratorium or even a new loan to Squirrel's former boss might put him back in business and get her back at the sewing machine. Many such loans might start enough wheels turning to get my oil refinery working nearer to capacity again.

That's why the standard prescription for rich countries after a breakdown includes government spending to jump-start demand, along with lower interest rates so that businessmen can borrow money to produce again. That's what the Western powers were recommending at the moment to a temporarily depressed Japan. But the Asian Tigers were being treated like perpetually poor African or Latin American countries.

That's why many traditional economists were surprised that the IMF, under American dominance, offered the Asian countries $70 billion in loans conditioned upon the same austerity/high interest structural adjustment formula they'd just imposed in Mexico. The result was a similar depression.

As applied to Mexico, the plan was mean, unimaginative, slightly risky, but comprehensible. As applied to Thailand, it didn't make any sense to me at all. I was also surprised that the big banks, having so recently won their liberation from government regulation, were now forming alliances with state collection agencies and allowing government officials to be their spokespersons in the negotiations with Thailand, Malaysia, Korea, Indonesia, Mexico, and so on about terms for loan repayment.

Would Walter Wriston fall back into a childlike role vis-à-vis the US government just because he got himself into a little trouble? The Wriston I interviewed had become even more libertarian in retirement.

As I was leaving his office, he tried out a bold antiregulation idea on me. He said that he'd been reading about the period in American history when each bank could issue its own money. Contrary to the common notion, bank failures were no more numerous then than now, he asserted.

Since the establishment of the Federal Reserve, US banks have been forbidden to print their own banknotes. But they have the privilege of issuing US currency, within certain limits. By a math I can never quite understand, a reserve requirement of about three percent allows the banking system, as a whole, to lend out or create almost ten times as much money as it takes in.

(My $29,500 deposited at Millbrook could underwrite about $295,000 in loans.) As long as they keep within that limit, the US government stands behind the money that banks create. When a bank agrees to give a home buyer, or a Thai finance company, or the Mexican government a loan, it opens an account for the borrower. The money the bank declares to be in that account becomes US currency. Every one in the country is required to accept it. In this manner, banks create far more dollars than the US treasury prints. They play the central role in expanding or contracting the amount of money and credit available.

The currency creating privilege is what makes banks quasi-official institutions. By suggesting that we go back to a time when the country didn't have one exclusive currency, Wriston was striking at the government's ability to control the money supply through reserve requirements and at the government's basic justification for regulating banks.

The idea of Chase issuing its own currency was so Wild West that all I could think of was three masked men backing out of the Bank of Dead Man's Gulch, guns drawn, with a million dollars in large, worthless, blue and green banknotes. I knew I'd been asking Wriston very naïve questions and I figured he was kidding me along.

But a few weeks later, the *Wall Street Journal* printed a column by Walter Wriston which they headed "Money: Back to the Future?" In it, Wriston explained that certain kinds of electronic smart cards amounted to non-US government currencies.

> Their broad issuance and use could return America to something very close to the free banking of the last century, when every commercial bank issued dollar bills, backed sometimes by the skill of the management, sometimes by doubtful state bonds, and sometimes by gold or silver. . . .
>
> None of this is necessarily a cause for panic. There is very little, if any evidence, that government has managed our currency values any better than the commercial banks did in pre-Fed days.

I guess he wasn't kidding me.

Walter Wriston had led two generations of bankers out of the wilderness of government regulation toward a Jerusalem of free financial markets. Like the other Moses, he himself had not made it over into the promised land. But his chosen 60,000, still on the march, had stirred up so much sand that, after the Asian crash, a third of the world was buried in economic depression and the sand was starting to sting the chosen themselves. Then, two years before the second millennium, a country finally did go broke. Russia simply stopped paying its creditors.

Lashed by the sands around them, in dread of the unknown ahead, some of the chosen slowed their steps and turned their eyes back toward the security of bondage. Walter Wriston will never turn backward—not in this lifetime, anyway. But by the fall of 1998, many bankers were themselves calling for global regulation, or at least some traffic lights, to slow down the flow of capital.

That was the state of things when I went to my first IMF meeting in Washington.

Washington, DC—one year after the Asian crash

After the Thai currency crash turned into a bad loan crisis that spread throughout East Asia, after Russia defaulted on a piece of sovereign debt, and at a moment when it appeared that Brazil might be next, the International Monetary Fund and the World Bank held their annual joint meeting in Washington, DC.

The IMF is a bureaucracy that was created in 1944 to handle ongoing adjustments to the fixed-exchange-rate currency system established for the post–World War II world at Bretton Woods. [See page 287.] When the Bretton Woods system was abandoned in the 1970's, the inconspicuous agency might have disappeared, but instead it took on the new and constantly expanding role of heading off loan repayment crises in the free-market/floating-rate era. According to the World Bank's chief economist, just under 100 countries had gone through crises involving IMF intervention in the 25 years since the end of the Bretton Woods system.

In both its old and new incarnations, the IMF was supported by government money. But like the Federal Reserve Bank, it partakes of a mysterious duality. It is, at one and the same time, a government agency paid for by the public and a private service organization whose constituency is international banks.

The new post–Bretton Woods IMF operates by lending government money to countries that might otherwise default on private foreign loans. Though the IMF has 182 sovereign members, its loan policy is set by the members who contribute the most money—the wealthy European nations, Japan, and the US. That meant that the condition for receiving a loan was to adopt the shopping list of "reforms" or "liberalizations"—privatization, low budget deficits, flexible labor force, and no capital controls—enunciated by the bankers whom we met at the Waldorf. In IMF circles this set of principles is called "The Washington Consensus." Its central tenet is the freedom to lend and invest across all borders with no impediments.

But at that precarious juncture it seemed, for a brief moment, that international financiers might be willing to accept, or even themselves create, some significant constraint on the free flow of their own capital.

Normally, the IMF/World Bank conference is a posh and self-celebratory reunion. As a matter of convenience, the finance ministers, treasury secretaries, and other representatives of the G-7 and G-24 (Group of 7 or 24 rich nations) meet at the same time so they can coordinate policy and see old friends. But you could tell from the brief opening remarks of IMF Director Michel Camdessus that things were different this year.

Well, Mister Chairman and ladies and gentleman, it's a great pleasure, pleasure, to join Jim Wolfensohn [President of the World Bank] in welcoming you this morning to the opening of the program of seminars for this year's annual meetings of the World Bank Group and IMF. Traditionally, well, but, ah, [a nostalgic, French-accented sigh] there is something too nice in using the word "traditionally" today, as a matter of fact, at the very moment when so many things around earth are questioned, destabilized, and submitted to, to so many intellectual or financial or many other forms of turmoils. . . .

The international monetary system, I must say, for almost twenty years has been a, a kind of item which was there as a good thing to talk about even if many people were asking themselves if the system existed. But now we have the impression that the system is such—under such a stress, that no doubt it exists and requires reflection and probably fixing . . .

When I see the work that has, which *is* being completed in so many fora around, I believe that at least, that what I call the Golden Rule of *Transparency* [to be explained] will emerge as solidly established after this annual meeting.

It will be particularly instructive to see how the seminar participants from the private sector, the persons who are working each day in the marketplaces around the world, are coping with the crises in countries. How they are making investment decisions—hopefully they continue doing [so]. . . .

And now, Mister Chairman, ladies and gentlemen, I hope that you will understand if I must excuse myself as I have another competing meeting of the G-24 countries which will start in [a "would you believe it?" laugh-sigh] in next few minutes and I think Jim will have the same obligation also. But I did want to have an opportunity to welcome you to this program, to thank the many distinguished people who have agreed to serve as moderators, panelists, and keynote speakers, and to wish you well in your important work. Thank you very much.

In the four days of simultaneous panels, many speakers gave business-as-usual analyses. If they acknowledged the Asian crisis it was as a bug in the beta version of the global economy. But at the best-attended lectures, well-known economists reminded the audience that what started as a mere currency devaluation in Thailand had lasted much longer and turned out to be more catchy—"contagion" was a frequently repeated word—than anyone among them had predicted.

At one such session I noticed an avuncular-looking man, whom I thought I knew from somewhere, listening quietly at the back of the auditorium. I was about to say hello when I realized that his face was familiar because he was George Soros, who, through the hedge funds he runs, is perhaps the largest investor and foreign-exchange speculator in the world. He's also a thoughtful philanthropist who'd tried, through his personal foundation, to ameliorate the suffering that accompanies unregulated capital, particularly in Eastern Europe. At this forum Soros appeared to be giving a good ear to one of the many speakers who told us that the world financial system needed not only minor repairs but "a new global architecture." That phrase became almost a mantra.

Many of those who acknowledged a problem claimed that there was nothing wrong with the way capital moved around the world. The difficulty was its recipients. Countries like Thailand had weak fundamentals, loosely regulated banks, and accounting and disclosure standards that obscured the financial condition of enterprises from would-be lenders and investors. For these people the answer was summed up by Mr. Camdessus' word, "transparency." Third-world capital recipients must adopt the transparent or what-you-see-is-what-you-get financial reporting practices of the West. "Transparency" became the counter-mantra to "new global architecture."

Actually almost everyone at the conference, including me, by the way, would say amen to transparency. Of course enterprises should adopt uniform truth-in-labeling codes and publish enough financial information so that potential depositors, lenders, investors—and curious citizens?—can tell what's really there.

But I'm not sure that transparency would have helped much before the Asian crash. The crucial figure for many Asian businesses was their high debt-to-equity ratio. They had simply bought too much money for their size. But that was already transparent to the banks, since they were selling them the stuff.

One indication that bankers understood that weakness of Asian businesses is that they charged them much higher interest than they could charge in Europe or the US. High interest is supposed to cover possible losses. But if the losses are sure to be covered through IMF bailouts, than the high interest is a pure windfall.

That's why several speakers talked about "bail-*ins.*" By this they meant that the IMF and the rich governments that it represented should make it clear that all future third-world bailouts would be structured so that international banks had to absorb some part of the losses from their own bad loans. Otherwise they would feel free to lend unwisely again, no matter how transparent the borrowers' information.

A few of the IMF and World Bank's best known panelists went so far as to reexamine the efficacy of capital controls as a way to restrain the overenthusiastic lending. With a notable exception, the East Asian countries had followed IMF recommendations to rescind regulations that slowed or limited foreign money coming into their countries. But China, the one East Asian nation that still retained rigid capital and currency controls, was also the one country that had escaped the Asian contagion. Then Malaysia, which had fallen sick early in the crisis, defiantly reinstituted capital controls.

Those speakers who were willing to reconsider hypothetical capital controls seemed to find the actual Malaysian controls an embarrassment to their arguments. They were either too broad, too narrow, too late, or too compromised by the arrest of Malaysia's neoliberal and popular finance minister on suspiciously timed charges of sodomy.

The most interesting objection to Malaysia's controls was voiced by Jagdish Bhagwati, a super-bright economist known for his support of absolutely free trade. (I would support it too, I think, if it existed.) But free trade and free capital mobility were not the same thing, he reminded us, because trade in real goods and services is not subject to the same kind of speculation as is trade in securities and currencies.

Bhagwati joked sardonically (or maybe nervously) that he ran the danger of being made into an unlikely hero of the left for defending capital controls in the same way that US President Dwight Eisenhower had become a left-wing hero for his warning about the military-industrial complex. Therefore I shouldn't unjustly tar Bhagwati with left-wing sentiments. Nevertheless, I think I detected regret that he hadn't stressed the distinction between free trade and free capital mobility before the unregulated capital movements caused so much suffering.

Bhagwati opposed Malaysia's capital controls for the disconcerting reason that reimposing controls once you've opened your country is like trying to quit the Mafia once you're in.

"You don't go up to Mr. Gambino and say, 'Look, I'm going to leave.' You call up the FBI and you enter the witness protection program. You don't, like Mr. Mahathir [prime minister of Malaysia], just say 'I'm going to do it.'"

Bhagwati's practical conclusion was that the countries that hadn't abandoned capital controls should not be pressured to "get in the game." They should be allowed to continue to exist safely "off the radar screen" of the investors. But those that had already reformed would have to play out their hand.

———

In one of the white vans that shuttled between IMF headquarters and the conference hotel, I sat next to a tall man who looked like James Coburn. He wore a dark turtleneck and slacks, his badge said World Bank Staff, and he said he'd gone to the conference just to look at the exhibits. He hadn't attended any lectures. These clues led me to assume, with relief, that he was part of the support staff. I was at a point when I couldn't absorb any more abstractions from economists.

"What do you do at the World Bank?" I asked.

"I'm a lawyer," he said. "The bank draws up a lot of contracts."

"Like to rent these vans or for the catering?" I was still on the wrong track.

"No." There were indeed staff lawyers who handled things like that, he explained, but "No, the bank lends money. We draw up the contracts."

"Are they actual contracts like for a *real* bank loan?" I think he stiffened at that. "I mean, you actually write in loan conditions?"

"Of course."

"Like you tell them they have to privatize?"

"Yes."

"But that must be expressed as a sort of a generalized goal, I guess."

"No, it isn't," he replied with injured dignity. "They spend months until they come up with a list of the things that must be privatized."

"Like dams or oil companies?"

"Yes."

"And they're listed by name?"

"Of course."

I was thinking of the Petroleum Authority of Thailand (PTT) which was the silent partner in my Map Ta Phut refinery. What kind of a price would you get for a third of an oil refinery when the handful of potential buyers know you have to sell by a certain date?

"Supposing a country doesn't meet its obligations on time?" I asked. "Does the IMF foreclose?"

"The enforcement mechanism is if they haven't fulfilled their contract you withhold undispersed portions. [I must have made a belittling face.] It can be very unpleasant," he assured me. "It may mean that the government can't pay its employees. . . . It can be very uncomfortable for me to deal across the table with people who are not being paid."

If it's uncomfortable for a lawyer to deal with another lawyer who's not getting his paycheck, imagine how uncomfortable it is for a head of state to face departments full of civil servants and regiments full of soldiers who aren't getting their paychecks. Once a nation's currency deteriorates to the point where it's meeting the payroll with loans, it may be risking ouster or even an overthrow to reject the terms of the next loan installment. No wonder governments accept IMF conditions. The lawyer who looked like James Coburn had given me a less abstract sense of the kind of enforcement power behind Bhagwati's financial Mafia.*

"Is PTT for sale?" I scribbled during an IMF session called "Global Integration" and passed the note to an Australian economist based in Thailand.

"Yes," she wrote back. "Most of its assets are scheduled for auction."

"Won't they get much less than if they could wait until the demand for oil rises again?"

"Exactly!" the scrap of paper returned. "That's why the Asians say the IMF forces them to sell to Western companies at fire-sale prices."

Once again, I was amazed how direct money people are. When Michael Price visits a company CEO, he doesn't talk about sports and mutual friends, then slip in a parting word about how nice it would be if we could see some better returns. He tells them how many shares he holds, what size dividends he wants, and what will happen to them if the money isn't forthcoming. Investors thirsting for juicy national phone companies or oil companies don't send academic economists to explain the general merits of privatization. They send the IMF detailed lists of offers you can't refuse.

Half a Year Later

In the 1980's, Citibank had to set aside three billion dollars as a reserve against loan losses from Walter Wriston's era. The final losses weren't enough to cancel out the profit from all of Wriston's high-interest third-world loans. Still, it was the first year since 1813 that the bank declared no dividend for shareholders.

---

*In an interview with Michel Camdessus on the occasion of his resignation 14 months after the IMF meeting here described, the *New York Times* reported on Wednesday, November 10, 1999:

> "We created the conditions that obliged President Suharto [head of Indonesia] to leave his job," Mr. Camdessus said. "That was not our intention," he said, but quickly added that soon after Mr. Suharto's resignation he traveled to Moscow to warn President Boris N. Yeltsin that the same forces could end his control of Russia unless he acted.

But a decade and a half later, US banks came out of the Asian crash with just about no losses at all. This may be partly because of more sophisticated lending. But it's mostly because, by that date in the global era, international investors had refined the mechanisms for getting governments to cover their losses.

After the LDC crash of the 1980's, the US Treasury came up with Brady bonds, a somewhat cumbersome way for the government to assume the potential losses while the debtors were being squeezed to pay. But by the late 1990's, the IMF and rich governments knew the drill. Their quick emergency loans, ostensibly to aid the debtor countries, were structured so that the money bounced right back to the international banks. In Southeast Asia, Chase and the other lenders were not only paid back quickly out of 70 billion dollars of taxpayers' money channeled through the IMF, they also earned sizable fees for handling the privatizations and other property transfers that were mandated as IMF loan conditions.

Yes, it had been touch-and-go at the time of the IMF conference that I attended. But six months later, the Asian crisis had blown over and the emerging markets were reemerging—at least for investors.

The latest (as I write) IMF and World Bank reports acknowledge that output is still down and living standards still seriously depressed in much of Southeast Asia. The time had passed, they admitted, for the rapid "V-shaped" (steep down but steep back up) recovery that they predicted early in the Asian crisis. But the recession in Thailand had probably bottomed out, they thought. And corporate restructuring, especially in South Korea (where there are massive strikes protesting it at the moment of this writing) should produce more efficient businesses, offering even better investment opportunities the next go-round. Interestingly, the most recent IMF and World Bank papers (again as I write) predict deeper recession for Latin America than Southeast Asia next year.

As to "new global architecture," capital controls were once more taboo even though Malaysia, which had imposed theirs too little/too late (or too big/too soon), seemed to be recovering faster and less painfully than Thailand or Indonesia, while Chile, with similar controls, withstood Latin American currency crises much better than its neighbors. You could still, however, hear occasional talk about "bailing *in*" the lenders. But the US trea-

sury secretary warned that tough rules would discourage investors from going into developing nations at all. So while the idea was still floating around,
nothing concrete was done.

At the time of the meeting that I attended, the IMF seemed to have temporarily lost the credibility to restore investor confidence. This led to palpa-
ble panic, not so much that Southeast Asia could sink into permanent
decline, but that the world's creditors would find another enforcer and the
IMF would revert to a minor bureaucracy. But with the crisis receding, there
seemed to be agreement among financiers that the emergency plans had
been adequate and the IMF had implemented them effectively.

That may seem like a generous judgment, considering that almost all the
third-world nations that followed IMF (Washington Consensus) precepts
had been reduced to a state of recession and about a third of the people living in those countries subsisted on incomes of under $2.00 a day. In In-
donesia alone, over a hundred million people fell below that country's
poverty line after the crash. In compliance with its IMF austerity program,
the Indonesian government closed 250,000 clinics, infant mortality rose 30
percent, and six million children dropped out of school. (It's too soon to tab-
ulate the increase in malaria and untreated tuberculosis that will follow from
the required cuts in preventive health care.) But the IMF isn't charged with
human welfare. Its mandate is to see that loans are paid back.

To me it seems inappropriate that a private industry's bill-collecting functions should be performed by government agencies. What do we have to do
to get a government that will chip in 70 billion dollars when its ordinary citizens are threatened with a loss of income? (IMF Southeast Asian bailout
loans would eventually total more than 125 billion.)

IMF/bailout supporters could, of course, argue that the international
credit system serves us all. I'm not convinced of that, but I must admit that
some of my own bank deposit went into the sum that Chase stood to lose in
Asia. That made me a creditor too. But I didn't need an IMF bailout because
my bank guarantees to return that money to me in full. That's why depositors accept such modest interest rates.

Legally, morally, and capitalistically, a bank's loan losses should come out of
its shareholders' dividends. After all, they took a risk in the hope of big returns.

But let's be realistic. When banks faced defaults in Asia, Latin America, and Africa, they didn't pass the losses on to their shareholders. They got governments to collect for them from millions of poor, powerless people who neither borrowed the money nor ever stood a chance of sharing in the banks' profits. Finance isn't about taking risks *on,* it's about laying risks *off.*

It's funny, I never felt bitter toward the working bankers I met at Chase. Their job was to get money into places, lend it at the highest possible rates, and get it out at the first hint of risk. Of course they wanted no barriers to the free flow of capital.

It was only at the IMF meeting, as the academics explained how this financial "liberalization" was going to benefit us all, that their methods of money-pushing began to look like gunboat diplomacy. Did those 19th-century capitalists hire a hotel full of academics to explain to the Chinese that the opium trade would be mutually beneficial?

No, they didn't hire academics, but they did bring along missionaries. And in that era I might have been stupid enough to hate the missionaries more than I hated Cecil Rhodes. Because I have to admit that it was at the IMF conference, with its cocktail parties and that urbane Monsieur Camdessus, that I finally longed to see the bankers and investors suffer, just once, some of the personal insecurity and loss that their schemes inflict upon others.

But that's a mean and ignoble feeling. Besides, they've got it worked out so that if they suffer, you and I will suffer more. In that regard, at least, we're all linked in a global village.

So let's look at where we stand, without the bitterness. Though medical clinics, schools, food, and factories disappeared in the Asian crash, the world's big piles of money remained more or less intact. That's what US treasury officials meant when they congratulated themselves for having narrowly averted the crisis—that time.

But insensate piles are oblivious to close calls. As long as they're intact and growing, piles of money keep on exerting their primitive pressure to be invested. Money managers never stop searching for the next emerging market. But the globe is finite, so money was already moving back into Asia. That means that while Squirrel, Alfalfa, and even the illegal Burmese pipefitter may find employment during the next growth phase, they'd better brace themselves to pay during the bust.

I don't know how many times a region can be squeezed before, like at Sunbeam, it's once too many. The entire continent of Africa seems to be used up right now. The banks concentrate almost exclusively on collecting on old loans.

But Sunbeam might have gone another round if it weren't for Dunlap's hubris. And Southeast Asians may be able to pay for several more boom-and-bust cycles under the right austerity plans.

If and when Third Worlders can't pay, the bankers and investors will bring their losses back home. As for the round that's just starting, it doesn't seem likely that the banks will be bailed *in* this time. So the options in the next overlending crisis are once again peasants pay and/or Western taxpayers pay.

Of the hundreds of people I met on my money travels, very few still live in the same houses and hold the same jobs. Wherever my money went, it changed the landscape and it changed lives.

I was excited when I saw 9,000 people, mobilized by a Chase loan, building a refinery in Thailand. But a Caltex company wife who'd been there earlier remembers when there were still small farms and houses on the site. She didn't feel guilty when they were torn down, she says, because the company brought jobs, hospitals, and other opportunities. It was more than a fair exchange, she felt then. "But after the crash the jobs and the hospitals were gone but there were no little farms to go back to. How will these people live?" she asks now.

It's odd that a woman who had no part in the decision to move capital in or out of Southeast Asia (and probably little to say about moving her husband there and back) should feel responsible for what happened. Something like a hundred million people were reduced to extreme poverty in the short time that I happened to be following my money around the world. But the money isn't going to turn back and try to undo the damage.

Whether as a bank deposit or a stock investment, my money is going to keep ping-ponging across the planet changing people's lives. Not all the change is unwelcome, of course. Squirrel had been glad to get away from the kind of picturesque village the company wife described. Even after the crash she still didn't want to go back, but she might have liked the financial flows to be more even and predictable. She would have liked the growth phase to last long enough to set up her market stall. It would be nice to be able to plan.

Unfortunately, I've now seen enough of unregulated capital flows to predict that if Squirrel ever does get back on her feet, there'll be many more sudden sharp turns to knock her over again. The money is so skittish, and the pressure that propels it from one highest return to the next is so great, that it usually can't be stopped until after the rubber band breaks.

I was surprised at the start of this research when I found banks "awash" in money. At first I didn't believe the loan salesmen who claimed to have so much trouble getting rid of it. I should have realized the depth of their problem when I heard the bankers at the Waldorf insisting on their right to lend unlimited quantities of the stuff even in risky, poor places. But the notion of too much money was still strange to me then. When I made my mutual-fund investment I saw that attracting money was a minor activity for the managers compared to finding places to put it. So I wasn't surprised that after the Asian crash the bailed-out banks and investors were as adamant as ever that no nation's law must impede the flow of their capital. They had to hold their ground. They were desperate.

Money that could be earning more money is as demanding as rot. Anywhere it collects—banks, mutual funds, insurance companies, Mrs. Pearls' trust fund—it expands and exerts unbearable pressure. For good, for bad, or for no practical purpose at all, that money must be invested and its returns reinvested. Unlike the fisherman I met in Penang, money managers can never say "You stop when you have enough."

That's what creates the constant change I find so exhilarating, but that's also what creates so much insecurity for so many people in the world.

———

I began my travels wondering if there was any such thing as a new global economy. The answer is of course, yes and no. Something definitely happened in the late 1960's and early 1970's that sent a greatly increased stream of money coursing from the rich countries to the poor countries. Eurodollars and the vast Euromoney market are new, amazingly self-regulated vehicles for carrying that money. In that sense, there is a distinctly new global economy.

Still, there have been similar episodes of "globalism" in the past. In fact, at the end of the 19th century, when Africa was the hot emerging market, the planet was probably more open to the free flow of capital than it is now. There were fewer capital controls and no communist countries before World War I.

Each previous great wave of capital has been associated with a revolutionary new technology. The telegraph changed the speed of commerce at least as dramatically, in its time, as computers have in ours. The instant long-distance media before the telegraph was smoke signals.

Each wave was also characterized by a new ideology, or at least a new way of explaining why it would be good for everyone. In the last global era, the industrialized countries offered "civilization, Christianity, and commerce"* Today, investment capital brings the benefits of the free market, the mass media, and democracy. (Both sets of gifts turned out to have their advantages and disadvantages.)

Each great wave of globalism has had a similar beginning. They all rose out of mature economies when established enterprises were yielding lower profits and there just weren't enough ventures at home for all the venture capital. Yet the money was accumulating in fewer, bigger piles, and whoever held it had to produce returns.

So off it went, like my money. In the short time I'd been following world finance, I'd seen my bank deposit rushed into and out of Mexico, South America, and Asia. Meanwhile, my mutual fund was running out of opportunities in the US and moving on to Europe, where there was still shareholder value to extract. But the earth is finite. When the impetus for new ventures peters out, the money gets caught up in increasingly frenzied speculation—buying and selling the same old things over and over—and eventually the wave recedes.

That's hard to imagine. Global integration seems to go in only one direction. At the height of previous global eras, people were sure they had transformed and unified the planet forever. In a way they were right. Boundaries shifted, languages changed, and more people knew more about each other at

---

*It was sometimes called "legitimate commerce" to distinguish it from the slave trade, which had been a major commercial activity of the preceding global era.

the end of each global episode than at the beginning. The world is definitely coming together. Still, the capital waves of the past eventually contracted, usually quite painfully, the international economy got smaller, and millions of people dropped back out of touch.

But I like being part of a global economy. Meeting so many different people and bringing back some of the useful things they showed me, like jellyfish and green papaya salad [see Appendix: Jellyfish Recipe] gave me a taste of the one-world I once envisaged.

Of course, today's "global village" isn't organized around humane or egalitarian principles. Getting around in that village was a lot easier for me than for most of the other people that my money set in motion. After all, I traveled with a credit card and much of the world's business was conducted in my language. Now that I'm back home, my cherished souvenir—the badge of my global citizenship—is all the e-mail I get from Asia. But the migrants who worked on my shrimp farms and oil refineries aren't getting e-mail. Fewer than half the people in the world have ever made or received a phone call. And it's the half that doesn't get e-mail and doesn't make phone calls that's usually hit the hardest by the wild oscillations of capital. The goodies in this global village are very unequally distributed.

It's easy to see why there are rising movements around the world to reject all aspects of anything called "global." Yet for me, the resources, human and material, that I saw in my travels awakened all the old international optimism. Though it may not be easy politically, we have the means to transform the global village into that Eleanor Roosevelt one-world.

In the meantime, we have to tame today's careening capital flows, both to make them less turbulent now and to avoid, or at least cushion, the usually painful end of a global era.

Actually we're not quite global yet. Currency crises reflect connected but still separate economies with money moving between them. Investment booms and capital flights mean that the modern superhighways connecting those separate economies are kept open for quick egress. But the sign of a truly integrated world economy isn't a series of regional currency crises. It's a global depression. At least that's been the climax of previous global eras. I believe, or I'd *like* to believe, that that's not inevitable.

Most financiers aren't ideologically against government. As we've seen, the banks and other big companies that used my money routinely called upon governments to help them. What they oppose, not ideologically but pragmatically, are any laws that limit their options. But during the Asian financial crisis, things were moving so quickly and the collapses looked so contagious that some financiers at the IMF meeting I attended feared that this was the onset of a worldwide crash. At that point, a few seemed ready to accept regulations that would slow things down.

Several plausible measures were proposed at that IMF conference. These included limited capital controls, and "bail-ins," which meant letting banks know in advance that they, themselves, would have to absorb some of the losses from their future bad loans. This, it was thought, would get them to modulate their international lending. There's also a long-standing proposal floating around for a tax (sometimes called the Tobin Tax after the Nobel Laureate who first suggested it) on currency transactions. The idea is to set a tax small enough so that it doesn't discourage the currency exchanges necessary to carry out trade, but large enough to take the profit out of speculative transactions.

These are all what I would call traffic lights. They're intended to affect the speed, more than the direction, of money movements. As we saw at the Chase Fed funds desk, banks don't always oppose traffic lights, at least not in their own neighborhoods after there've been a couple of crashes. But when the Asian crisis was contained without losses to the banks, they dropped such notions and turned back to the desperate business of lending and investing freely.

Apparently it will require a great public effort to get even a yield sign installed where our children play. But the public has an interest not only in the speed of capital flows, but in their destination as well.

I had been dazzled by the skill, wit, and cooperative energy that was brought together to build a refinery in Thailand. But it wasn't very democratic, or even sensible, as it turned out, to let Caltex and its banks override the Thai government and decide what should be done with 1.9 billion dollars' worth of raw materials and human energy. It was equally undemocratic (and even more unwise) to let Michael Price hire Al Dunlap to dismantle Sunbeam.

These were, I realize, private decisions about the use of private capital (a *very* small part of it mine). But in both cases, thousands of people who had no input to the decisions were harshly affected. (The people with the least say are almost always the ones with the least to fall back on when the plans go wrong.)

When I think back on Bangkok, it reminds me of Dickensian London: so much suffering and so many possibilities. But since the people I met were real, they probably aren't going to be revealed, by the end of the story, as the long-lost relatives or the rightful heirs. They're going to suffer and get back on their feet by themselves. The austerity programs imposed by the IMF mean that they have even less of a social safety net than in Charles Dickens' times.

To be honest, I'm half-embarrassed to make a naïve appeal for kindness. It's firmly believed (or at least firmly asserted), at the time I write, that the unregulated activities of banks and investors will, collectively, lead to "development," and that will take care of most problems. It can be a little rough along the way, the adherents of this laissez-faire philosophy acknowledge. But "to make an omelet you have to break eggs." Leave Chase, Price, and Walter Wriston's 60,000 traders alone, says the theory, and things will work out far better than through any well-meant intervention. Haven't things gotten better since Dickens' days?

Yes, but if daily life has gotten more secure in the last century, it was in countries where unions were organized and capital was somewhat regulated. Now, just when, or perhaps just because, money is again accumulating under great pressure, economic trends have moved back in the other direction.

Today's unregulated capital waves are bigger than ever, faster moving than ever, and operating without brakes. If one, two, or three oil refineries are profitable in an area, someone will build the fourth and fifth. The only legitimate way to determine that there are enough is to wait until a couple go bankrupt. If capital is getting high returns in Asia, pour in more. A crash is the sign that it's time to move the money somewhere else. That mechanism—go until the rubber band breaks, then do one less—may seem neatly self-correcting to some economists, but its real-world effects are too disruptive to be tolerated. The scale of modern economic development is so vast that the overbuilding phase does environmental damage that lasts long after the overcapacity is "corrected." Then, as we saw in Asia and Mexico, the correction phase shuts down so many productive facilities that people have even less to live on than they had before. Yes, things will eventually swing the other way again. Yes, there will be new investment in Asia and Mexico. But without any control or limit on the flow of capital, there's nothing to stop the overdevelopment and crash from repeating. The swings are too fast, too wide, too extreme. Money makes the world go around, but it also stops it periodically.

Perhaps I didn't have to go around the world to come up with the simple idea that capital should be controlled more democratically. But at least now I understand the mechanisms that connect financial flows to daily life. Those mechanisms are still at work, of course.

I could make a new bank deposit or a new mutual-fund investment and set off today on another financial odyssey. Or, I could continue to follow the old money that now flows in the bloodstream of a Chase that merged with Chemical and then injested JP Morgan.

When I started, my money was fleeing Mexico and pouring into Asia. I stayed long enough to watch Asia boom, crash, and become a *re*emerging market. "This is where I came in," I said at that point. But just because I stopped to sum up doesn't mean that the money slowed down. As a matter of fact, I read yesterday that Sunbeam is selling off those little companies Al Dunlap bought. That means more discombobulation for whoever is still left. My book may end but my money keeps moving. And every reader, whether he finds himself in an "emerging market" or a "mature economy," is feeling its effects.

As people increasingly make that connection, I'm sure that the concept of regulating capital flows and humanizing the economy will come back into vogue. But no matter how obvious or reasonable an idea, we still have the problem of implementing it. The question at this point is, "Who will bell the cat?"

While no one should look to me for investment advice, I thought some read-ers might like to know how I made out financially. For almost five years I col-lected somewhat under 2.5 percent interest, on average, from the Bank of Millbrook. Of course I was spending my money down all that time, and even-tually I bounced a check to my landlord. But the bank covered for me.

When I saw what had happened I felt terrible, and phoned offering to wire the money or catch the next train to Millbrook. But the clerk suggested that I simply mail an ordinary check to cover the overdraft. I added some ex-tra to keep the account open. Though my research is finished, it makes me feel secure to retain a tie to the Bank of Millbrook.

I'm not as sure what I want to do about my mutual-fund investment. I just phoned shareholder services and learned that as of last night, the $5,000 I invested in Mutual Shares is worth $7,791. That's considerably less than it would have been without the disastrous Dunlap year. Still, if I'd invested the same $29,500 with them that I deposited at the Bank of Millbrook, it would be worth about $44,000 now (three years later), even with one year's return averaging just above zero.

Though some of my Millbrook money was used by Chase, the bad loans they made in Asia never threatened the security of my bank deposit. The Chase shares in my mutual-fund portfolio are doing so well that they offset some of the Sunbeam losses. Viewed from this height, the global economy doesn't seem quite as unstable or as uncomfortable as it did from the ground.

THANK-YOUS

When I started this book, Robert Zevin, then head of investments for US Trust of Boston, explained some of the financial mechanisms that would enable me to follow my money. In that sense, it was he who convinced me that the project was possible. Even more important were his assurances when I was at my most confused that I really did understand what his fellow financiers were telling me because it was just as simple as it sounded.

Authors are usually advised not to show people advance copies of the chapters in which they appear since no one ever feels fairly represented. But because I was dealing with unfamiliar technical material, I took a chance and showed the oil chapters to Al Center and the banking chapters to Turhan Turana. Both men responded immediately with small, specific corrections that had nothing to do with their own personas, and both cushioned their suggestions with tactful praise. How lucky I was to meet two kind people who just wanted to help me get it right.

Scores more who appear in these pages helped me from the same selfless motive. I hope they can tell by the writing how grateful I am. But many who gave me equal time and help didn't make it into the final book. Among those I'd particularly like to thank are Anita Murray, who (a complete stranger at the time) housed me and oriented me to Singapore, Christopher Ng in Singapore, Sakool Zuesongaham in Thailand, and Willie Jones and Councilman Herman Lodge, who showed me around Waynesboro, Georgia, a town much harmed by my investments.

Over the course of four years, Doug Henwood patiently answered questions like "So you mean X goes up when Y goes down?" without ever suggesting that I was hardly the person to write about economics.

Jeremy Brecher, one of the authors of *Globalization from Below*, read the manuscript and responded with simple, doable suggestions.

As time closed in around me, there was only one person to whom I felt I could show the work in its embarrassingly unfinished state. That was my daughter. She edited every single chapter, bringing her fine feeling, intellect, organizational skill, and tact to the work.

My editor, Wendy Wolf, and my agent, Joy Harris, shielded me from discombobulations and helped keep the writing on track. I'm the only author I know who can't blame anything on her agent or publisher.

The John D. and Catherine T. MacArthur Foundation provided a generous grant for research and writing.

Jellyfish is neither fishy nor gelatinous. The processed product comes in springy amber ribbons, "crisp on the outside but soft enough to stretch your finger through," as exporter P'ng Lai Heng told me. Almost all the work of preparing jellyfish is in rinsing off the processing chemicals. Once that's done, jellyfish is a handy, high-protein noodle that avidly absorbs the flavor of sauces. In Southeast Asia it's usually served with a soy sauce-sesame oil dressing as an appetizer or part of a salad.

Jellyfish Salad in Soy Sauce–Sesame Oil Dressing

1 lb. package of processed jellyfish
Bowl of boiled water

4 tsp. soy sauce
2 tsp. sesame oil
1 tsp. sugar
a splash—about 1/2 tsp.—of white wine vinegar or rice vinegar (optional)

Rinse the jellyfish with hot tap water. It will shrink at that stage. Then soak it in a bowl of cold water for at least twelve hours. I keep it in the refrigerator overnight.

Mix the soy sauce, sesame oil, sugar, and vinegar in a bowl. Scoop up the desired amount of jellyfish, steep in boiled water for a few seconds, drain, pat dry, and turn a few times in the dressing. After a minute or two, take the jellyfish out of the dressing and chill it in the refrigerator for 15 minutes or until ready to serve.

Dressed jellyfish makes a nice appetizer garnished with sesame seeds and surrounded with cucumbers and tomatoes. Malaysian hawkers use jellyfish in a refreshing salad called *pasembur,* which also contains beansprouts, cucumber, jicama, squid, and tofu sprinkled with crushed peanuts.

The few jellyfish recipes I found all called for a standard soy sauce-sesame oil-sugar dressing, but I couldn't get the balance right without that splash of rice vinegar. Hot pepper flakes are another good addition. I also liked jellyfish in an olive oil dressing flavored with garlic, oregano, and again a bit of vinegar, but normal vinaigrettes are too acidic. If you're not using soy sauce, remember to add a pinch of salt to the dressing. Properly rinsed jellyfish isn't salty.

I originally tested jellyfish out of a sense of obligation to Mr. P'ng. But it's become a favorite low-calorie snack. Guests love it too. The trick is not to tell them what it is until after they've tasted it.

The Thai office of Germany's Friedrich Ebert Foundation provided me with information on Asian working conditions and with pioneering studies of Bangkok's working population. The foundation can be reached at Turismo Thai Building, 3rd floor, 511, Soi 6, Sri Ayudhaya Road, Phayathai, Bangkok 10400; e-mail: gabfes@asiaaccess.net.th.

Some elements in my picture of postcrash Thailand come from *Taming the Tigers: The IMF and the Asian Crisis,* by Nicola Bullard with Walden Bello and Kamal Malhorta. This and other papers on the effects of international capital flows in the third world are available from Focus on the Global South, c/o CUSRI, Chulalongkorn University, Phayathai Road, Bangkok 10330, Thailand; e-mail: admin@focusweb.org.

The quotes I used from Alan Greenspan were reported in *FOMC Alert,* a publication of Financial Markets Center, PO Box 334, Philomont, VA 20131, US; e-mail: info@fmcenter.org. The center monitors actions of the US Federal Reserve Bank.

For more information on the effects of both shrimp farming and oil refining on worldwide coastal ecology, contact Mangrove Action Project, PO Box 1854, Port Angeles, WA 98362-0279, US; e-mail: mangroveap@olympus.net.

Marcia Stigum's *The Money Market* (Business One Irwin, Homewood, IL) is a remarkable reference book without which it would have been much harder for me to understand what I was seeing at the Chase Fed-funds desk. William L. Leffler's *Petroleum Refining for the Nontechnical Person* (Tulsa, Oklahoma: PennWell Books, 1985) was clear even to a person as nontechnical as I am.

In the course of this research I've had to read a lot of tedious prose. But the *Economist* and the *Left Business Observer* are so well written that I'm keeping my subscriptions. Though they generally supported opposite economic policies, they surprisingly often came up with the same statistics. Those are the figures that I tended to rely on. The *Economist* is available on newsstands. The *Left Business Observer* can be reached through its editor, Doug Henwood, at 250 West 85th Street, New York, NY 10024–3217; e-mail: dhenwood@panix.com.

INDEX